THE RISE OF DIGITAL SEX WORK

ALTERNATIVE CRIMINOLOGY
General Editor: Jeff Ferrell

The Rise of Digital Sex Work

Kurt Fowler

NEW YORK UNIVERSITY PRESS

New York

NEW YORK UNIVERSITY PRESS
New York
www.nyupress.org

Library of Congress Cataloging-in-Publication Data
Names: Fowler, Kurt (Professor of criminal justice), author.
Title: The rise of digital sex work / Kurt Fowler.
Description: New York : New York University Press, [2023] |
Series: Alternative criminology | Includes bibliographical references and index.
Identifiers: LCCN 2022059273 | ISBN 9781479824151 (hardback) |
ISBN 9781479824205 (paperback) | ISBN 9781479824199 (ebook) |
ISBN 9781479824182 (ebook other)
Subjects: LCSH: Prostitution. | Computer sex. | Sex-oriented businesses.
Classification: LCC HQ118 .F69 2023 | DDC 306.74—dc23/eng/20221222
LC record available at https://lccn.loc.gov/2022059273

CONTENTS

Introduction

"I Got This New Job"

> *Avoiding all work*
> *'Cause there's none available*
> *Like battery thinkers*
> *Count your thoughts*
> *On one-two-three-four-five fingers*
> *Nothing is wasted*
> *Only reproduced*
> *You get nasty blisters*
> *Du bist sehr schön*
> *But we haven't been introduced*
> —Blur, "Girls & Boys," 1994

Roxy had questions, so we decided to meet. The Kill-Time was on the north side of town, a cement cube with a stocked bar that ran the length of one side. The front of it was covered in corrugated metal in an attempt to give it an industrial style, but the effect came off as if someone had quit halfway through. The bar top still had some shine, but years of spilled drinks and sweaty palms had corroded it to a mottled black.

The dance floor was painted concrete and full of college students and young professionals flowing together like a tide that would crash against the bar between songs. All the patrons were vying for the attention of a lone bartender who was busy pressing cold bottles into disembodied hands clenching cash.

But Roxy was an oasis.

She cradled her drink in both hands, unaffected and untouched by the throbbing crowd—unlike me. At six feet tall and dressed like an undertaker, people usually keep their distance from me, but this place was a subway at rush hour. I winced as a sophomore elbowed me in the kidney.

"Sorry, sir," he mumbled.

I grunted back, feeling a little older after the "sir."

I surveyed the area for anywhere else to stand. The other end of the room held a stage propping up a DJ booth decked out in long foil fringe with the words "Big Bop Bangout" in party-store letters hanging from the lip of the façade. A bass line thumped from black-carpeted speakers suspended from the ceiling, and a young man crooned about girls who like boys like they're girls, while the stage lights flashed to the beat. A vodka-flavored sweat hung in the air, making every surface slick.

The room itself was alive and straining under the pressure of too many bodies in too small a space. Roxy glanced at me, jutted her chin towards the exit, then turned on her heel and headed for the door. Her long red hair flowed down her back in waves and brushed her shoulder blades, framed on either side by the low back of an emerald green jumper.

The crowd parted, and in one smooth motion she tossed her plastic cocktail cup into a wastebasket and tucked her purse under her arm. A security guard held the door open and nodded as we passed through. All the while, the singer droned his polemic of "it always should be someone you really love" to a dance floor packed with true believers.

"So, I got this new job," she said over her shoulder, side-stepping the line of people that circled the building.

"Oh?" I asked. In the time I had known Roxy she had worked mostly food industry jobs with small stints in fields like interior design or fashion.

We perched on a small outcropping that ran the length of the building's blacked-out picture window. In a previous life it was probably a window-box garden, but now tiny cigarette seedlings sprouted from a bed of sand, planted by exhausted dancers.

The opposite side of the walkway was hedged by a black wrought-iron railing with an assortment of bicycles padlocked to it, all protruding in different directions in every variety of size and color, a modern-art tangle of metal and rubber.

"I wanted your professional opinion on something," she said and snapped open the latch on her purse, producing a pack of cigarettes. She flipped open the lid and gestured towards my face. I squinted an eye, considering it, but waved it off. She pulled a cigarette from the pack and placed it between her lips, flicked a lighter, and received a fruitless spark.

"Crime stuff?" I asked. Since I had a couple of degrees in criminology, my friends would message me in the middle of TV cop shows to ask questions.

"Yup!" she responded, shaking her lighter and muttering past her unlit cigarette. For all her grace and beauty, Roxy kind of looked like a shady mechanic when she talked with a cigarette in her mouth. She flicked the lighter again, cupped the flame, and touched it to the end. She took a long drag, closed her eyes, and exhaled a plume of smoke, then tilted her chin to look at me.

"I'm a sex worker." She said it with furtive excitement and the tentative confidence of someone who had lied on their resume but was still savvy enough to get the job. "I just need to know what I should be worried about. Mainly how to avoid the cops. Everyone says it's illegal, but exactly how illegal is it really? It doesn't seem dangerous, but am I missing something?"

I leaned against the web of bicycles opposite her and let out a long breath. My first thought was "be careful," but—not wanting to seem alarmist—I shook my head and said, "I honestly don't know. But the good news is I can find out."

The answer satisfied her, and she punctuated it by twisting her spent cigarette into the sand, extinguishing it with a little puff of smoke.

"I mean, the important thing is that you're safe, obviously, like from dangerous clients or other people taking your money, sexually transmitted infections, that kind of stuff."

A smile pulled at the corners of her mouth. "That's not really a problem. I have a partner, but it's more like she's showing me the ropes and introducing me to clients," she said.

She explained how she had met her partner, constructed a work persona, learned the process of acquiring clients, interacted with them through messaging apps and websites, and took steps to protect herself. She described a whole world I knew nothing about. My only experience with sex work was a few chapters in various criminology textbooks and a handful of references from popular culture, and none of that sounded like what she was describing.

"Huh." I nodded and motioned to her purse. She opened it and produced a fresh cigarette, lit it, and extended it to me filter first. I took a long draw and thought for a moment. As I exhaled, I handed the cigarette back and she flicked the ash and took a drag.

I took a step back and looked at the bikes chained to the railing, my gaze tracing the web of interconnected metal, and asked "So you have a partner. Do you know any other folks in the same line of work?"

She pulled one last time on the cigarette, then added it to the other filtered flowers in the sand.

"A few. Wanna meet 'em?"

The Community: "Certain Populations"

Edward's blue eyes reflected the glowing screen of his phone as he scrolled through his messages. Leaning back in a black leather computer chair, he flipped the phone over on his desktop and rolled his eyes, sighing. "I wouldn't know how to do this job without an iPhone," he said in a thick German accent.

He was sitting at his bedroom desk, the sleeves of his black hoodie were pushed halfway up his forearms, and he raked his fingers through his hair, pulling it towards the ceiling. Edward and I looked strikingly similar, which was unexpected for me. We both had carefully coiffed hair that made it look as though we had just woken up, and we both had on a black band t-shirt that peeked out from behind a hoodie. Both of us were tall and thin with the sole exception to our likeness being his thick, horn-rimmed glasses. We looked as if we could pass as the other's alter ego.

There is a cultural expectation about what a sex worker looks like, and I was not prepared for one that looked just like me. Indeed, the workers I met defied those stereotypes time and again. Edward laughed and let out a low groan.

> Oh my god, this is such a lecture-y speech. . . . I don't want to make a big sweeping statement about how sex work has changed because in many ways it hasn't, but it does seem that certain populations of people who maybe wouldn't stand on a street corner for various reasons, are now more able to dabble in forms of sex work that they otherwise wouldn't.

The fact [that] I can sit at home and send out an email or text and post online, which is essentially a public forum, where I can get anybody to find me, is an incredible time saver and saves me from leaving my house and prevents a lot of potential risk associated with street-based work. . . . Sex workers have always been on the forefront of modern technology. They're usually first to adopt anything and use it to protect themselves, to advertise, to whatever, for safety and for business.

As Edward hinted, these "certain populations" represent a traditionally understudied group.[1] But the implication was clear: mostly white, mostly privileged people were using the Internet to gather firsthand information on the risks and rewards of sex work. And perhaps the cultural notions of pimps, drug addiction, and shady johns were not the whole story when curious spectators began to peek behind the curtain.

The workers I spoke to described how they came to enter sex work; how they created and shaped personas in real and digital spaces; how they perceived and responded to on-the-job risks with security measures; and how technology has rapidly changed society, providing new opportunities while also presenting new dangers. The providers who sat down with me were overwhelmingly white, female, and college educated[2]—clearly part of Edward's "certain population." Yet they came from a variety of backgrounds, and their diversity came in the form of styles of work, culture, disabilities, and geography. Though most of the workers were cis white women, I was also able to speak with transgender workers and providers of color, all from a spectrum of ages and sexual orientations. All the workers were from Western nations (including Australia, Canada, England, France, Germany, South Africa, and the United States) and hailed from a variety of locales (urban, suburban, and rural), but their common setting was the Internet, which they used to facilitate sex work.

As an overarching term, "sex work" encompasses a variety of activities, including, but not limited to, escorting, dominatrixing, webcamming, fetish photography, stripping, and burlesque. Yet all of these types share a consistent theme: the exchange of value (most commonly money, but including gifts and services) for some form of sexual gratification (both in person and now digital). But though the work can be delivered in a variety of ways, workers described similar processes concerning their entrance into sex work, the management of their business, and security concerns. This is a very broad definition of sex work and can include both legal and illegal activities, but my sample was purposely designed to reflect that workers all face similar issues and resolve them with similar methods regardless of the type of work they engage in.

In order to begin contacting workers, I used four entry points. The first two were local sex workers and activists on the East Coast of the United States—both with separate friend/acquaintance/work networks. The other two entry points were digital—in the form of social media posts to a virtual sex-worker community. The first post was made by me and the second by the moderator of the virtual community. These multiple entry points were used to increase diversity and minimize bias that may occur in the selection of the initial participants.[3]

Sex workers can be difficult to reach through conventional research techniques, so a purposive snowball technique was used to contact the providers I spoke to. A snowball sampling method includes finding existing providers and then having them recommend additional workers to interview. But still, the question of how the population responded to me looms large. Does the fact that I am a white male mean that only a certain type of worker would be comfortable talking to me? Even those who made posts and introductions seemed to all share similar demographics. This made the sample of people I spoke to relatively homogeneous, but also says something interesting about digital interactions.

Methodologist Douglas Heckathorn showed that hidden populations have two discrete qualities. First, there is no sampling frame from which to draw any inference on the size, parameters, and characteristics of the population. And second, hidden populations often include stigmatized or marginalized groups, and therefore security and privacy concerns can make gaining access difficult.[4] This would indicate that even with the anonymity of virtual meeting spaces, only workers who felt secure enough in their work and life would choose to reach out to me. All of these factors would favor white, middle-class, privileged workers—who accounted for the majority of the fifty workers I ultimately spoke to about their experiences.[5]

This book is organized into eight chapters, each addressing a step in the sex-work process. This chapter introduces a variety of the providers I spoke to, as well as describes the overall character of the community and presents the major themes of the stories workers told me. Chapter 1 gives an overview of previous research and how cultural views can dictate scholarly approaches to investigating sex work. Chapter 2 examines the recent advancements in technology and how they impact workers now and in the future. Chapter 3 looks at the process of entrance and the various situations and contexts that accompany it. Chapter 4 describes how workers adopt a range of work personas for their jobs. Chapter 5 investigates the cultural perceptions about the risks of sex work and the specific risks providers say they must address. Chapter 6 explains how providers address the risks of their work by creating security protocols to protect themselves. And chapter 7 concludes by considering how society often harbors inaccurate views of providers and how a more precise understanding could impact policy and improve the situation of workers.

In order to better understand the situation of workers, I spoke with a variety of providers from around the world. The average age of the workers I spoke to was twenty-eight, with the youngest being eighteen and the oldest being forty-six. The overwhelming majority identified their gender as female, including two interviewees who responded with "trans-female." Three identified as male, and of those one added the qualifier of being nongendered. The last two identified as being nongendered with an inclination towards fem.

The majority of workers identified as white or some combination. Four indicated that they were Asian, and one provider each identified as African American, Hispanic, and Jewish American. Most of the providers identified as bisexual, and workers who identified as queer made up the second-largest category. This was followed by those who identified as straight, including one provider who identified as "unfortunately straight" because she missed out on more "opportunities." Pansexual, homoflexible, heteroflexible and three self-described categories ("fluid," "anything goes," and "does not apply") made up the remainder of the people I spoke with.

When it came to the type of work providers participated in, most were escorts, followed by webcam performers. Many of the providers I spoke with also participated in fetish modeling and BDSM sessions. In addition, I spoke with two burlesque performers and one worker who counted her production work in pornography as part of her sex-worker career. Two participants had taken part in street-level sex work, but they were part of a group of providers who named a combination of work styles that mixed virtual and in-person work.

As I was developing the interview guide, I consulted three current and former workers to assess the cultural sensitivity of the questions I was asking.[6] I was told that workers are particularly resilient, but certain subjects may make them uncomfortable. Questions regarding specific amounts of income should be avoided. Similarly, questions about educational backgrounds, family history, and previous abuses were rejected.[7] There were two reasons for removing these. First, a lot of existing research on sex work attempts to causally relate it to deviant behaviors or indicators of low socioeconomic status (such as level of education or a history of domestic abuse). If information on these relationships is desired, there is plenty of research to explore. Second, and more importantly, if sex work is to be examined as work, previous qualitative studies into employment and careers do not customarily attempt to connect choice of employment to deviant behavior or histories of victimization (no one asks librarians what trauma led them to a career around books). Given that the goal of this book is to understand how sex workers do their jobs and what their relationship to Internet technology is, most of these questions are irrelevant. This approach seemed to be validated when one provider thanked me for not asking questions about previous abuses and not "digging around" to find out why she had decided to become a sex worker.

The question of whether stories collected by a social scientist can be trusted as either accurate or reliable is one every researcher should ask. Often, qualitative research like this is judged by its ability to conform to four requirements: credibility, transferability, dependability, and confirmability.[8] Credibility represents the confidence a researcher has in their project and speaks to the authenticity of the participants' experience. And if the data provides enough detail to allow comparison between similar situations, then the research sufficiently addresses the concept of transferability. However, variation in the stories of providers, yet consistency in the themes and concepts identified by the research, becomes a form of dependability that can result in both increased understanding and confidence in the quality of the data and its analysis. But once the presence of these first three qualifiers is determined, the lens then flips to the reflexivity of the researcher to assess the confirmability of the data. The researcher asks, Did I get it right? Am I biased? Can I ever fully grasp the experiences of a person who is different from me?

Reflexivity involves the critical attempt to understand and account for the role the researcher plays as the conduit through which the data are interpreted. Social science has a long tradition of striving for objectivity, but over a century of research has often produced unobserved white, male, heterosexual, cisgender bias masquerading as objectivity.[9]

Every human has unidentified biases, and even if we were aware of them, there is no way to fully eliminate them.[10] As a white cis man, I have more than my fair share of biases, but when I asked a provider if it was okay to be talking about her life and work with me, she looked me square in the eye, smiled, and said, "It's cool. We can smell our own." I had to pause and think about what that meant for me, both as a researcher and as a person. Before I was a criminologist, I was a musician—still am. I had spent years touring in the back of a van, playing music in every bar and basement this country had to offer. I had stood next to burlesque dancers as they blew fire or sprayed sparks from an angle grinder pointed at their crotch. But a few cocktails aside, no one has ever offered to pay to have sex with me, nor have I ever offered.

But maybe the experiences of workers were not so foreign to someone like me. I did have experience performing for others, creating an inviting atmosphere, making people feel comfortable. I have wrangled hecklers. I have cajoled venue managers to pay up when they have suddenly forgotten that we were hired as entertainment. I have slept in parking lots and penthouses. I have shared drinks and laughs with people not exactly suited for polite society. I could be hungover and dry heaving from the night before, but when the house lights go down and the stage lights come up, the show must go on. Maybe I am not one of their own, but I was at least part of Edward's "certain populations."

Reflexivity is often conceived as the subjectivity of the researcher. But methodologist and cross-cultural researcher Roni Berger argued that reflexivity should not be seen as a limitation of qualitative research.[11] Instead, it should be embraced in order to aid in the fruitful "co-construction" of meaning between the researcher and participants. It is the rejection of objectivity as a goal in favor of self-discovery that

can fuel new breakthroughs. Rather than reflexivity being an awareness of what must be negated during research, instead the researcher
should be an integral part of the process. Of course, this approach can
create new challenges, and responsible scholars must always be mind-
ful of the consequences of the reflexive "I" when approaching empirical
interactions.[12]

But knowing this, how could I identify the areas of myself that needed
specific attention—achieve the heightened awareness of where my own
biases might peek through? I knew that my race and gender cast a long
shadow, and even when I was vigilant, I could get caught up thinking
others had those same perspectives. I had always had access to high-
quality education, and my degrees in criminology meant that I was an
expert on a criminal justice system from which I had never truly felt the
sting, as others have. And as a cishet-presenting man, I had never had
my sexuality criticized or, frankly, even questioned.

But when Berger discussed the suitableness of this co-creation, she
said that the researcher must be someone who is seen as sympathetic
to, or understanding of, the concerns of the group being studied. And
I realized I had been standing next to workers for most of my life. But
they were hidden, or, maybe more accurately, I did not see them. After
meeting Edward, I discovered that though my "research lens" was not
exactly equivalent to the lives and experiences of the workers I spoke
with, maybe it was complementary. And the strength of a reflexive co-
construction of meaning is that, ideally, the findings become more than
data; they become an expression of reality understood by both parties.
And if this co-construction is done well, the findings would be accessible and applicable to a range of people, and valuable in understanding
the complex interaction among workers, technology, and the business
it facilitates.

Overwhelmingly, workers pointed to digital resources as the key feature
in their experiences. Most acknowledged the fact that they were part of a
worldwide community of sex workers, but hesitated when they described
their own role in that subculture. Many described feelings of loneliness
and isolation, but still felt as though a support network existed online that
they could tap into. And though providers shared a lot of demographics,
each was unique in the story of their lives and work. When they would
recount stories, the focus was on personal experiences, but they would

frequently switch gears and discuss sex-work problems and issues in the abstract and wanted to be sure to include workers from other parts of the world or less privileged backgrounds. But despite these feelings of solidarity, Edward pointed out that when it came to digital communities, there were still some obstacles to overcome: "The community among male sex workers is virtually nonexistent compared to the robust network of communication and community building and safety resources that women seem to have. Most social-service organizations focus on women. They use female pronouns when they talk about sex work. Yeah. It sucks. It's sad." As Edward explained the differences between male and female providers and their various contexts, he rolled his eyes and leaned his head on the back of his chair. "I think men like to give women things," he said, shrugging. "They see women as little dolls or whatever, pretty little things who need nice things and who shouldn't stress." He flipped his phone over, tapped the screen, and looked up. "Whereas I get clients who *could* support me, and they're like 'oh no, no, you got to work really hard. You got to be your own man. You got to be independent.'"

Edward's eyes grew wide and he threw up his hands in mock outrage. "I don't want that. What the fuck, man!? I'm a pretty fucking doll! That's the thing, and I think it goes to conceptions of gender. The only industry where women make more than men."

He put his hands down and shook his head. "As a male feminist, of course that's what I do. Idiot." He laughed and added, "Should have gone into finance. I don't know what's wrong with me."

Sex Work and Its Frames: "Society Works Really Hard to Deny That We're Sexual Beings"

Nancy drummed her sparkly red nails on the kitchen table as we talked. She had matching red hair that brushed her shoulders and pale porcelain skin that made her blue eyes shine. Nancy was a forty-six-year-old escort and called herself a "reverse hobbyist," with a bit of a wry smile. "If it's a hobby for guys, why can't it be a hobby for women?" she asked with a raised eyebrow. She explained that the risks of sex work are woven in with current cultural contexts and personal privileges.

"I really see myself in that light. Right now, I wouldn't even have to have a felony, but it only takes an arrest for me to lose everything," she said. "I feel like there's a lot of stereotyping, which is very hard to overcome." Nancy was knowledgeable about sex-work research and knew that there was a connection between cultural trends and how society viewed providers, but she also saw how there could be benefit in those assumptions changing.

> I'm not ashamed at all of the work. I met some really terrific guys. Some have turned into friends. . . . I do agree with prosecuting trafficking and underage [exploitation]. I do agree with coming down on pimps who are pocketing most of the money, using the girls, making them work without any of their terms being filtered in. I think that if you look at Nevada and the model they have, number one, I think the government is missing out. . . . Just think of the taxes they are missing out on. . . . Not that I'm moving to push it in that direction, but I think Nevada does a really good job, for the most part, in that the girls do need to have all their medical info right out there, that the places have to meet a certain standard of cleanliness and decorum and all that.

Nancy recognized that there were multiple models to follow when approaching being a provider, but that possibilities were always limited by the current cultural understanding of sex work. It was twentieth-century physicist and science historian Thomas Kuhn who suggested that research is contained within a set of concepts dictated by our current understanding of the world around us.[13] He called these parameters a "paradigm," and sought to explain how science and society develop over time through a series of cyclical revisions rather than a progression of linear discoveries. All this means that research into sex work has always been tied to the current cultural views of sex work.

Researcher and professor Ronald Weitzer suggested that most sex-work research is broken into two paradigms that roughly coincide with history.[14] The first, Weitzer argued, was an "oppression paradigm," wherein sex workers were framed dichotomously as either the victim or the offender—either as victims of a patriarchal system that exploits them or as undesirable offenders who corrupt the moral fabric of communities and families. As society progressed in the twentieth century, sex workers began to speak to their own experiences as providers and began to emphasize the empowering aspects of their work. This led to the second paradigm being introduced as an "empowerment paradigm." This paradigm was advanced mostly via the personal ethnographies of current and previous workers and activists attempting to shift the overall cultural narrative of sex work away from only focusing on negative aspects to accentuating personal agency and the positive benefits of their work.

Both of these paradigms left little room for nuance, and in his 2011 book, *Legalizing Prostitution*, Weitzer presented a new paradigm to enable better understanding of the various "occupational arrangements, power relationships, and participants' experiences" involved in sex work.[15] A "polymorphous paradigm" would have to include the various contexts in which providers live and work. This idea is similar to the ideas suggested by the women and gender studies researcher Wendy Chapkis in her book *Live Sex Acts*, where she argues that "sex [is] a cultural tactic which can be used both to destabilize male power as well as to reinforce it,"[16] and where she goes on to say that "the prostitutes cannot be reduced to one of the passive objects used in a male sexual practice, but instead can be understood as a place of agency where the sex worker makes active use of the existing sexual order."[17] Both Weitzer and Chapkis emphasize that these contexts can lead to both positive and negative outcomes, and that the situations that both lead to and sustain sex work need to be understood as multifaceted social constructs.

Though these three paradigms cover a lot of sex-work research and speak to the cultural views of society when they were produced, some research aims to address the health concerns of sex work and avoids addressing the overarching cultural debates. Public-health officials frame sex work as a health vector. Most of their research is concerned with "harm reduction," a concept within public health described as "a new synthesis, a paradigm to guide action—in the Kuhnian sense, a scientific revolution."[18] Put more precisely, harm reduction describes policies and interventions intended to reduce the social or personal consequences of harmful or illegal behaviors. It originated in the Netherlands in the 1970s when several government commissions found that "as drug use became prevalent in all social strata, drug law enforcement itself became a social and political problem."[19] The public-health paradigm aims to view sex work as an agnostic offense and is more concerned with limiting the damage that can result from exploitative or dangerous situations.

Nancy drew a lot of parallels between sex work and culture. She was completing a master's degree in social work and was keenly aware of how society viewed sex work. "I think society works very hard to ignore the fact that we're sexual beings," she said with a nod. She told me that social work and sex work had a lot in common, as both are concerned with how individuals interact with the society they inhabit, and sex and sexuality are part of that experience.

This book aims to understand sex work from this viewpoint—not as an absolute of oppression or empowerment but as contextual. Prospective providers make decisions based on their own social position and privilege, their background and demographics, and the acute circumstances of their situations. And the precarious balance of both agentic and deterministic factors forms a complex tapestry revealing the unique journey of each worker.

"At the core, at our base biological makeup, we are driven to be sexual human beings," Nancy said. "It's a human service job." I asked what that meant and she said, "They're seeking to fill a need. I'm just the instrument by which they're doing it. I think that if people were less uptight about it broadly, in society, that the sex-worker industry would be a lot better for it too."

Digital Style and Symmetry: "An Outlet to Help Them Socialize"

The faded red shipping container looked like an oversized Christmas decoration nestled against the brilliant green backdrop of a tropical jungle. Inside, Darla sat cross-legged on a king-sized bed flanked by a large dresser vomiting clothes all over the floor. A twenty-nine-year-old cammer, she was thin with angular features complemented by dark chestnut hair that spilled down her back. She was explaining how to handle trolls who find their way into her chat room while she performs on webcam: "A good sense of humor helps. So say somebody comes in to pester me— to be a dick. Just be a dick. They're trying to get a rise out of me, and sometimes the rise isn't what they're expecting." Like telling the other members of the chat room that she would flash the camera if they got rid of the troll who was pestering her. "If you come at things sideways it really defuses the doucheyness," she said with a broad smile. It sounded as though it could be her life mantra. Darla was exclusively a digital sex worker. Her remote location and general dislike of being around people meant that camming was a perfect fit for her.

Darla paints and sculpts, but she considers her camming to be another kind of art. Her partner even plays a role in her performances, as her inclination for exhibitionism matches his desire to be a voyeur. They would have brainstorming sessions to figure out what kinds of routines got the most attention and attracted the best clients. "[My partner and I] have actually discussed trying a number of different things that we want to see but haven't really seen because the industry hasn't quite gotten there yet. There's the spoof porn, everybody's seen them, they're horrible," she says with a shrug. Darla wanted to see artistic advancement in the realm of pornography. But she said that a lot of the recent trends are based around satire, and most of these spoofs are so cringe worthy that they don't advance the art form at all. "For me," she said, "this is something very personal. I'm an artist. . . . This is just another kind of art for me."

Sex work can take many forms, and providers largely saw this as a positive. There was a market for every kind of specialty, and workers liked to take advantage of the variety to cater to the clients they preferred to see. But it was their ability to connect with clients via the Internet that facilitated the majority of these market exchanges. And digital inequality mimics other social inequalities by dividing along demographic lines.[20]

But, "variety" also meant more than the demographics of the provider or the category of service. Within every kind of work there were nearly endless subgenres of style. For example, Darla liked to spend time on adult gambling sites where workers play games and clients pay to compete and receive a prize if they win: "So, [xxxbox] is actually a video game website where girls go and play video games and a client lays down a specific amount of tokens, which are exchanged for cash later. Then they play a game with you and if the girl loses, they have to choose something, like get naked or play with my boobs or whatever. And then we go to the next game. So it's kind of like gambling on whether you're gonna see boobies or not."

Providers all had different styles, both in the category of their work (escorting, camming, fetish work, etc.) and in its style (fun, dominant, romantic, serious, etc.). Between workers there was variation, with some providers specializing in one thing, whereas others offered a variety of service styles. But all the workers agreed that what they were doing was legitimate sex work and that they were trying their best to deliver quality services when clients were both reliable and respectful.

At first, it was the digital workers who pointed out the benefits of not having direct contact with clients—different from the experiences of their in-person counterparts. But in nearly every case, after some consideration, all the providers explained that sex workers had far more in common than they had previously thought. Whether it was weeding out problem clients or seeking aid from digital communities, all workers shared the majority of concerns. This was a form of "digital symmetry," the common elements that transcend the category and style of interaction, be it in-person or digital. Darla explained that the presumption that digital workers have less of a connection to clients just isn't true, and instead that in-person and digital work shared many elements. She maintained a personal relationship with many of her steady digital clients, even going so far as to know their children's names. But all the workers recognized the advantage of, as Darla put it, "that screen that separates us." And providers were careful to maintain boundaries for their own protection.

All the workers I spoke to used digital resources to gather information, advertise, connect with clients, and increase their own safety and security. And the majority of all workers admitted, both directly and indirectly, that without the technological advancements presented by the Internet, they would have been reluctant to consider sex work. The introductory process was almost exclusively digital for all workers, though in-person providers eventually cross the threshold into seeing clients . . . well, in person. That screen that separates them was seen as an advantage by all workers, even if it could create new problems that would need to be addressed.

Darla admitted that wrangling with clients who get too caught up in the illusion of her performance could be difficult. Though she worked exclusively in digital spaces, she still found that (like her in-person counterparts) she had to walk the fine line of managing client expectations while enforcing her own boundaries. "Sometimes they see things that aren't there, even with the separation of the screen. They start fantasizing and imagining and then they just get completely sucked in. A lot of my clients are very awkward in real life. They're really nerdy. They play video games, they don't get out much, they work a lot, they just get awkward. Because they don't socialize enough in their real lives. And I'm kind of an outlet to help them socialize. And sometimes they have a hard time separating what they feel for me over the Internet and who I actually am." Ultimately, Darla saw her work as a positive, both for herself and her clients. She enjoyed the variety and creativity of her work and thought she was helping clients by encouraging them to socialize. As long as she could remain safe in her work and be creative in her expressions, she wanted to keep doing it, and joked that she had recently made an investment in her business.

She had on a mischievous grin and leaned far to her left, straining to grab the doorknob of a closet just out of reach. The door swung open to reveal a large plastic shoe rack, divided into five rows and four columns, each with a clear plastic pocket containing a different vibrator or dildo. She waved her hand in a flourish and exclaimed, "It's my wall of sex toys!" then laughed maniacally while rubbing her palms together.

Entrance: "More like a Job"

Kelly was a thirty-four-year-old escort from the southern United States. Her auburn hair was tied in a ponytail and she was wearing a white tank top with "Super Fun Time," a local amusement park, printed on the front. Her story of entrance was what a lot of people imagine when they think of a stereotypical entrance to sex work, but it stood out as unique among all the providers I spoke to.

"I'm going to be totally honest, so sometimes it's not going to sound very nice," she started.

When I spoke with providers about their experiences, most took the opportunity to "start at the beginning" and told me the stories of their entrance into sex work and how it became a viable option for them. Kelly was stern, but a slight hint of a southern accent softened her delivery. She wanted to make sure I did not have any preconceived notions before we started. She was well read on sex-worker scholarship and was suspicious of researchers because she felt they often had an agenda that drowned out the voices of workers.

"I was nineteen. I was really high on Xanax and another girl basically pimped me out when I was blackout high. Then to process that—deal with it—I kept doing it after in a weird way." As Kelly spoke, she often ran her fingers through her ponytail, twisting the end and laying it across one shoulder. "One thing led to another and then I got more used to the idea of it being an actual job part of my life instead of just something that I did to have bills met."

I asked how that transition was made, from being "pimped out" to a "job." She paused for a moment. "I would say probably when it got to the point of realizing that I did have other work options, that they weren't paying me enough money to really live life, that's when I decided that it was a job and I was choosing it."

Kelly offered a juxtaposition from the overwhelming majority of providers I spoke with. Most providers discussed an entrance process that started with a "turning point"[21]—a moment or event in someone's life that can start them down a new path. This was followed by a period of information gathering—doing some research or seeking out others with knowledge to assess whether this was a choice they wanted to make. The final stage in the entrance process was either an active or a tacit acknowledging of their personal contexts and privileges—often indirectly addressing issues of race and class by using phrases like being from a "good family" or having a "good education." But what many providers did not like, and would have been happy to see the community dispel, was the argument that providers are placed on a hierarchy of workers, a term they have not so affectionately dubbed "the whorearchy." "There's a perceived hierarchy, but I don't understand it. I don't know how it makes sense." Kelly felt that sex work garnered enough stigma without workers judging one another for their work choices. "Prostitutes are like, 'Oh cam girls, fuck them.' And cam girls are like, 'Oh prostitutes, fuck them.' Or porn stars, 'Oh porn stars are awful.' You know. It's—there's just so much conflict within the community, and I don't understand it. It's something that I've thought about a lot, but it just doesn't—I don't see why there's this conflict."

Kelly wanted to take a "realistic" view of her job and thought that others often put on "rose-colored glasses" when discussing their careers.

But reframing the work as a choice was an important step for Kelly, and it also accompanied the themes other workers discussed in their entrance stories. Providers overwhelmingly noted the use of the Internet to both enter sex work and maintain their business. This use was accompanied by the cultural contexts that shape the way technology is used to solve problems, gather information, and increase the choices of workers. Kelly described how the use of the Internet reframed sex work from something she felt she had little control over to a job: "Before, I was just falling into things. When opportunities presented themselves or when I met a guy who had money and we'd develop sort of sugar daddy–type relationships.[22] . . . Then 2010 is when another friend of mine [said], 'Oh, you should, you know, start getting on some of the sites online and stuff,' and it was so organized and so easy to do. Then from there it wasn't hard to learn how to screen and start scheduling my days and it seemed more like a job." I asked about the "stuff" Kelly had found, and she told me that most providers had a variety of online resources to help them run their business, if one just knows where to look. I asked where I should be looking, and she shrugged and told me to check the links page of her website: "You'll see fifteen links or something and those will be all the main ones people use." Most workers talked about technology this way. Few had details or explained specific functionality, instead opting to use the same search engines and social media sites most people use to gather information or connect with others. But this did not stop them from recognizing the importance of those platforms.

> If I didn't have my website or I didn't have a way to screen people before I met them, I would be relying on other people to do that for me. You never know if you can trust them because they have a financial incentive to get people in your door. I'd rather do those things myself and with the Internet and the different platforms that are set up, it allows me to do that. Yeah, I think at this point if I didn't have that, I wouldn't do it. I wouldn't want to work in like the red-light district in Amsterdam where it's just like, "Okay, I'm here." I wouldn't want to do it if I wasn't able to screen people in advance and do all my own stuff basically because I can control it all.

Kelly's story was unique—as with all of the workers I spoke to—but the details of her entrance stood out against those of the other providers.

The key component to the movement from sex work Kelly considered exploitative to what she considered her job was not the work itself but the contexts that allowed choice to subvert exploitation and technology to enable agency. In her own words, she can control it all.

This emphasizes that, as noted above, sexuality, sexual contact, and, by extension, sex work are contextual.[23] This means that outside factors, including race, gender, socioeconomic status, and a variety of other privileges, could impact whether a provider decided to become a worker. Though the providers I spoke to performed a variety of kinds of work at different levels of contact, frequency, and intensity, the key concern for this book is not the method by which services were delivered. Instead, the focus is on the perceived choices and agency of workers, and how technology interacts with those choices.

When providers discussed their entrance, their stories varied in the details of how and why they became a worker, but the consistent theme was the cultural contexts that facilitate the use of the Internet to gather knowledge, solve problems, and sustain their careers.

The Girlfriend Persona: "It's More Beneficial for Both Parties"

Jordan, a thirty-five-year-old escort from Canada, was dressed like the emcee of a winter festival, wrapped in a flowing gray sweater with pale blue hair and square glasses.

"I'm not an actress. I have no interest in being an actress. I have no interest in faking shit," she told me.

Remaining true to her authentic identity was a priority for Jordan, but many providers explained that for reasons of safety, both physical and emotional, they often "put on" a persona for work. All but a few people I talked to altered their persona to convey a sense of legitimacy, connect with clients, and provide a form of emotional labor. Sociologist Arlie Hochschild coined the term "emotional labor" in reference to "the management of feeling to create a publicly observable facial and bodily display."[24] However, over the years different researchers have expanded the scope to include making impressions desired by businesses or eliciting certain emotions from interpersonal transactions.[25]

Many workers specifically pointed out emotional labor as part of their job performance. Jordan said that offering an emotional connection can help attract the kind of clients she wants, if she presents a persona that offers those relationships: "I've learned over the years that the client base that I want to attract are the ones that go for ads that offer a connection or authenticity or, things that more appeal to an emotional connection. . . . It's kind of who you want to work with and how you want to work is the language that you're gonna use."

Technology also played a crucial part in facilitating the creation of work personas, attracting clients, and fostering communities. Though providers worked alone more often than not, it was this connection to the broad digital culture of sex workers that gave them support, opportunities to vary their business, and a sense of belonging that would have been all but absent previously. Jordan swept her bangs out of her eyes and explained, "Twenty years ago I probably wouldn't have stayed in the industry for so long because I wouldn't have connected with other people and learned from them and had that sense of community." Once workers identified the kind of persona they wanted to accentuate in advertisements and early client interactions, they determined how those personas came into existence, what specific features were highlighted, and how much effort went into constructing and maintaining that persona. And a big part of that construction was deciding how much of their personal selves to reveal to clients.

They described wanting to foster an authentic connection with clients, and this resulted in having very specific tactics for how they constructed their personas. At first, Jordan said that she did not even bother to put on a work persona and that she just had a stage name that protected her identity. But then she paused and thought about it.

> So I do have a persona—to the point where I have a work name and I have some things that I don't share with clients. But at the same time, I am, I think, more open with clients. And that's also what attracts them is that I am pretty open about the fact that I've had mental health issues or I work within the social services. They don't get enough information that it becomes very personal. But I share enough to create that connection. Or I share enough sometimes [for] what that person might need. Some people get to know my real first name. Some people don't. But I've never had this stage persona where I completely shift 180 degrees because, to me, I can't do that.

Wanting to create a connection was a common theme in the stories workers told. Jordan described the combination of emotional labor with her work to create a "Girlfriend Experience" (GFE): "So heavy emphasis on the emotional connection with someone. I find a lot of people are lacking in physical intimacy," she said, pushing her eyeglasses up her nose. "Some people—I have one client that just comes and wants to be held while he cries. And that's totally cool. There's a lot more physical intimacy, emotional intimacy, rather than just . . . a one-time session and that was it."

These authentic connections obviously came with caveats about keeping themselves safe and creating boundaries with clients. Sociologist and sex-work researcher Elizabeth Bernstein coined the term "bounded authenticity" in her book *Temporarily Yours* to describe this concept.[26] The work persona of providers was meant to enable a sense of authentic intimacy with clients that is limited to the confines of the economic exchange.

For Jordan, that authenticity extended beyond trying to convince or trick her clients into thinking she was enjoying herself. Instead, she used her authenticity to give the client "a more realistic expectation of what sexual pleasure looks like." She said, tugging at the shoulders of her sweater,

> I don't often fake orgasms with clients for that reason. And I've had a few where they've been like, "Am I not pleasing you?" Because they're used to this overtheatrical, overdramatical reaction from workers. And that's just not who I am. I'm not gonna do a "When Harry Met Sally" sort of interaction. Because, A, I can't do that. And B, what the fuck is the point? I'm teaching you that what you're doing is pleasurable when it's not necessarily. I think that it's more beneficial for both parties if they have a more realistic expectation of what sexual pleasure looks like.

She shifted in her seat. "I'm finding that it also feeds into the connection part, as well as that they're getting to know my personality and what I like."

However, Jordan explained that part of the balance of a work persona was compartmentalizing the risks by acknowledging that you are withholding things for your own safety: "Even though it's completely scripted in terms of what I want clients to see. Some of it is authentic, but I definitely filter out stuff," she said. Most providers agreed that the work persona they put on was just themselves with certain aspects tweaked. Some changed a lot of aspects, and some very few. And those who changed the fewest just presented their own persona with a different name. The right persona could attract the types of clients they were looking for, gave them the ability to grow relationships with suitable clients, and, perhaps most importantly, mitigated some of the risks workers could face.

Risks: "Those Violent Tendencies"

Deana, a twenty-three-year-old cammer-turned-escort, wore huge, puffy headphones that were framed by flowing chestnut hair, and when she smiled, her brown eyes were obscured through half-closed lids. She told me that before becoming a provider all she had ever heard about sex work was that it was wrong. But her views started to change when she gathered information about sex work during a university gender studies course.

"It was kind of like your basic intro to sex workers . . . [which conveyed the idea that] this isn't immoral. And I was like, yeah, it's not. That vibes with me," she said with a little shrug.

Deana has lived all over the world and done a variety of sex work, including cam work in Canada and erotic photography in Europe. But eventually she settled in South Africa, where she began escorting full-time. She bounced her chin on her open palm when I asked her about the risks of her work. "Being a white person in South Africa, you just kind of cruise around. No one would suspect you; I don't oftentimes worry about the risks of that. [The cops] don't keep an eye on me. I think that they just go around on their beat and abuse sex workers that work on the street. That's what they do with their time."

When providers talked about their jobs, they often alternated between what most people *think* is a risk of sex work and the actual risks. Though they never wanted to diminish the risks that others might face, many said that they personally felt safer than other workers because of things like their middle-class status, digital prowess, or white skin. Deana nodded and added, "It's those undertones of violence that you realize that—it's something that keeps me inherently safer, I think, being white. Which is such a fucking hectic thing to try and wrap your head around." Often, the recognition that privilege played a role in their broader safety—such as insulating them from stigma or harassment—would be followed by an acknowledgment of more universal risks—like STIs, and how to mitigate them. When Deana started to talk about sexual health, she sat up straight in her chair and began to count on her fingers her various safer-sex strategies: "The risk of HIV is a lot higher here. . . . There's the risk if a condom breaks that you'll get pregnant. I have an IUD. I have rapid STI tests, which you can get for discounts here. They're [inexpensive] for a full HIV, syphilis, gonorrhea, with the swab, so I have the option."

Privilege played a largely unspoken role in the narratives of providers. If they did talk about race or class, it was most often as an abstract construct, rather than a personal reflection like Deana's. But these concepts loomed large in almost every discussion I had. My interviewees would use phrases like "well educated" or "from a good background" to talk about the amalgam of qualities that landed them in a privileged position in society. When the concepts of race and class did come up, many providers worried that others did not have the same privileges. This meant that the calculation of risk can be different, depending on the contexts of the individual worker. Deana told me about how she has used her privilege to assess whether prospective clients pose a security risk.

> I've walked out on escorting clients because I felt unsafe. So I've definitely made that call if things get hairy or if I just can't listen to them anymore or they offend me or say something that I just think might pose a security risk, then I'll either not meet up with them in the first place or I'll just leave. I've had people just be very condescending to me, and you can tell in the way that people speak to you, and they're like, "Oh baby you wouldn't understand anything like that." People that just want to pontificate to me to where I just know that I couldn't just sit with them for long enough to be like, fuck this.

Deana was one of the few providers who explicitly identified being white as a major factor in deciding whether or not a situation was risky for her.

Because of her race, she had to worry less about police interventions or being exposed to dodgy clients. I asked what she thought about the fact that she was less susceptible to risks and benefited from her race. Deana was always dependably candid. "I get paid probably the most of a lot of sex workers here, kind of the privileged end, which I think is very class-based and racialized." She went on, nodding her head. "There's definitely a privilege to being a white, middle-class sex worker."

When researchers examined the relationship between risk, privilege, and digital access among sex workers, they found that providers use the Internet to reduce their risks, but as soon as advancements appear in one area, they want to see them distributed across all other areas and every variety of worker.[27] Providers saw the reduction of risk through the use of technology as something that should benefit everyone regardless of privilege.

Deana pointed out both the positive and negative ways in which race and privilege affect sex work, and she worried that others do not receive the same benefit she does, saying, "The women of color that I know in sex work, there's definitely an element of being less safe." Providers acknowledged that they weighed risk and reward on the basis of the specifics of the situation and how it intersected with their own personal privilege. This led to the common refrain of "sex work is dangerous, just not for me." But Deana wanted to accentuate how much the community of sex workers has in common and pointed out the racial issues with clients rather than focus on the differences of workers: "We all get paid eventually by rich white guys," she said. "Rich white men are a very volatile group to work with on a regular basis, and you see those violent tendencies in them and the way that the world just reinforces everything that they do and how they are entitled to everything, and that's what makes them scary." It was clear that Deana had concerns about how social factors like racism, sexism, and classism played into her work, but she tried her best to combat these issues where she could. She attempted to use her own privileged status to normalize sex work by speaking openly about it and admitting that it is her job, if she could safely reveal that information. "I try to keep it very open, try to be open about it to try to combat that stigma," she said.

But the use of the Internet for sex work can create unforeseen new problems that workers had not prepared for. Deana told me a story about the unknown risks that can accompany new technology. She had someone on the Internet use the metadata of one of her social media posts to track down her personal information.[28] She spread her hands and said that overall the Internet has helped keep her safe, but part of the equation is knowing how to use it to one's advantage. "I couldn't do this without a smart phone. It would be impossible. Everybody uses [encrypted messaging apps], which is a very important part, security-wise. I have used technologies to take metadata off of my photographs that I send to people. I have used technology to give myself an alternate number for people to text. I have used temporary email addresses. I drop a lot of pins,[29] pin dropping is a very easy thing to do to, whoever I'm telling I'm at a gig, generally within my sex worker network, I'll tell somebody else."

Providers had complex feelings about the risks of their work. Most often, they acknowledged that risks were present in the abstract, but struggled to connect the concerns of workers who did not share their privilege to their own experiences. They would begin by describing a risk that all workers face, then describe a specific tactic for mitigating that risk. Finally, they described how new technology helped to facilitate their safety through the spread of useful security measures, screening protocols, and the support of the digital-sex-worker community. Ultimately, providers pointed to these new security protocols as being the most important part of both keeping themselves safe and ensuring the future of their work.

Security: "Meeting Strangers on the Internet"

Lydia, a twenty-three-year-old escort, was careful. When she first contacted me to talk, she told me she had reservations about in-person interviews. Recently, she had had to stop seeing a client because she had concerns for her safety. "It was a good advanced booking. And Friday night came and he texted me, he was getting sick. What am I gonna do, 'Oh, how dare you get sick'? So we rescheduled," she said in a long southern drawl that pulled each sentence from her mouth in a long, unbroken thread.

At first it seemed as though the appointment would be a positive one, but Lydia began to notice that this new prospective client just did not feel right. When they finally met for their appointment, the client attempted to assault her. Luckily, she was able to diffuse the situation. "I was continually saying 'no' that entire time and physically pulling away and getting physically pulled back and it wasn't violent in any way—but it really made me concerned," she said with a downward look. The client wanted to book another session, and Lydia agreed, but as the day moved closer, she reconsidered. "So, when Tuesday came, . . . I was just kinda like 'Oh, I'm probably hungry, let's just go out to dinner,' like in a public place so I don't have to be alone in my apartment with him. So he was like, . . . 'I don't have any going-out clothes,' and I was like, 'Well, I'm really sorry. I'm starving and I'm too tired to cook, so I think we'll just have to meet up later.' And honestly, I haven't talked to him since. And I think that he knows."

Even though Lydia said she did not feel the situation was dangerous, she felt she had to be extra careful. Security for providers worked best when it was preventative rather than responsive. Workers had to pay attention to small details to avoid problems before they started. Lydia told me this was the case because she had to assess a new client without a lot of time or exposure to him, and that could create concern: "[T]hat doesn't mean he won't turn violent or stalker or something like that. I just don't know him that well and that's kinda frightening because when you only see somebody an hour out of every month or maybe every week you don't really know them that well."

When providers talked about security tactics, it was very different from their discussion of risks. This was the case because they knew that security was their own responsibility. Workers perceived risks in large and small ways, but security was a process that included valid and reliable steps that could be described and replicated. Lydia would ask prospective clients to provide her with personal information to verify their identity. I asked how she learned her security measures, and she hooked a thumb at the computer screen. "If somebody doesn't want to give me the required information, I'm just gonna say, 'Look you're gonna have to find somebody else a little more newbie than me' because . . . if they don't want to give that to me, you know, that's their prerogative, but it's also my prerogative to ask for it. And if they don't want to furnish it then I'm not gonna see them. Yeah, I'm not putting my safety at risk for, you know, a fucking hour of sex. Fuck that." Even workers who admitted that their security procedures could be lax still had ways to gauge whether a situation was dangerous and had steps to minimize that danger. This could include "intuition" as to whether a client would be dangerous or incompatible, or even judging prospective clients by their syntax and grammar. But by far the most common security practice was similar to Lydia's: the preemptive screening of clients.[30] Screening, the practice of collecting information about a client in order to judge their safety or suitability, was a common feature in all forms of sex work. Lydia explained her screening process early in our conversation, emphasizing that it is a common practice.

> I'm pretty forthcoming about my screening information. I have it listed pretty much where any intelligent person would expect to find it. I also list in my profile that if they want to schedule a date with me, to please [message] me with their intro *and* their screening info. I do this for a few reasons. One, I have all the info in one place for easy review. Two, I can begin the screening process sooner—quicker screening equals quicker play time. Three, it's indicative of who reads and who doesn't . . . and I don't want to attract people who aren't self-serving enough to read my profile and research who I am and what I offer.

Most providers ask that new clients give them some basic information in order to verify their identity. Different workers required different information, but Lydia described the basics that most workers ask for. "First name, phone number, and email along with two to three recent references," she said, nodding. "Optional includes last name, age, and race. References being ladies they've recently seen."

The entire process is rather self-explanatory, but the rationale behind it is to minimize any security issues before they get to the point of requiring police or other outside involvement. Most of the providers I spoke to were suspicious of police, even in countries where sex work had been decriminalized. Most often, they pointed to the possibility of harassment, arrest, or even assault or rape as the source of their mistrust of law enforcement. "I'm more scared of cops than of problem clients," was a common refrain among workers. Most believed that police pay closer attention to them than to clients, Lydia explained. "The cops will watch us the most. You know, because women are more unreasonably treated in the courts when it comes to sex, unless they claim trafficking or something. Then it's fortunately an offense against men, you know, and it's a shame, but that's just how it is right now." Though providers frequently said security was important, they emphasized that mostly their job was safe, as long as they followed their own rules and screened out bad clients in advance. Workers were careful when explaining these points because they did not want to diminish the concerns of other providers in different situations who might not have as many privileges or resources.

Lydia wanted people to know that using the Internet for security helped make sex work a viable career as long as the workers could be safe. "As somebody who cares a lot about women's rights, it's important for women to know this is a career path, if that's what you want to do. And it needs fixing." But what do those fixes look like? For Lydia, putting the power in the hands of providers was the best way to keep workers safe. "Growing up in the Internet age myself, I know about safe sex, meeting strangers on the Internet, meeting in a well-known public place, etc., etc." She nodded thoughtfully. "This is how you do it."

A New Model: "I Don't Want It to Be Work"

Janine, a thirty-year-old escort, sat on her white linen couch and toyed with her long blonde ponytail. At the ends of sentences she would flip it over her shoulder like a punctuation mark.

"I've moved, I think, nine times in the last seven years." She had started escorting only a few months previously, after another recent move. "I've been bouncing around the area my whole life, but I've only lived in this particular neighborhood for the last couple months."

Janine wanted a place of her own. She had only had roommates since graduating college a few years earlier, but felt as though it was the right time to be self-sufficient. The only problem was that she found that rent and utilities essentially ate up three-quarters of her income. She rolled her eyes and told me, "I'd like to be able to do things like go out to eat, get my nails done, be able to take a cab once in a while." So she looked into some other under-the-table-style work, but neither dog walking nor babysitting really appealed to her. So she began to think about other opportunities.

Janine was an avid dater. As soon as she would land in a new town, she would investigate the nightlife, using dating apps to fill her social calendar. She even went as far as keeping a spreadsheet of all of her different partners, but the results of her research were less than stupendous. Most of the sex she was having was pretty terrible. "So I thought, 'You know what? If I'm going to have lots of bad sex, I want to get paid for it.' So that's what happened. . . . It's just like casual sex, except there's an agreement that he's going to pay me," she said with a laugh. So Janine weighed her options, did some research, and then waded into being a provider through an ad on NearMart.[31] "I looked around for a little while, and I actually did two, what I kind of called 'test runs' to see if I thought that I was able to handle it," she said, flipping her ponytail over her shoulder.

Janine considered this a new lens—to view sex work as a process that providers were honing for their own benefit. But it raised some important questions, such as, What exactly is being sold? What role do technology and community play in the sex-work landscape? Are legal policies around sex work being shaped to help workers or further ostracize them? How can the community address the looming specter of stigma? And if sex work is so different from the overarching cultural narratives about it, what is it really like?

Janine explained, "I mean, this isn't *Pretty Woman*. This is real life. It's important to be able to say the right thing, and to help that person feel more comfortable." She nodded and pulled her ponytail from behind her back and rubbed it between her thumb and forefinger. "So having good people skills, I'd say, and I've been lucky that in my legitimate day jobs, there's always been an element of customer service that has served me well as an escort."

Concerns around the "authenticity" of the connection workers were trying to facilitate was something providers discussed often. Janine wanted to figure out a way to relate to her clients even though her clients come in a variety of styles. "So I mean, just in the two dozen clients that I've seen, I've had the full spectrum." She took a pause and thought through the list. "The virgin all the way through the sixty-year-old who told me, he's like, 'I've had prostate cancer.

Here's what turns me on, and here's what I can do and here's what I can't do,' and everybody in between." She has had to find ways to bring clients into her world, which opened up a level of vulnerability for her, but still wanted to foster that connection. She told me about a regular client of hers who showed up while she was rooting for her favorite football team.

> I was finishing watching the World Cup game, a nail-biter of a game, and so he shows up and he knocks on the door, and I go downstairs, and he's like, "Did you just hear someone yelling?" I was like, "Yes. That's me. I'm yelling at the TV." And there was literally ten minutes left in the game, and I was like, "I'm really sorry." I was like, "Do you just want to sit on the couch and finish the game with me?" I was like, "It won't count towards your hour," and he's like, "Yeah." He's like, "I would love to." So we sat and finished the game. It was fun, and then we went and we had sex, and it was not a lot of work at all.

Enabling these kinds of interactions with clients was important to a lot of workers, but Janine acknowledged that there is an inherent contradiction when attempting to produce authentic connections. An attempt to be authentic is in and of itself performative, resulting in a paradox. And interestingly, she saw the exchange of this bounded authenticity as a two-way street, doubting the compliments and self-esteem that result from her interactions with clients. "I have never felt better about myself or my body, but I keep thinking, 'Maybe this is all an artificial sense of goodness when it comes to my self-esteem and self-image,' and I said, 'Well, even if it's artificial, if I feel it now, then that still means something.' It still means something to wake up in the morning and to get dressed, and to go to my day job and to feel like a beautiful woman, whereas four months ago, I would not feel that at all."

But the benefits that Janine enjoyed from being a provider, of course, came with some drawbacks. Providers named two areas that desperately needed attention to improve the sex-work industry. The first was to reduce the stigma associated with being a provider. Janine frowned when I asked her how she thought the stigma of sex work could impact her life moving forward: "I am prepared, unfortunately, to have to lie about it to future partners," she said. But she anticipated that anyone she would be involved with would be sensitive to the decisions she has made. "I'd hope that a partner that I'm with on a long-term basis [would] be the kind of man who [understood] why I made these choices, and that it's just another chapter in my life."

The second way providers wanted to see the perception of sex work change was in the legislation that gets passed. The discussion around the spectrum of differences between criminalization and legalization could be confusing, and providers had a variety of opinions on the matter. Janine felt that she needed to do more research before she could comment on it substantively. "I don't think I know enough about it. . . . The answer saying, 'Oh, it should be like pot. Legalize it and have the government regulate it.' I think that answer is too easy." But she had already formed some early opinions based on her experiences. "I think that for an independent provider like myself, it would be great if I could take a couple training classes on safety and get some kind of license," she said with a shrug of her shoulders. "I mean, I think that that would be a good step forward."

Providers wanted people to know that being a sex worker was a legitimate career, that their job was very similar to other types of service work, that many of them enjoy what they do and feel that their work is a benefit to society—and that technology has opened up avenues for providers to make their own choices and run their businesses as they please.

Janine flipped her ponytail over her shoulder one last time and said, "It should be fun for both parties. In the ideal world, I think that's what it would be." Overall, Janine thought that her experiences were positive and that the negative aspects of her work were due to external factors creating friction—well, most of the negative aspects. She let out a little laugh. "I mean, of course, with clients I have zero expectation of reaching orgasm. But I don't want it to be work. I want my cake and I want to eat it, too. I want to get paid and I want to have sex."

Conclusion: "Different How?"

When I next saw Roxy, her feet were propped up on the rungs of a stool in the little Mexican place on Ninth Street. The entire front of the restaurant was French doors that were open, and the sounds of the city drifted in on the summer night air. I took the stool next to hers at the bar as she rummaged through her purse for a lighter.

"So how's the project going?" she asked without looking up.

I gave a noncommittal grumble.

"What's up?" she asked, holding the little orange lighter up in triumph.

"It's just different," I said and took a pause.

The bartender placed a glass of ice water on a napkin in front of me and then turned to Roxy. "There's no smoking in here."

"Huh?" she replied, taking the unlit cigarette out of her mouth so she could hear better.

"There's no smok—"

"Right right, sorry," she said, waving the white stem in the air like a conductor in front of an orchestra. She turned to me. "Wanna sit outside so I can smoke?" I nodded and we grabbed a table on the sidewalk out front.

I ordered a blood orange margarita and Roxy wiggled her fingers in front of her face and groaned, "Blaaah blooood" in her best Transylvanian accent. She smiled that she had made me smile and snapped the lighter, holding it to the end of her cigarette. "So different how?" she asked.

I lost a lot of assumptions speaking with providers. The people I met were not simply victims or offenders, at least not that I could tell. They were people—both regular and remarkable—who make choices based on agency and context. They have been poked and prodded by social scientists for over a hundred years, and though that research is important, many sex workers said that their lives and work were still fundamentally misunderstood. And that the rise of digital sex work gave providers new avenues to pursue the work and manage their business. The presence of new technologies played an integral role in all the parts of their stories. It framed their entrance narratives, facilitated their work processes, and subverted traditional social institutions. Providers could use technology to abate risk and increase their security. Though many of them noted that the Internet has also created some new problems, an overwhelming number of them said that they would not even consider doing this work without it.

"Huh?" I mumbled, lost in thought.

"You said talking to people was different. Different how?" she asked, waving the smoke out of her face.

"I think I figured I was gonna hear a lot of the same stories, drug addiction, abuse, homelessness. But it wasn't like that. Like, at all. I'm not even sure where to start," I told her.

"Well," she said, pulling a fresh cigarette from her pack, "I guess start at the beginning?"

1

Sex Work and Its Frames

"Things Get Whittled Down"

Octavia pulled up to the vegan sandwich place on Fifth Street on a trendy silver ten-speed. She slid into the booth next to me as the waitress asked her if she would like any lunch. She ordered a kale salad and a bottle of water, while I poked at a Caesar salad with a mysterious substance that was lying about being chicken.

"Hey, we're both wearing our cool kid uniform!" she said.

"Hmmm?"

"A black band t-shirt and black hoodie," she said, gesturing back and forth between us.

I chuckled, thinking back to "we can smell our own." I asked what band reminded her of her experiences as a provider.

"Well," she said, "Rage Against the Machine is a personal favorite."

I couldn't help but laugh and thought of their infamous "fuck you, I won't do whatcha tell me" chorus. Not many discussions on the rich history of sex work start with Zach del la Rocha lyrics, but maybe more should.

Octavia had a wealth of knowledge on the scholarship of sex work, not only because of a long and successful career as a burlesquer and sex educator but also due to her doctorate in human sexuality. She ran her fingers through long purple hair that flowed over her shoulder, and her dark eyes, as always, held a hint of mischief. She readily saw that there was a disconnect between the concerns of workers and the goals of researchers. "Sex workers are not being listened to as sources, but then their labor is expected for research," she said, shaking her head. And she was right: research into sex work has taken quite the evolutionary journey in the last century and a half and often can frame sex work in confusing and contradictory ways. Though there have been advancements in the last few decades, with the voices of activists and allies being elevated through social media and academic discourse, stigma still persists.[1]

Octavia leaned back in the booth and furrowed her brow. "So I would say, yeah, academia has a mixed track record."

It was prominent sex-work researcher Ron Weitzer who observed that the bulk of sex-work research fell into two overarching categories that roughly coincided with history: an "oppression paradigm" and an "empowerment paradigm."[2] Each paradigm has a unique view of the cultural frames that are used to make sense of the emergence and persistence of sex work in society. The first, an "oppression paradigm," framed workers as either offenders or victims, dichotomizing them into either the purveyors of moral degeneracy who harm families and communities or the targets of a patriarchal system that commodifies female bodies. Later, the "empowerment paradigm" emerged as a counterpoint. Here, researchers and activists claimed that workers can choose to do sex work freely and that choice is an act of defiance against overarching patriarchal systems. The empowerment paradigm focused on workers' agency and their ability to make choices about clients, prices, and activities autonomously. It framed the negative consequences of sex work as a result of criminalization, stigmatization, and its relationship to broader society, rather than the work itself.

Octavia waved her hand in front of her face and pitched her voice up a few notches. "But it's the world's oldest profession." Kipling's often misquoted opening line to describe the work of Lalun, the main character from his short story "On the City Wall," has become a familiar trope in discussions of sex work.[3]

"So, historically speaking," she continued, "I mean, [sex work's] probably not the world's oldest profession. It's probably, you know, giving people food," she said, laughing and rolling her eyes.

Though "the world's oldest profession" has become part of the vocabulary of sex-work research, the passage that follows is rarely considered: "In the West, people say rude things about Lalun's profession, and write lectures about it, and distribute the lectures to young persons in order that Morality may be preserved."[4]

Sex work is a social phenomenon, and research into it cannot be separated from the culture that surrounds it. So, in a way, research on sex work says as much about society as it does about providers. This all feeds the notion that sex work is not a monolith and not easily classified using one overarching philosophy. It was a concept Octavia was very familiar with. "Personally, I have gone head to head with some clinicians and academics, who just have that same paternalistic idea that everybody is a victim. I remember there was a protest [outside of a newspaper] writing about how strippers are all drug addicts and are all traumatized and they only go into this because of trauma, which is not true, plenty of people have trauma that don't go into stripping. A lot of the people who go into sex work do so because they have to pay their bills, you know. . . . Some of it is practical." In response to these two binary paradigms, Weitzer suggested a third paradigm to frame sex work as a social phenomenon couched in a variety of sociocultural contexts. He called this paradigm the "polymorphous paradigm" and defined sex work as being comprised of various "occupational arrangements, power relationships, and participants' experiences."[5]

This framing can result in more nuanced analyses of sex work because it accepts that sex work contains a variety of interactions, which should be judged on the basis of the people involved and not by a static ideology. Sex work happens while life is happening, and provider experiences need to be understood within the mosaic of their lived experiences. Octavia explained that one of the biggest challenges of the work is attempting to make all the pieces fit together, especially when sex work carries such a large stigma. She told me the story of a friend and fellow worker who wanted to pursue a master's degree.

"It's a psychology program, my understanding is they won't come out and say it, but if you were open about your sex work or your sex-work activism, you won't be accepted into the program." She looked down and shrugged. "I have friends who can't be open about their sex-work experience, because the system will just invalidate anything they say and then they'll do a study where they ask for sex-work participants," she said, throwing her hands up.

The question of what role sex work plays in the lives of providers can also, conversely, encourage researchers to focus their efforts on specific problems. A wide variety of studies on sex work since the 1980s and 1990s has aimed to reframe sex work as a public-health intersection. I would argue that this constitutes a fourth paradigm that rejects both of the historical ideologies of sex-work researchers, but also curbs the discussion of contexts by focusing only on the public-health concerns associated with sex work. A "public-health" paradigm would leave questions of morality or agency aside and instead focus on "harm reduction,"[6] strategies that emphasize decreasing negative health outcomes for both workers and communities and that see sex work as a vector for intervention to stop or slow the spread of things like drug abuse or sexually transmitted infections.

Octavia's years of experience were expressed in an enthusiasm for sharing knowledge. She would shift back and forth in her seat, rocking like a school kid who could not wait to tell you a joke they had just learned. "If you look at it from a public-health perspective, those kinds of organizations, they're very clear that they're in favor of decriminalization, that it leads to the best outcomes." She scooted to the edge of her seat before adding, "There are plenty of medical journals that will tell you that decriminalization is the best method for addressing sexually transmitted infections."

Each of these four research paradigms reveals a different lens through which to view not only sex work but the society and culture that surround it. They provide the language to define a social concept; the methods to study it; and ultimately the solutions to address it. As society changes, so do its priorities, and the research of an era fits its time and place. The study of sex work is a relatively new phenomenon, but the evolution of society and the natural thirst for inquiry have tied sex workers and researchers together in perpetuity. This was a point that had not escaped Octavia. "You tell me, which job is more exploitative? Eh, probably both of them, like all jobs."

The Oppression Paradigm: "I Would Have Gone Mad"

The initial research on sex work began in the mid-1800s, when social workers attempted to protect women who had "fallen from grace."[7] Routinely, this research excluded the voices of sex workers, which complicated the possibility of discussing the agency and choices of providers, instead favoring the certainty that prostitution is morally corrupt. In F. Arnold Clarkson's early examination of the history of prostitution, the opening sentence presumes that prostitution is "an important problem for modern society,"[8] whereas William W. Sanger, in his extensive global survey of sex work, bluntly begins with the premise that prostitution is an "evil . . . so notorious that none can possibly gainsay it."[9]

Historic research into sex work was entrenched in its own cultural conceptions of the meaning and morality of sex, starting from the biased position that sex work clearly must be a social evil. And the issue of framing sex work from the perspective of the contemporaneous cultural climate is not a new one; for example, the Spanish conquistadors of the sixteenth century translated the Aztec word "*ahuienime*" as "prostitute" or "whore,"[10] which mischaracterized the *ahuienime* as sinful people rather than as "bringers of joy," as the Aztecs saw them.[11]

These earliest attempts at research were short on empiricism. But this did not keep the scholars of the time from recognizing the importance of investigating sex work. Even Sanger noted, "The day has arrived when the shroud must be removed; when the public safety imperiously demands an investigation into the matter."[12] However, even he registered that research is restricted by the social climate of its time. Addressing the polite social standards of the Victorian era, he wrote, "The world decided it an outrage against propriety to inquire into a vice which many secretly practice, but all publicly condemn."[13] Because of the inhibitions of propriety, early works like Sanger's and Clarkson's were limited to historical surveys or interviews with the judges, police officers, and priests who worked with providers, rather than the workers themselves.[14]

The moral panic of white slavery in the late 1800s was used frequently to disparage sex work, the prevailing narrative being that the women who entered sex work were being trafficked against their will—by means of the first advancement in technology to aid in the spread of sex work: the automobile. The Mann Act in 1910 hoped to ensure the protection of white women from sexual and commercial exploitation by making it illegal to transport women across state lines for the purposes of prostitution or debauchery.

The Mann Act received considerable pushback from American feminists, who had been keenly aware of the success of British activist Josephine Butler, who fought for workers' rights against mandated medical examinations.[15] Butler, and her American counterparts, argued that these types of laws maintained a double standard that held providers, but not clients, culpable for the business of sex.[16]

By the beginning of the twentieth century, a second wave of anti-prostitution activists had appeared. However, with the prevalent view of prostitutes as unwitting victims of white slavery, sex work slowly came to be viewed as a "social evil,"[17] wherein the influence of vice made women unable to steel themselves from the temptations of dance halls and bars. In this new definition, the saving grace would be that sex work would eventually be phased out as society became increasingly moral. Nobel laureate and settlement activist Jane Addams represents one of the first important people to frame the cultural transmission of sex work as a social entity, not merely as a personal moral failing.[18] Addams's book *A New Conscience and an Ancient Evil* took a more sociological view of sex work and attempted to reframe the focus on society as the generator of the titular evil, rather than the workers themselves.

But it was during the civil rights protests of the 1960s and 1970s that sex work reemerged as a social and political cause. By 1979, famed sociologist and feminist Kathleen Barry had taken up the mantle left by Jane Addams and refocused the oppression lens of sex work on the economic exploitation of women as the main social influence that traps women in "female sexual slavery" and the link between the overarching patriarchal structures and the perpetuation of sex work.[19] By the mid-twentieth century, prominent abolitionist feminists dominated the discussion on sex work and its relationship to broader society.[20] Abolitionist feminists opposed the "lies" that sex work can be work; that there is room for choice; that there are substantive differences between trafficking, "outdoor" sex work, and "indoor" sex work; that sex work is a victimless crime; or, paradoxically, that it is a crime perpetrated by women.[21] This viewpoint is firmly grounded in the idea that any objectification of women, either through speech or action, is to be proscribed. And the cultural and technological advancements of the mid-twentieth century readily illustrated these objectifications. Commercial improvements in film and video saw an increase in the production and distribution of pornography, which brought the specter of sex work off the street and into the homes of citizens.[22]

Abolitionists argue that sex work reinforces the patriarchy's oppression through two primary mechanisms. First, it trains women to normalize sexual objectification by men through repeated sexual abuse. Second, it maintains women in conditions of perpetual poverty.[23] Abolitionists contend that sex work is better understood as domestic violence than as work,[24] that it is paid rape,[25] or that sexual commerce (including trafficking and pornography) meets the legal criteria for torture.[26]

Carole Pateman's influential work *The Sexual Contract* lays the philosophical groundwork for the modern abolitionist movement. In Pateman's view, society was founded on the social contract, but this contract establishes benefits chiefly for men. Therefore, the sale of female bodies is both a tacit confirmation and a public affirmation of the existence of the patriarchy. In this view, the mere existence of sex work is a fundamental harm to women. And any efforts to improve the safety, health, satisfaction, or agency of providers is futile since it will not address the gender inequality inherent in a patriarchal society.[27]

But modern oppression-paradigm research falls prey to many of the same pitfalls as its historic counterpart, omitting the voices of current sex workers in favor of the voices of previous workers who were identified as "victims." Tellingly, when famed pro–sex work activist Margo St. James, founder of COYOTE (Call Off Your Old Tired Ethics, the earliest pro-prostitution advocacy group), requested to debate influential abolitionist Kathleen Barry at a conference on human trafficking in 1983, she was informed that Barry believed it would be "inappropriate to discuss sexual slavery with prostitute women,"[28] echoing Sanger's initial concerns over "propriety." The exclusion of active sex workers from abolitionist research and advocacy is still a prevalent feature, the rationale being that providers in the midst of working cannot fully grasp the depths of their exploitation. As one former provider turned abolitionist put this, "When I was in prostitution I would always say, 'I'm fine, I love what I do.' I had to, or I would have gone mad. . . . It is only when we get out, if we are lucky enough to get out alive, we can admit the hell, the horror of what was happening to us."[29] Yet this view undercuts the agency of providers who have chosen this work, infantilizing them, creating a feedback loop wherein active workers' perceptions and judgments about their own experiences are not considered valid unless they align with the abolitionist perspective.

For Kathleen Barry's foundational modern abolitionist study, *Female Sexual Slavery*, she spent four years interviewing victims and drew several parallels between human trafficking and sex work. From a theoretical perspective, Barry ardently contends, there is no difference between sex trafficking and prostitution. She claims that "street pimp strategies and goals do not differ significantly from those of international procurers" and that the differences between the two are merely semantic, in that one involves the crossing of international boundaries.[30]

The modes by which Barry identified potential research subjects and verified their stories are laudable, as she went to great lengths to confirm the authenticity of the interviews she was conducting. Nonetheless, in the oppression paradigm, the omission of active sex workers from the sample population, in favor of theorizing on social or legal implications, was thought to be not only acceptable but ideal.[31] In order to define sex work within this broader philosophical view, abolitionists had to change their language and terminology in an ontological sense to convey the victimization, dehumanization, commodification, and fetishization of women.[32] In the oppression paradigm, it becomes appropriate to cast sex workers as "sex slaves" or "prostituted women," reifying the social foundations of victimization and disavowing the personal agency of workers. In short, sex work is something that happens to women.[33]

The Empowerment Paradigm: "A Powerful Emancipator"

By 1973, COYOTE was working feverishly to reframe the conversation around prostitution, which had traditionally carried with it a negative stigma of sin, crime, and illicit sex, and instead explored new terminology and concepts, categorizing sex as work, choice, and a civil rights issue.[34] Soon, other groups began to form across the country, such as FLOP (Friends and Lovers of Prostitutes), HIRE (Hooking Is Real Employment), and PUMA (Prostitute Union of Massachusetts Association).[35]

Empowerment activists of the time rejected the word "prostitute" with its implications of shame, immorality, and exclusion, and instead introduced the term "sex worker" to convey the idea that the selling of sex was no better or worse than any other form of labor.[36] Carol Leigh introduced the term in the early 1980s.[37] Leigh was attending a conference on prostitution, and during the proceedings the panelists used the term "sex use industry," which made Leigh uncomfortable. She stated, "How could I sit amid other women as a political equal when I was being objectified like that, described only as something used, obscuring my role as actor and agent in the transaction?"[38] Leigh suggested the term "sex worker," as it "acknowledges the work we do rather than defines us by our status."[39] The embrace of the term "sex work" marked the beginning of a movement.

The empowerment paradigm defines sex work as a reappropriation of (mostly) female sexuality, giving workers the power to do with their bodies as they please.[40] This new empowerment paradigm was rooted in the same contractarian theory Pateman described, but is more in line with philosopher Thomas Hobbes's view, establishing that choice is the critical aspect to agency, and deterministic forces are not the central factor in the social contract.[41]

Based on this agentic contractarian idea, the empowerment paradigm argues that sex work is not inherently exploitative; it is merely the lack of choice and the reduction of agency that can make it morally questionable. Therefore, it is easy to draw parallels to other kinds of service work, such as physical therapy, massage, or counseling; as long as agency is retained, the work can be organized for the mutual benefit of everyone involved.[42]

Despite the early attempts by empowerment activists and academics, the issue of stigma has remained, both within culture and within scholarship. Even when empowerment themes are prevalent in research, bias against sex work can creep into the writing, such as the ideas that sex work is coercive or that it has a pervasive connection to human trafficking.[43] The empowerment paradigm attempts to embrace the idea that people choose sex work as they would choose any career, weighing utilitarian costs and benefits and selecting the most appropriate fit.[44]

In this paradigm, rather than sexuality being the sole province of male power, sex is contextual, and even when sexual experiences are outside the "norm," they are empowering to women who are taking part in the exploration of their own sexuality.[45] Both paradigms agree that within an oppressive patriarchal system, women's sexual role is that of procreation and service to male desires. However, empowerment scholars and activists claim that any venturing outside of that role is met with punishment in a patriarchal system, and is therefore an act of rebellion. Any expression outside of this traditional role is seen as a "powerful emancipator."[46]

Empowerment theorists agree with many of the tenets set down by radical feminist oppression theorists: that women as a group are more likely to be poor, underpaid, overworked; that they are victims of male sexual violence, yet state and federal policies abound to regulate women's bodies and not men's actions; and that their sexual activity is both criminalized and stigmatized outside of heteronormativity.[47] However, empowerment theorists attempt to differentiate their viewpoint by challenging the idea that sex in all its meanings and functions is defined by patriarchal authority. Sex, instead, must be recognized as a "cultural tactic" in an atmosphere of conflicts fighting for legitimacy, echoing the assertions of Michel de Certeau that in a culture all actions are political.[48]

Wendy Chapkis defines this version of feminism as "Sex Radical Feminism" in her work *Live Sex Acts: Women Performing Erotic Labor*, which describes sex and sexual activity as context dependent;[49] that is, perceived meanings can be interpreted by an overarching culture, a subculture, or the context in which the acts are happening.[50] This is different from broad, sweeping "sexual libertarianism," a universally positive view of female sexuality presented as the foil to abolitionists, insisting that sex and sexuality are not based in oppression but are the source of women's greatest power.[51] Instead, sex radical feminism reorients sexual behavior as a dynamic choice focused on individuals.[52] Moreover, affirming the work of the prominent third-wave feminist and author Patrick Califia, sex radical feminism takes the view that sex and sexuality should be rooted in the consent of those involved, rather than broad proclamations of their cultural harms (or benefits).[53]

The move to an empowerment paradigm included a spate of new autoethnographic writings in the form of "in the life" publications by sex workers themselves, emphasizing individual experience.[54] In *Good Girls/Bad Girls: Feminists and Sex Trade Workers Face to Face*, Laurie Bell begins by noting the false dichotomy between these two ostensibly separate groups. Evident in the writings of sex workers is a palpable stigmatization, wherein they feel pressured both personally and socially to conform to idealized feminist categorizations that exclude sex workers. Instead, sex workers, when given a seat at the table, implore unity between groups, aptly claiming that "feminism is incomplete without us."[55]

The close relationship between choice and empowerment was a persistent theme in the empowerment literature. In a more recent study of digital sex work, providers found increased independence and autonomy through the use of technology, as well as the desire to participate in cyberactivism. Digital providers also created and participated in digital social networks to disseminate information on safety, security, and other informal social resources.[56] Providers routinely told me that digital gathering places not only helped them collect information on best practices but also fostered a sense of community that supported them both professionally and personally.

The Polymorphous Paradigm: "Distal and Proximate Factors"

The polymorphous paradigm recognizes that sex work is comprised of various "occupational arrangements, power relationships, and participants' experiences."[57] Sex work is not a monolith, and often the cultural discussion surrounding it in the news, media, political debates, and public discussion simply acts to reinforce the stereotypes maintained in the two preexisting paradigms. However, there is a growing subset of scholarship that is dedicated to understanding how sex work is structured and experienced by workers, clients, and others;[58] this scholarship argues that concepts like "victimization, exploitation, agency, job satisfaction, self-esteem, and other dimensions should be treated as variables (not constants)."[59]

Sex-work research has tended to focus on women of low socioeconomic status, and the work is often compared to other menial or low-paying, exploitative jobs, like those of nannies or maids.[60] People move in and out of these jobs frequently, turnover can be high, and people's work experience can have a lot of variety. Similarly, sex work can be very adaptive and includes a collection of entry and reentry experiences. Providers become versed in new and different types of work as they progress through their careers.[61] New research on sex-work entrée suggests that this very adaptive ability has helped digital sex workers explore new intersections of technology and sexual commerce.[62] Once the definition of sex work is expanded to include a more nuanced view of its variety and types, people can have a clearer understanding of the "work" aspect of sex work.

Pornography

From the earliest printed literature depicting scenes of sex and sexuality, and the first forays into photography, which included displays of overt eroticism,[63] whenever a new technology is introduced to society, there is an erotic counterpart.[64] And when technology provides new avenues for sex work, there are always groups of people willing to capitalize on them.

In a 2009 overview on the state of scientific research concerning the Internet's impact on human sexuality, psychologist Nicola Döring found that there was still much we do not know about how and why people consume Internet pornography. Though a vast array of studies has investigated this, few have studied the criteria for habits of consistent use, desistance, variety, or preference. Similar to early studies on sex work, the initial research on the effects of online pornography tended to focus on negative outcomes, such as addiction, possession of illegal media, or the impact of poor role modeling. However, recently researchers have begun to acknowledge positive aspects of consuming online pornography, "such as increased pleasure, self-acceptance, inclusion of handicapped people, improved communication between sexual partners, in addition to the widening of traditional gender roles and sexual scripts." Yet, as Döring points out, these "have been the subject of only a few empirical or theoretical studies so far."[65]

Similarly, sociologist Sharon Abbot studied the motivations for pursuing a career in pornography by interviewing actors. She found that initial motivations for entrance, such as quick money or "being naughty," quickly fell away. But, achieving fame, growing accustomed to the income, or gaining membership in a stigmatized group can sustain actors' careers. Gender also appeared to make a difference, as Abbot found that men experience less stigma and more opportunity to move to tangentially "legitimate" work (such as editing or directing), whereas women were more likely to have previous experience in some form of adult entertainment, finding it easier to move between forms of, but not completely out of, adult work.[66]

In 2010, sociologist and feminist theorist Jill Bakehorn used limited participant observation by working as a production assistant on the majority of film sites she observed for her exploration of women-made pornography. She found that most interviewees approached their work as a form of activism; as opposed to mainstream pornographers, they paid attention to the representation of women and people of color in their work. Most interestingly, Bakehorn's study found an important middle ground between the oppression and empowerment paradigms, concluding that pornography, when handled properly, can be both empowering and a form of activism, while remaining critical of the shortcomings of the mainstream adult industry.

Escorting

Initially, explorations into sex work as an academic topic focused primarily on street-level survival-style sex work. The historical writings on "prostitutes," written from their community-purity standpoints, evolved seamlessly into contemporary scholarship, which focuses on the relationship between drug abuse and sex work.[67] This indoor/outdoor dichotomy is merely an extension of the previous research paradigms. Research on outdoor sex work emphasizes the social determinants that can coerce someone into sex work, whereas in research on indoor sex work, the choice to improve economic conditions and upward mobility was most often highlighted.[68]

Researchers Janet Lever and Deanne Dolnick attempted to shine a light on this dichotomy by combining statistics from the Los Angeles women's health risk study, which drew from a large sample of street-based sex workers, with interviews with indoor workers to examine the relationship between emotional labor and variety of sex work.[69] They found that indoor sex workers were "more likely to establish an ongoing relationship with regular clients," illustrating the need for a better understanding of these different varieties of sex work and methods to study them. Similarly, a research team from the University of Victoria reinforced the polymorphous paradigm in a study examining the predictors of entrance into sex work as compared to two other low-income occupations. The study found that deterministic factors like childhood poverty, abuse, limited education, and employment experience all played a role in entrance; but these factors do not always adequately explain the lived experiences of individual workers.[70]

Because sex work is so widely criminalized, physical safety from violence perpetuated by both clients and police officers has been examined by several researchers,[71] who reveal the victimization patterns of women who work on the street level and the coping behavior of this particularly vulnerable population. The research showed that though these women had an increased occurrence of victimization, a pattern of informal social-support mechanisms had been constructed to help them cope with the trauma of possible client violence, and a continuum of strategies could be utilized to minimize those risks.[72]

But violence is not limited to only street settings. Barbara Brents and Kathryn Hausbeck,[73] two sociologists at the University of Nevada, looked at the types of violence that can occur in legalized brothels—interpersonal violence against sex workers, violence against community order, and sexually transmitted infection as violence—and the policy implications of the legality of sex work in Nevada. Their research concluded that legalization brings about a level of public scrutiny, regulation, and bureaucratization that ultimately discourages violence and community disorder, while decreasing the risk of disease outbreaks among all people involved in the supply and demand of sex work.

Providers who spoke with me were not often enthusiastic about a lot of public or legal scrutiny, but did think that legislation that put agency in the hands of workers was always a good idea. But the question loomed large: How? The answer for the workers I spoke to was always connected to digital resources. The nested culture of sex work is the mechanism through which technology is adopted and adapted by providers, giving them access to new resources to live, work, and keep themselves safe.

Digital Sex Work

The Internet now plays a vital role in the business of sex—just as it does in all other businesses—reshaping it and creating new sets of questions that must be addressed if we are to better understand the needs of providers.[74] With its humble beginning of sharing pornographic images in early Internet chatrooms,[75] the Internet is being used at ever-growing rates to access and advertise all varieties of sexual services.[76] It increases exposure to clients while decreasing the likelihood of victimization or violence.[77]

With more people having access to digital spaces every day, all kinds of providers have come together, supported by the security and anonymity of virtual meeting places. They have created networks to share new procedures for improved security, strengthen their business, and modify existing sexual identities through digital communications with clients and peers.[78] But more broadly, the Internet's ability to share information, form new communities, and shape identity has made it a fundamental part of the experience of being human, so much so that the possibility of Internet access as a basic human right has been widely and seriously debated.[79]

One of the strengths of researching the relationship between sex work and technology is the abundance of data that the Internet produces. Researchers from the University of Leicester were able to sample from a population of roughly twenty-five hundred sex workers from the United Kingdom due to access to an online incident reporting system.[80] They discovered that most participated in "independent escorting," with the majority of the sample using positive descriptors to explain their work. Likewise, two researchers from George Washington University analyzed content from message boards to better understand the socialization of new clients. They found that new clients learned the "techniques . . . motives, drives, rationalizations, and attitudes" of their specific subculture through a form of digital social learning.[81] Researchers from Shippensburg University were able to analyze 2,925 female provider profiles from a popular advertisement website to assess whether sexual orientation could predict the amount a provider would charge to visit a client, termed their "in-call rate."[82]

Using data provided by the Internet is a relatively new research method. But its value lies in the fact that it can speak to nearly every aspect of the human experience. Researchers do not need to be limited to merely advertisements or profiles. Instead, personal blogs can speak to the emotional issues of workers, private digital gathering places can reveal how information and aid are distributed among members, and social media can be a mouthpiece for the concerns of the community as a whole.

The Internet helps researchers explore the quickly evolving relationship among sex work and emotional labor, stigma, and access to resources. Some have already taken advantage of this new data with empirical explorations of "sugar babying,"[83] web-camming,[84] and fetish modeling,[85] to name only a few research areas.

However, researcher and activist Angela Jones noted that though research into the relationship between the Internet and sex work is a growing area of interest, most researchers focus on the facilitation of sex work via technology, rather than the series of complex relationships between technology and sex work.[86] The providers I spoke with were always quick to note the utilitarian benefits of new technologies, but many pointed out that issues like protecting their identities, dealing with platform managers, or handling "time wasters" (clients who want to engage in a lot of talk before or between appointments, essentially monopolizing a provider's time) are issues that may have "real-world" counterparts but are far more prevalent in their lives now.

In short, digital sex work is a new frontier that encompasses more than web-camming or advertisements. Successful research into digital sex work should help the public understand the variety of workers' struggles and aid the global sex-worker community by providing the resources it needs—and, importantly, inform the ongoing debates on the best legal policies regarding sex work.

Trafficking

Trafficking is an extremely difficult topic to study, as the subpopulation is very well hidden and the definition of what constitutes "sex trafficking" can be elusive.[87] Western media often confuses trafficking in different forms of sex work with human trafficking,[88] but using a one-dimensional paradigm to frame sex trafficking hinders understanding by oversimplifying the issue. Numbers and values are often conflated, and the scale of the issue can be difficult to assess.[89] Rescue organizations can frame victim-survivor narratives as one-dimensional emotional pleas, thereby creating a form of "secondary exploitation."[90] As a result, trafficking is a popular topic for abolitionists, because it anchors their ideological definition of sex work in a grim, undeniable reality. But the blunt instrument of activism can sometimes obscure the nuance of empirical investigation and discovery.

Weitzer specifically addressed the need for evidence-based research about sex trafficking.[91] However, the landscape surrounding sex-trafficking research is filled with methodological difficulties and unsubstantiated claims. There is a dearth of historical empirical research, which makes it difficult to measure changes over time, since the data is "simply not available for drawing macro-level conclusions."[92] Further complicating the issue are unreliable "official" statistics on the number of people being trafficked, specifically into the United States. Some estimates claim that the numbers are as high as "hundreds of thousands," but several meta-analyses put the estimates closer to 3,817 to 22,320, while still admitting, "There is enormous uncertainty about the national scope of the problem."[93]

All this being said, forcible sex trafficking is a major concern and an abuse that no person should ever have to endure. But the first step in understanding any problem is gathering valid and reliable data to analyze and present empirical solutions. The workers I spoke to were all concerned with the heartbreak of trafficking, but wanted to emphasize that their work was different from the abuses suffered by trafficked people. And when trafficking researchers focused on workers rather than victims, it muddied the understanding of trafficking, complicated legislation, and confused the public.

Taken in their entirety, these studies represent a small portion of the ways in which researchers are attempting to empirically investigate the diversity of sex work. The polymorphous paradigm, with its more precise, yet inclusive, definition of sex work, helps to limit broad generalizations, while providing a more accurate picture of the "constellation of occupational arrangements, power relationships, and participants' experiences" that constitute sex work.[94] And these studies contain a range of methodologies that can be used to gather and analyze data according to the needs of the population. As sex-work research has evolved, scholars have recognized this assortment of sex-work styles and have attempted to suggest policies and interventions that address their specific research population and not perpetuate the cultural ontology of sex work.

The Public-Health Paradigm: "A More Elite and More Specialized Audience"

Beginning in the 1980s and carrying through the following decades, there was a trend in research that rejected ideological labels, both positive and negative, in search of answers to concrete issues. Rather than scrutinizing theoretical explanations for the sources and persistence of sex work, researchers focused on the physical and material concerns of the sex-worker communities. Their efforts mainly focused on the issue of HIV/STI transmission,[95] personal mental health, and information-sharing mechanisms. In a public-health paradigm, sex work would be viewed like any other employment demographic. In a dramatic shift away from the broad moralizations presented throughout the history of sex-work research, the public-health paradigm recognized sex work as a social reality and approached it from a harm-reduction framework.[96]

HIV/STI

To examine the connection between HIV/STI rates and sex work, public-health researchers have developed precise definitions of all of the various factors that contribute to this relationship. Not only is it important to understand what constitutes "sex work" or "high-risk behavior"; even cultural and social contexts must be understood for a harm-reduction analysis. Some countries and cultures where sex work is legal or decriminalized and carries less stigma allow for access to health and social services, or provide some semblance of economic security. Conversely, sex work in criminalizing countries can be used as a survival technique, and stigma and legality can limit access to vital social resources. But most countries are not on either side of these extremes, instead existing somewhere in the middle, making generalizations about individual harm-reduction policies difficult.[97]

Though providers are frequently the focus of HIV/STI public-health campaigns, there is evidence that workers do not have higher rates of either HIV contraction or HIV transmission than the general public. A study published in the *Lancet*, one of the oldest and most well-known medical journals, presented strong evidence that street-level sex workers show an increased risk of injection drug use that can contribute to the contraction of HIV/STIs.[98] However, these studies focus mainly on specific locations and varieties of sex work.[99] In the several public-health studies where providers are examined more comprehensively, reducing the selection bias of drug use and treatment, sex workers tend to have lower rates of HIV/STIs than the general population. The key mediating variable that lends credence to the public discourse on sex workers infecting the "general population" is repeatedly shown to be drug use.[100]

Because of this association with drugs, the sex-worker community has often been labeled a "bridge" population, where sexually transmitted diseases make their way into the general population.[101] However, there is scholarship to support the idea that sex workers, concerned with their personal health more than that of their clients, can act as educators encouraging safer-sex practices and normalizing condom use as part of the culture.[102] For example, in the mid-1990s, sex workers organized and led "John schools" in response to the AIDS epidemic to educate both clients and the public on safer-sex practices.[103]

Finally, the idea that sex workers are a monolith continues to be inaccurate. Sex work includes a vast array of people and behaviors, and providers have multiple roles in families, mainstream employment, social institutions, and community organizations that modify their relationships to public-health issues.[104] So, in short, though public-health interventions often focus on sex workers, there is a litany of other factors that play into the effectiveness of these policies. Unfortunately, though, stigma can play an important role in hindering public-health initiatives to reduce HIV/STI transmission because sex workers rarely disclose their occupation.[105] Ironically, many providers withhold this information because revealing it could deny them access to much-needed medical or social services. Some workers I spoke with told stories of hiding their occupation from their landlords, their employers, or even their own doctors for fear of either rejection or reprisal.[106]

Research by Jacqueline Comte from Université Laval points out that the history of sex-worker research is often skewed in the direction of easily accessible or visible populations, and as these populations change, so does the focus of the scholarship.[107] The majority of research focuses on street-level workers, or those caught up in the criminal justice system. Though studying these populations is valuable, the research is not necessarily generalizable to sex work as a whole. And sadly, it is this very research that continues to contribute to the cultural narrative on sex work and its connection to stigma, deviance, and social degeneration.[108]

Stigma

A great deal of research has focused on stigma as one of the main concerns of sex workers.[109] Famously, sociologist Erving Goffman identified stigma as "blemishes of individual character perceived as weak will, domineering or unnatural passions, treacherous and rigid beliefs, and dishonesty, these being inferred from a known record of, for example, mental disorder, imprisonment, addiction, alcoholism, homosexuality, unemployment, suicidal attempts, and radical political behavior."[110] In essence, according to this definition, stigma links perceived poor moral quality and specific behaviors or statuses. An example would be the perception that someone smoking a cigarette must not care about their health. An increasing amount of research is focusing on the outcomes associated with criminalization and stigmatization of sex work and how they shape working conditions, health, and access to resources for workers.[111] There have been several examples of how stigma and sex work intersect in the public-health sphere. Studies have shown that providers often face abusive language, breaches of confidentiality, humiliation, and outright denial of care in public-health spaces.[112] And, stigma has a profound impact on the mental health of workers. When providers feel they are only viewed as a vector for HIV transmission and other public-health problems, this can further ostracize them, driving them underground and negating targeted public-health policy initiatives.[113]

Though stigma is a common theme both among providers and in the research, many workers have pointed out that they are able to emphasize personal agency when attempting to balance the negative effects of stigma.[114] Jacqueline Comte points out that "in fact, many sex workers are torn between the feeling of pride they have regarding their work and the feeling of guilt that dictates to them that they should not be doing such work."[115] Instead, when the research lens shifts and focuses on the privileges of Western middle-class workers participating in indoor/independent sex work, most providers report that they freely chose to work and have never been forced by a pimp or third party.[116]

Furthermore, research on the privilege of middle-class workers has highlighted the positive aspects of sex work, including the ability to "make money faster, enjoy more free time, and be self-employed."[117] Though some workers' privilege can help insulate them from certain stigmas, external structural issues still remain. Negative stigma towards sex workers permeates every level of social interaction. Workers across cultures, nations, and socioeconomic statuses all name stigma as a major concern.[118]

But importantly, this stigma can also affect identity. Chosen careers affect personal perception, and people construct communities, sharing information and social networks, around both chosen and unchosen groups.[119] And it is these digital meeting places and virtual communities that can help redefine many of the stigmatizing terms and definitions that make up the overarching cultural conversation around sex work, replacing them with language composed by the workers themselves. In this regard, sex workers have used Internet technology to negate stigma, increase community, and reaffirm their identity.

Psychological Health and Identity

Concerns over disease transmission or stigma can also have a profound impact on the mental health of providers. Additionally, researchers have looked at the relationship between the stigma associated with sex work and how it affects the perceived identities of providers, their self-esteem, and the specific coping mechanisms they use to manage the presentation of self. The research has found that many women workers shape their identities according to cultural, political, and religious constructs of "femininity."[120]

Yet, the emotional labor of keeping both work and personal identities hidden from people not "in the know" can be difficult.[121] And often providers would justify this additional effort by associating it with more conventional ideological goals, such as earning money or providing for loved ones, both to minimize the impact of stigma and to rationalize the additional emotional labor. Workers were reframing these behaviors to better fit mainstream values in an effort to alleviate some of the mental stresses.[122]

Though physical threats to the health of sex workers can be more visible, emotional risks weigh just as heavily on providers.[123] Living with the uncertainty of disease outbreaks and potential violence can have an adverse effect on the mental health of many workers.[124] Though this aspect of sex work has, until recently, been underrepresented in the literature, attention to it signifies an important move forward in understanding the variety of ways sex workers manage complex social interactions with few options for help from conventional social institutions.[125] Further study on the role Internet support groups and anonymous digital gathering places play in providers' access to mental health services and community support could help augment the current trend in caring for the mental health of sex workers.[126] In the current research, "traditional" concerns around violence are often being replaced by concerns over the strains of added emotional labor and how digital communication can intensify client interactions, possibly increasing the risk to providers.

Many of the issues surrounding psychological health and identity have shifted dramatically in the last few years with the spread of the Internet.[127] Elizabeth Bernstein's work in the famous Tenderloin District in San Francisco examined the creation of intimacy with clients in bounded settings, and identified a transitional moment in the history of sex work in which sexual commerce adopted new forms of technology and transformed itself to address concerns over business and security. "For many indoor sex workers, it has become easier to work without third-party management, to conduct one's business with minimal interference from the criminal justice system, and to reap greater profits by honing one's sales pitch to a more elite and more specialized audience."[128] Bernstein's research catalogued some of the first instances of the use of the Internet to ensure safety, not only from troublesome or dangerous clients but from police interaction. In the late 1990s and into the next millennium, sex work saw a major schism between the providers who had no access to technology and those who did and could thereby move their business from the public "outdoor" sphere to the private "indoor" sphere, away from police foot patrols increasingly concerned with "public order." "With the advent of the Internet, solicitation of sexual companionship via advertisements allowed escorts to maintain greater control of their occupation and clientele."[129]

Following the 1990s, access to technology only increased. However, this increase in security and agency has had unforeseen consequences for the nature of personal and professional sexual identity.[130] Though the Internet is an extremely useful tool for exchanging information, its real value lies in the perceived quality and authenticity of relationships.[131] An "authentic" interaction between client and provider can introduce interesting questions about personal identity into sex-work research. Some more recent studies have observed that the early proliferation of technology fundamentally altered the nature of the commercial exchange between worker and client. Bernstein's concept of "bounded authenticity" describes how within this movement, clients were no longer, necessarily, looking for sexual mechanics but instead were seeking a specific "girlfriend experience" that emulated a legitimate relationship.[132]

Clients are already using new modes of technology to rate and assess the value and performance of sex workers, and often "authenticity" is a desired metric.[133]

Participation in pretty much any sexual commerce can result in stigmatization, and even when there are efforts to reduce these stigmas, policy-based conversations can lead to "othering" and can further erode a person's perceived identity (more on this in chapter 5).[134] Finally, participating in these commercial exchanges that feign intimacy can result in a broad range of experiences; and even counterfeit intimacy can result in interpersonal bonds that both parties involved must negotiate and manage.[135]

Harm-reduction initiatives that happen at the policy level, aimed at benefiting sex workers as a whole, represent a macro-sociological approach to risk reduction. And these initiatives can take the shape of decriminalization campaigns, community-based child-protective organizations, or educational programs.[136] But by and large, providers acknowledge the public-health risks of their work and respond by fostering communities that have strong ties to activist organizations, unions, and charities in an effort to put as much power in the hands of workers as possible.[137]

Conclusion: "I'm Largely Optimistic about It"

Octavia took a swig of water. "For most of history, it happens in the ivory tower and then things get whittled down through a series of pipes till, eventually, it reaches people." She set the bottle down and smiled. "And I think that now, with the rise of more independent media and the sex workers' rights movement, we're seeing it go from the research to the people faster, and people are able to access information they would not have been able to before."

To say that the four historic paradigms described in this chapter represent the evolution of sex work would be reductive. The many kinds of sex work—including a variety of workers from different backgrounds, varying levels of public and private displays, and early adoption of technologies—are the true legacy of the "most ancient" profession. Sex work has never been a monolith, and when both culture and scholarship focus on specific aspects of the work, it is a declaration of society's specific viewpoints, not a description of reality per se. To say that modern workers who use the Internet progressed from street-level work to their current position would deny the history of privileged classes engaging in sex work. Courtesans and "kept women" throughout history have used race, class, and technology to aid in their work and maintain that privilege.[138]

Instead, these four paradigms should be understood as attempts to place certain kinds of sex work within the cultural contexts of their time and place. In other words, the techniques, drives, motivations, rationalizations, and attitudes surrounding sex work are framed by the culture that they are a part of.[139] Often, sex work can be used as a mirror to reflect the broader social attitudes about gender, sexuality, morality, technology, and public health. These viewpoints are framed by the paradigms of the day, and though scientific questions of validity and reliability are important, scientific paradigms cannot answer questions of "truth." Thomas Kuhn noted that though recognizing paradigms as frames for the production of knowledge was important, they do not necessarily result in a greater truth. "We may . . . have to relinquish the notion, explicit or implicit, that changes of paradigm carry scientists and those who learn from them closer and closer to the truth."[140] Instead, these four paradigms of sex work must be better understood as lenses that focus on what society, in its time and place, has deemed worthy of study.

I asked Octavia what she thought about the future of sex work and its research, and she laughed in spite of herself. "You know, I'm largely optimistic about it, just because we're getting more people speaking directly to their own experiences and giving voice to others." She had a few reasons to feel encouraged for the future. Some were specific, like the work of activists who are changing the perceptions of sex work, but there was still a ways to go. "The sex workers' rights movement is helping people conceptualize it. But, for most people . . . it's broached through a lens of like, 'This is a social ill that in an ideal world would not exist anymore.'"

Mostly, though, Octavia was optimistic about the next generation of young people. She felt that they were interested in learning more about the complexity of sex and gender rather than casting aspersions on people different from themselves. And she recognized that technology was an important part of facilitating these moves by fostering community in digital spaces. Many of these young people take the very aspects of themselves that are being stigmatized and instead defiantly proclaim them. "They say, 'This is the thing that could be held against me, and instead I'm going to be openly proud about the fact that it is a part of me.' It's a feature that's probably always been among young people, but especially today," she said with a smile. "I think that it's easier to find each other, it's easier to find terms to grasp onto, and to find community and support. I love young people these days."

2

Digital Style and Symmetry

"There's So Much More That Can Be Done"

Nicole's back was covered in an elaborate lace tattoo—a colorful design that had taken six years to complete. "I'd need to heal for two weeks and if I'm doing a gig where I'm rolling around on a bar floor, that doesn't really work. It was like one or two sessions a year," she said, raising an eyebrow. "It started out as coverup and now it's my entire back. It is just done—it's done! I never have to do it again. And that's really the best part because it's horrible!" She shook her fist with mock indignation and an oversized frown, but then laughed. "All this is going to tie into our talk. I made a lot more money this year than I have in the last . . . I don't even know how many years."

A twenty-nine-year-old cam performer, Nicole saw her online presence increase because of the COVID pandemic of 2020. Before the lockdowns, her career was diverse. She did in-person, local and touring burlesque, custom and fetish videos, and web-camming. But after her city shut down, she had to move her business 100 percent online. "I picked up another day on cam and just like made a lot more money," she said.

Like many of the more fortunate people during the lockdowns, Nicole was able to both continue to work and save money since there was inevitably less to spend it on. She decided to spend her newfound free time and income to get some old artwork covered up.

"I had the money suddenly coming in. I wasn't spending it on costumes or touring and traveling. And I wasn't needing to take [time away] to heal. I wasn't doing anything anyway, so I was like—well?" she said, scrunching her nose and giving a little shrug.

Behind her, sheer curtains were draped over the wrought iron frame of her bed, and Christmas lights slowly alternated colors behind her head. "This is basically like the cam room slash burlesque closet because it's this tiny little room," she said with one hand extended, motioning around, then hooked a thumb over her shoulder. "And then we have the room over there, which is like the storage room slash where I was teaching yoga."

Nicole would cam four days a week from her apartment to supplement the loss of her other gig money and would often come up with clever and interesting ways to keep people engaged during her cam shows.

"You're basically a television show. Especially because most of the things that make me money aren't necessarily sexual. I could just so happen to be naked, drawing pictures that are terrible and making a lot of money from that. You know, like a surprising amount of money from sitting in my underwear just drawing bad pictures."

Providers come in a variety of styles, and digital providers are no different. Most cam providers I spoke to worked from their own homes. But some worked for a studio or performed in other spaces. And though the specifics of how they did their job varied, Nicole told me that most cam providers followed a basic process that the various sites facilitate.

Performers have public and private rooms. The public rooms are like lounges where patrons come and text chat with each other and the workers. In these public spaces, patrons are not necessarily charged any money, but they can still tip performers, and providers (depending on the rules of the specific site) can choose to perform in the public spaces for these tips. Alternatively, cam performers could take specific clients into private sessions, where the user is charged a premium to be "alone" with the provider, and the performer splits the fee with the platform site. Opinions were mixed on which was a better strategy, and workers tended to gravitate towards the methods that worked best for them.

Nicole's years of experience became apparent when she explained how she runs her cam site. Her expressive blue eyes are always fixed on the camera, her voice clear and direct. "I liken camming to being a carnival barker or like a gameshow host," she said, spreading her hands. "You gotta amp people up to like compete against each other in the room. If you can get a tip war going in the chat room—it's ridiculous."

Some providers liked to hold the attention of small groups of people, whereas others preferred to rely on a stable of dependable regulars. Nicole had a combination approach in which she liked to keep her free chat interesting and fun and encourage people to tip her, but also had a series of regulars.

> So free chat is where anyone can log in with their account; they don't have to spend money; they can log on and talk to you. And see whatever you are doing. It's really tip-based. So you know, I'll set a goal where it's like this many tokens for topless and then once they hit that goal I'm sitting there topless chatting and anybody can—no matter if they spent money or not—can come in and talk to me topless.[1] So like when people are skipping from room to room, they see something like that and go "what the fuck is this girl doing?" And, like, they stay and watch and they're having a good time and tip you.

There's so much variety in what Nicole and other providers do that she often had to dispel misconceptions. "Nobody really knows what it is until I sorta explain it. I had a friend who was talking about me be like, 'Well she's a porn star.'" She bobbed her head back and forth, "No, that's not quite true. It's not quite untrue. There are times where it is just solo porn. But that's few and far in between."

Regardless of the different styles of work, providers were careful about upholding security procedures. Whether workers were in-person or digital, their work processes and concerns mirrored each other's. "Everybody's a little different but mostly similar. . . . Mostly it's kinda the same just pick and choose," Nicole told me. This "the same, but different" distinction was a common theme with providers; though client interactions or security concerns were not precisely the same provider to provider, there was a form of "digital symmetry" wherein workers used similar tactics to solve parallel problems.

She explained that she learned early on to take her safety seriously, even though there was the separation of a screen while she worked. "When I started, someone [told] me to like never tell your clients things like you love them, or like never pretend like, 'Oh you're my Internet husband' like that was a thing," she said, shaking her head, "and management was like, 'Don't do that because that's how you get stalkers.' The people in the industry really want you to be safe."

Though Nicole took the advice that was offered, the relationship between providers and the sites they use can be complicated. Though providers often named ease of use and autonomy as their big concerns when dealing with platforms, sites gain reputations as being easy to work with or exploitative—too micromanaging or unconcerned with the safety of providers and other users.

The Internet has become essential to a huge portion of sex work, but questions about its role in more than facilitation are still emerging. How is increased communication altering the expected relationship between worker and client? How is the Internet creating and enforcing hierarchies in new digital communities? How are the concerns of noncontact digital workers similar to those of in-person workers? What role will platforms play in the future, and what level of responsibility will they bear for clients and providers?

As for Nicole, she wanted a fine balance of security and freedom. A good digital platform should make her life easier while not feeling intrusive. She propped her chin in her palm and nodded. "I think people still think I spend more time masturbating on cam than I really do. Or that I make more money than I really do, 'cause again I don't spend a ton of time doing it." She spread her hands, palms out. "I'd rather have the free time to just have my shit taken care of."

Digital Frames: "That Sense of Community"

Jordan, a thirty-five-year-old escort, took a pull on her vape pen. "A lot of my day is spent on technology. Even though I'm not actively advertising, I'm still posting Twitter updates . . . or I'm replying to emails," she said, waving her hand in front of her face. "A lot of clients are texting now."

I asked if she used the Internet for anything besides interacting with clients. She took another pull and nodded. "To connect with other workers. . . . I probably wouldn't have stayed in the industry for so long because I wouldn't have connected with other people and learned from them," she told me. When I inquired about those different relationships, Jordan thought for a moment, adjusting her vintage square eyeglasses, and added that they weren't just with workers and clients; technology facilitates most of her communications about her business. "My tax accountant. My people that host my website. My friends that work in the industry that I might choose to do duos with. Even my friends in the industry that I don't physically work with but we might share referral links. There are all these indirect ties. . . . There's a lot of connections. And people may not realize those connections."

Providers used the Internet and its variety of associated technologies so much that they were folded into the narrative of their lives—as unremarkable as remembering to wear shoes or ride in a car. And the term "unremarkable" is literal. When someone says, "I woke up and checked my phone," it is unnecessary for them to describe the various steps involved in gathering the news, social media, and messaging applications they will be looking at. In its short history, the Internet has become an ideal example of James Spradley's concept of "tacit cultural knowledge"[2]—information so engrained in the lives and culture of people that it can often be overlooked. The phrase "check my phone" has come to include a variety of actions. And the Internet has so seamlessly integrated itself into society that often its use is incorporated into our behaviors without any expressed description.

These new technologies were adopted early and widely because their effectiveness was undeniable. In her book *Social Movements and Their Technologies*, Stefania Milan used the myth of Prometheus and his emancipation of fire to describe the liberating effects of technology on populations.[3] This "stealing the fire" to describe new technological advancement and its adoption by groups of pioneers includes the forerunners of digital sexual commerce. But the question of who gets to use this technology looms large. Prometheus stole fire from the gods, but who are the gods of the twenty-first century? Privilege as a largely invisible construct can shed some light on the issue of who gets access to resources, for example, how groups of people use the Internet to gain knowledge and solve problems. Both the US Census Bureau and the United Nations report that developed nations have higher rates of high-speed Internet usage than developing nations, and within those developed nations, whites, both as households and as individuals, use the Internet at higher rates than anyone else.[4] In 2000, half of all Americans used the Internet, and that number has increased to nine in ten Americans in recent years. But when these figures are examined across race/ethnicity, there is an appreciable difference between consistently high rates of usage by whites and growing rates by people of color.

The digital divide between races has steadily closed in the last decade, with 87 percent of African Americans using the Internet in 2018, up from 38 percent in 2000. This same trajectory is mirrored in Latinx Americans as well. But though percentages of Internet usage have consistently increased in the last decade, no group has displaced whites as having the highest percentage of Internet users.

Part of the social construction of race inexorably ties racial status to economic status and, by extension, class status. Rates of Internet usage by socioeconomic status (SES) also mirror those of racial differences. In the year 2000, 34 percent of individual adults who made under thirty thousand dollars a year used the Internet, contrasting with 81 percent of people who made over seventy-five thousand dollars. Similarly to the racial digital divide, the gap has been shrinking in the preceding years, with 81 percent of low-SES people using the Internet and a striking 98 percent of those in the high-SES category doing so. Though this digital divide is closing, again, it is worth noting that no group has higher usage than those in the over-seventy-five-thousand-dollar category.[5]

The Internet embodies the benefits of a robust investment in public information infrastructure. The "birth" of the Internet can be traced to the early 1960s, when the Defense Advanced Research Projects Agency was fixated on the idea of sharing vital research information between laboratories at UCLA and Stanford.[6] The central concept of the Internet was that these different networks (either technological, geographical, or social) could be separately designed and could interface with the whole in a self-prescribed way. This, in turn, would encourage a high level of autonomy by individual users and networks. This high level of autonomy and customizability explains precisely how and why sex workers became such early adopters of Internet technology.[7]

By the mid-1990s the Internet found its way into the homes of many everyday citizens. But the connectivity of the Internet was also accompanied by new and increasingly available audio and video technology that aided nonexperts in being able to become self-made writers and producers of original content.[8] The reason the Internet has had such an immense impact on human society is its ability to adapt and thrive with these new technological advancements.

New products routinely have an Internet-connectivity component. "The Internet of Things" was coined in 1999 to describe the network of items and objects that have a digital element,[9] creating a common ecosystem where control can be centralized and facilitated via the Internet. Researchers predicted that in a few short years the Internet would usher in a new paradigm of "nomadic computing and communications,"[10] wherein a central hub (like a powerful personal computer) would be replaced by smaller mobile digital devices able to access information and computing power, rather than supplying it (similar to a smart phone). This nomadic paradigm is evident in the lives and businesses of sex workers who use mobile Internet technology to attract new clients, heighten personal security, and interact with online communities.[11] However, there are still differences between the access and resources of mobile users as compared to more traditional computer users.

The rise of mobile Internet technology has helped narrow the technology gap in many developed nations, but digital inequality is still a difficult topic to address. Researchers and theorists have warned about simplifying the issue into merely "haves" and "have nots."[12] Instead, it is important to acknowledge that technology as a resource is a complex balance of access, skill, and expectations. Two researchers, Wenhong Chen and Xiaoqian Li from the University of Texas, found that mobile Internet technology is complicating these discussions further.[13] It raises questions: Is a mobile phone's browser equivalent to that of a desktop? How do wired and wireless speeds compare? Technology, and specifically access to the Internet, can be measured in many of the same ways most social resources can be measured, by focusing on "the addition of skills, attitudes, and types of engagement in current measures of inclusion, beyond the initial indicators of access and infrastructure."[14]

Since sex workers are a stigmatized group, their use of the Internet for building community is arguably one of its most important roles. Prior to the Internet, fostering community for providers could be difficult. And, of course, context played a major role in determining whom a provider could communicate with. Researchers from the University of Sunderland spoke to gay male providers and found that they had a difficult time creating community because sex work is so stigmatized. Virtual spaces for gay men could largely mimic their in-person communities, but when being a provider was added in, digital groups were the only place workers could seek community.[15]

The providers I spoke to echoed this sentiment as well. Mandy, a twenty-nine-year-old escort, started by "doing research" online. She read articles, subscribed to blogs of current workers and advocates, and tracked news stories about providers. Mandy said that she was completely on her own, and the only place she had to turn to for the support of a community was virtual meeting places. "I think the most important part technology plays is connecting with other escorts, and connecting with the broader community. All the advice on how to get started, and how to screen and things to watch out for, all the advice was online. The reason I joined [the message boards] in the first place is I felt really alienated and alone when I first started. So joining [the message boards] and getting to vent, and talk to other sex workers, that was the biggest benefit for me. Having a support community."

The crucial point of this new "digital model" is that providers recognize the advantages of Internet-based techniques over the traditional "indoor/outdoor" models of sex work and their commensurate norms. Sex workers create new ways of doing business simply because they are more beneficial than traditional models, reducing the risk of detection and increasing both anonymity and autonomy. But providers also point out that the Internet is valuable for more than advertising and communicating with clients. It also helps foster community and provide resources to a stigmatized group. Sex work as a culture has no tradition. Providers adopt techniques when they are effective. When those new techniques are accompanied by new technologies, providers adopt those as well—and then share with each other what works.

Jordan pointed out that communicating with other workers and feeling like a member of a group helped her feel less alone and provided support when she needed it. "[It's] that sense of community where it's not so socially isolated or so stigmatized if I know other people within the industry who, you know, have different paths in life too."

Digital Styles: "That's What They Come Back For"

Nicole tugged at the shoulders of her black sweater. "I'm getting like a lot more return clients that are just there to spend money and a lot of what I'm doing [is] jerk-off instructions."

"Oh?" I replied.

"It's literally just telling them what to do, how fast you move with their hand, what to do with their other hand, breath work like literally yoga. Where I'm like 'deep breath in, deep breath out' like all of this," she rolled her shoulders back and inhaled deeply.

I arched an eyebrow and opened my mouth to ask the question she had already begun to answer.

"So yeah, I would say like it's very close to like—is this sex work? Yes, it's absolutely sex work. It doesn't feel like it sometimes; it feels really strange and stupid and goofy."

Providers engaged in all categories of work: escorting, sugaring, dominatrixing, camming, fetish modeling, and burlesquing, to name a few. But even within all of those categories, different workers adopted different styles. Some escorts pursued more personal relationships with clients that could last years, whereas others preferred to only interact with clients once during a set appointment. Style could also include demographics and descriptors of providers. For example, some of the workers I spoke to identified as BBW (big beautiful women), a specific substyle in escorting and pornography, as well as other adult categories. Style included anything the providers wanted to accentuate about themselves, the services they were providing, or the method of delivery.

Sociologist Dick Hebdige pointed out that style carries with it a heavy significance—that often a subculture's stylistic choices are "a struggle for possession of the sign which extends to even the most mundane areas of everyday life."[16] The "humble objects" that inhabit our lives can have many meanings, and the way a person or subculture chooses to present itself is

> open to a double inflection: to "illegitimate" as well as "legitimate" uses. These "humble objects" can be magically appropriated; "stolen" by subordinate groups and made to carry "secret" meanings: meanings which express, in code, a form of resistance to the order which guarantees their continued subordination. Our task becomes, like Barthes',[17] to discern the hidden messages inscribed in code on the glossy surfaces of style, to trace them out as "maps of meaning" which obscurely represent the very contradictions they are designed to resolve or conceal.[18]

Hebdige famously used the example of French novelist and political activist Jean Genet being in possession of a "dirty, wretched object" that proclaimed Genet's homosexuality to the world:[19] a common tube of Vaseline found in his nightstand. These "secret meanings" are common in the world of providers.

Workers who describe themselves as "next door" are expected to have not only a certain visual aesthetic but also a set of behaviors indicating a more laid-back attitude and an easygoing experience. The workers who described themselves as "BBW" frequently discussed being shamed for their weight or suffering from low self-esteem until identifying as BBW in advertisements and interactions with clients framed these qualities in a positive light, often increasing their confidence.

Janine, a thirty-year-old escort, shifted on her couch, getting into a more comfortable position. "I was just home bored on a Saturday night, and so I was like, 'If I put up some racy ad'—I just wanted to see what kind of responses I would get, and of course, within an hour, I had like two hundred emails." She flipped her long blonde ponytail over her shoulder. "There were a lot of dick pics and guys offering to come over, and I was inundated with responses, and a lot of them were really graphic, and I was like, 'Okay. So this is what it might be like.'"

She explained that, due to being BBW, she initially thought she should not be charging a lot of money for an escorting gig, but later realized that the qualities she had been shamed for were something to accentuate in this new subculture.

> I thought that I needed to keep my prices lower because I was a BBW, and because I do not fit society's conventional standard of beauty. Little did I know that there are men with various specific tastes. I mean, I guess that works for any type of woman, whether Asian, or super tall or super short, or for any body type, there's a man who fetishizes it. . . . When I first got started, like I knew that I was very competent as a lover, and not just from sheer experience, but confidence—it's like before, I had always tried to minimize my thighs, and like emphasize other parts of my body so that maybe he wouldn't notice that I'm not really skinny, and I was always trying to make myself smaller and look thinner, and blah, blah, blah. Then, once I started marketing myself as a BBW, it was like these men, this is

what they want, so I had to start to emphasize that in a certain way, and be able to take off my dress and stand there in my underwear and feel 100 percent confident. Whereas before, I would have been terrified, and that was a big, big change for me. A really big change.

All of this points to the fact that the images, descriptions, and messages all shared by workers and clients include a variety of Hebdige's "secret meanings." And, as providers use more and more digital resources, the variety and style of services has become almost infinitely adaptable. Regardless of what a client is seeking or what a provider would like to offer, the subculture finds a way for them to communicate.

These developments have not gone unnoticed by scholars. The use of the Internet has helped promote physical safety, foster better wages, and assist workers with advertising, screening clients, and building their reputation.[20] The variety of uses of the Internet would often make for interesting stories from providers. Lucy, a twenty-seven-year-old cammer with an absolutely infectious laugh, explained that, similarly to Nicole, she liked to be as creative as possible when she was performing.

"It's almost like a television show. So, like here's the board that I use. People get prizes!" She motioned to a giant corkboard square with brightly colored three-by-five cards thumbtacked in a grid. She squinted and grinned while she explained that clients can win a prize and that is what keeps them engaged. "There's a chance someone will get one and that makes it addictive for them." She laughed in a cartoon villain voice and tented her fingers. "Like this one is—" She stretched out the words as she pulled the card from the board and flipped it over. "Slutty angler fish or twenty spanks!" she said, holding the card in the air. "You can actually see it right now!"

She jumped up and grabbed a tangle of blue nylon fabric and plastic hoops. "Its mouth is really big and you can see my tits so sometimes for fun I get naked and I open it." She pulled it over her head and started to shimmy it past her shoulders; the giant mouth flapped and a tiny LED light dangled from the top of the costume. I broke out laughing like a kid sneaking comics into church, covering my mouth with my hand and waving with the other.

"That's so incredibly creative and hilarious all at the same time!" I laughed.

"Most people love it," she said, flapping the giant blue mouth with white felt triangle teeth. "But I've had people be like 'This is the worst show ever!' and leave. If they could've slammed the door, they would've!"

The style of a subculture can be expressed in a lot of ways. Many providers had creative and inventive ways to advertise themselves and offer different services. A lot of in-person providers specialized in what they call the "girlfriend experience" (more on this in chapter 4), but many others dealt with specific fetishes or other unique requests, within the bounds that workers were comfortable with.

Isabelle, a thirty-four-year-old escort and fetish model, glided through her kitchen in impossibly high heels. She had a stable of clients interested in her fetish: fur coats. She smiled and told me, "I got into an argument with a dude . . . and he sent me my first fur coat." She moved to her closet and produced a long mink stole and draped it over her shoulders. "[He] was telling me all about fetish stuff and I was like, 'Oh, this is even more awesome than like straight naked people.' And I was like, 'Oh my god, I am totally in love.'"

She enjoyed the ease of digital work as compared to her escorting gigs, which took more time and effort. She wanted to continue doing work with her fur coats, but there was a problem. "It's not really profitable, so I branched into more general—like I just discovered the pedal-pumping fetish."

I held up my index finger and arched an eyebrow. "Wait, what?"

She nodded and smiled, "Pumping, like—cranking cars and pretending they don't start and revving the engines."

"So, like, an old-timey engine with the crank on the front, am I getting this right?" I asked.

"No no, it's like pumping the gas pedal," she continued. "I have this friend that's a mechanic and she owns like a vintage car," she said with a shrug. "I got so much positive feedback and then I posted clips, like I made pretty good money. The guys are really hungry for fresh pedal-pumping clips."

Most of the providers I spoke with were escorts, meeting with clients in person after some introduction and initial screening. But in-person work required almost as many digital resources as camming and other virtual work. Noreen, a thirty-two-year-old escort with bright blue eyes, was one of the few providers who waded into sex work by slowly increasing her exposure to more of the work as she felt comfortable. She started as a topless waitress and eventually became a full-service escort. She described her work as "curating chemistry between me and the client."

"Like, first off," she said with a smile, "music in the work room. Most importantly, some disco," she laughed and did a little dance in her chair. Similar to Mandy, referred to above, she described how the versatility of new technology can provide her with more than music during appointments. It aids in advertising, ensuring security with new clients, and building community with existing providers. "It's a really useful tool that I find revolutionized the efficiency at which I can communicate with my clients, and I can check them, and do my own safety and security [screenings] as well."

Most of what providers used these advances for boiled down to autonomy: the ability for workers to make choices for themselves and design solutions to their own problems. Ultimately, regardless of what kind of sex work providers participated in, the common theme was "give providers the power." They knew how best to utilize it and where it was most needed.

Kelly, a thirty-three-year-old escort, was a rare case among the providers I spoke to. She had been a provider since she was nineteen, but was coerced into it due to a friend who exploited her when she was addicted to Xanax. But things changed for her when she decided to use digital resources to give herself more agency. She broke away from her abusive situation, but continued to do sex work. She said that the Internet insulated her from people who wanted to take advantage. "Huge, massive, very, very important. If I didn't have my website or I didn't have a way to screen people before I met them, I would be relying on other people to do that for me."

But Kelly's concerns were not only about autonomy around security. She also saw digital resources as a way to legitimize her work—because not only has Internet technology spread to more people around the globe, but its ease of use has also increased. "It's so much easier to give yourself an online presence, and then you gain a bit of validity, and say like, 'Oh, that's a real person who's doing things, and it's legitimate.'" And most providers said that the spread has helped workers, even to the extent of saving lives. Vivian, a twenty-nine-year-old escort who had started out a decade prior doing escort agency work before she became

100 percent independent, said that the Internet "actually saved lives. It's got women off the street, we're able to verify [clients] now. We can communicate, so work like mine can exist. It's integral to my business model." The most common response when I asked workers about how the Internet, digital communication, and virtual communities played a role in their day-to-day lives was that, without these resources, sex work would be more dangerous and they would not have considered being providers.

And Nicole offered her clients something unique: an experience that made them feel connected to her. "What I'm doing that other people aren't doing, aside from having like my yoga voice, is I'm looking directly into the camera and making eye contact." She demonstrated by looking into her camera as we spoke and her bright blue eyes lit up the screen. "That's what they come back for . . . I'm looking at them and talking to them." Providers had a variety of experiences communicating with clients and interacting with their community, but this belied the fact that, overwhelmingly, providers had similar concerns about the process of doing their jobs. Even though, on the surface, workers appeared to be doing very different work, there were far more commonalities.

Digital Symmetry: "I Can Make Those People Go Away with a Button"

Yvette, a twenty-year-old cammer and escort, sat cross-legged on her bed, her purple and red hair standing out against the burnt orange walls behind her. She was explaining that security for webcam performers was different than for workers who meet clients in person. "It's less applicable to the kind of work I do than it is to people who escort, but—." She took a thoughtful pause. "Sometimes people who order customs or people who want [video chat] shows will try and get free things out of us."[21] Yvette sold private video chat shows in which she performed one on one for clients over her webcam after having been paid an agreed-upon amount. She had a young face that looked younger thanks to the Pikachu sweatshirt she was wearing but wore a serious and thoughtful expression.

I've had people who are like, "All right give me a [video chat] show, I will [send] you the money." And they have websites that are built to make it look like someone [sends] you money, but it's really just a fake email. You get a thing that looks exactly like you've received money from so-and-so. . . . And I learned that the hard way. . . . I've learned to check my account, I've learned to make sure that, before taking a custom order or like doing anything at all for anyone, that I receive payment first because people are so quick to want to cheat you out of things. But other than that, because I'm not meeting up with these people in person, like some other sex workers are, there's a little bit less of a stringent screening process. It's more like, "Are you going to pay me? Okay, you are? Fine. I'll do this for you."

Screening clients, as a security tactic, lends itself to escorting or almost any "in-person" style of sex work (more on this in chapter 6). This is the case because screening's first and most prevalent purpose is to ensure the physical safety of workers. But the Internet has created new situations, and with new advantages come new challenges. When providers discussed screening, it was almost universally defined as gathering information on prospective clients that workers interact with.

Digital workers also screen, yet they noted their screening implicitly rather than overtly labeling it as such. Gerry Anne, a twenty-six-year-old cammer, was an animal lover. She sat in front of a huge, bubbling fish tank inhabited by turtles, and it would not have seemed odd at all if she had suddenly broken out in song. She said that though webcam work had different risks than in-person work, there was still the possibility for harm to workers. "Obviously, doing cam-girl stuff is safer in terms of a lot of stuff . . . but I mean, there's still certain risks involved because you never know when somebody might try to stalk you online, or somebody might try to find your personal information, or whatnot. Plus, I mean, harassment even over the Internet can be just as bad as harassment in person."

What Gerry Anne described was a kind of digital symmetry, wherein the type of work was different but the concerns were similar to those of her in-person counterparts. When in-person workers interacted with prospective clients, if those clients were deemed dangerous or otherwise unsuitable, the worker ceased contact and refused to see them. Digital workers do something very similar when interacting with clients and making judgments about their behavior. If workers did not want to interact with a client, that person could be personally blocked or reported to the website and could have their membership revoked. Blocked members on websites were able to still use the site but were unable to view or interact with the particular worker who blocked them. Reported users may be kicked off the site permanently if they are deemed dangerous or abusive. In short, digital symmetry is the common elements that transcend the style of interaction, be it in-person or digital. Gerry Anne continued by describing her criteria for blocking problem clients.

> Anybody who ever said anything vaguely threatening or harassing got blocked. They weren't allowed to see my site anymore. And if I thought that they were enough of a risk I might report them. Like, if they made any kind of death threats or anything that might be considered a threat of violence. . . . Anybody who made any kind of fat-shaming comments, they were blocked. I don't need that kind of shit. Anybody who started asking too many questions about what I did in my—for lack of a better term—civilian life. . . . I didn't let anybody know where I lived. . . . I do allow friends to come to the site, because hey, if they wanted to see it, why not? Plus, it's always nice to have some friends to talk to if I ever got bored.

Often, digital workers would use screening measures to judge whether the sites they used were suitable. If digital workers were satisfied with the platform they were using, they usually pointed to the fact that they were able to curate their workspace and were satisfied with its level of screening and control.

Deborah, a twenty-five-year-old cammer, always laughed with three low, rhythmic, chuckles, as if she were about to pull a prank on the rival campers across the lake. She used screening metrics to judge the quality of sites she would agree to work for. She wanted to know that the websites she used contained specific protocols or features that ensured the safety of her personal information and financial security. For example, cammers would often work for a hosting site that would host their videos and give clients a platform through which to pay providers. Clients would attempt to find ways to see workers' media for free by paying to gain access but then canceling the payment at a later time. This was known as a "charge back," Deborah explained.

I will not work on a site that does charge-backs. Because of that, I don't have to screen clients at all. Charge-backs are when somebody has filed a credit card fraud. They say to their provider that this was a fraudulent charge. What's interesting about it is that there are plenty of sites that do charge-backs. But, statistically, charge-backs are challenged by the business, and the business wins 80 to 90 percent of the time. So, when a business is taking a charge-back from a girl who just did an hour-long cam show and now can't pay her rent, they're probably getting that money back, and not having to pay her share. So I will not work a site that does charge-backs. I determined that at eighteen.

Deborah needed assurances that a client would pay for the services she was delivering. Furthermore, she had to trust that the website processing the payments and holding her vital information was protecting her in a satisfactory way. Screening contains an element of trust that is transferred, and in this way digital workers' concerns mirrored those of the in-person providers. They needed their identities to remain hidden and required assurances that clients could and would pay for services.

The other main factor digital workers screened for, beyond safety and guarantee of payment, was the ability to pay. Nicole drank approximately seven cups of coffee while we chatted, and she told me that she feels responsible for her loyal clients. After all, they are paying her rent, so she owes them "some happiness." Part of that responsibility is making sure her clients are satisfied. But, if a client decides to become a problem, "I can make those people go away with a button."

Nicole used a web platform where providers were able to examine the profiles of the user client base. Clients were then ranked using a two-part criterion: first, a point system, and then second, the amount of money associated with their profile. Workers are "tipped" during shows via tokens that are commensurate with money. Workers collect tokens and then exchange them for payment from the website. Clients can request to have a private show with cam performers, which then costs additional tokens depending on the pay scale the worker sets. At first, Nicole was going to describe how she does not screen clients, but then realized it was something she did so routinely that she did not notice.

Well I was gonna say you can't [screen], but you can. [The site I use] has—you click on their name. . . . You can see how many points they have. The higher the points the more they have spent on [the site]. Some of them can figure out how to hide those things so they stay hidden. So those are the people you're like, they can either have a lot of money or none at all. Sorta like a poker face, you talk to them and figure it out. . . . So, if there is a basic member talking to you, you can click on their name and see they have been on the site for three years and never bought tokens. You can kick them the fuck out because you know they are not going to [purchase a private performance].

Nicole could gather information on clients in real time as she interacted with them, and the screening-by-profile approach helped digital workers avoid time wasters, increase the value of their work, and avoid problem clients, similarly to in-person workers. Though escorts often took longer to screen prospective clients, cam workers still used the same metrics, just within the microcosm of the website.

Both kinds of workers still had to be vigilant about the validity of the information they were receiving and used individual tactics to bolster their confidence in specific decisions, as when Nicole described that "some of them can figure out how to hide those things" and she had to use a "poker face" to gauge whether they were a good client.

If someone is asking you for a private show you can click on their name and there is a section where you can write notes about them. My notes are usually their name, how much money they spent, and what they wanted and their attitude. Sometimes my notes are "don't do this one if you are in a bad mood." You know, if you're in a bad mood he'll get the fuck on your nerves. He'll spend a lot of money when you really need it, go for it, but just know he will try your patience. So, I screen them myself. And you can always end a show at any time. . . . So if you start to get in a certain mood, and it's always better to log off or just not log on at all if you're in a bad mood.

Though digital workers said that their concerns were different from those of in-person workers, the risks and responses were strikingly similar in both cases. Digital workers still face risks, both physical and emotional (more on this in chapter 5), and their response was to attempt to preempt any problems with payment or abuse through screening. Workers also applied these tactics not just at the level of clients but also at the level of administrators.

For workers who only provide digital services, screening was most often described in terms of seeking the most profitable or reliable clients. Providers did note that the possibility of danger exists, but they were more concerned with keeping agency in their own hands. Workers interacted with technology frequently, and it was their early adoption of new technologies that informed their calculations on the risks and rewards of sex work.

Digital Behavior: "I Take Care of My Own Battles"

Charlene, a thirty-five-year-old escort with a penchant for tidying up and accusatory red fingernails, had a "no bullshit policy." "I just ask for the work information and that's it," she said while wiping dust from a bookshelf. "And if a guy can't produce that, or if he gives me any lip about it, fuck him, he's out." She hooked her thumb and pointed it at the door. Charlene liked to be the one in charge of situations, and that included digital interactions. But she was always on the lookout for ways to both cut costs and keep choices under her control. "Some girls say, 'Hey do background checks' and stuff like that, but that type of stuff costs money and sometimes it can be inaccurate. I follow a few groups and blacklist sites and stuff like that, and some names are pretty popular and kind of ring out to you."

Finding ways to control the flow of digital interactions was important to providers. There were a variety of ways to use the resources at their disposal, and no one way was the "right" way to do things. Instead, workers were always looking for the methods that worked best for them, and then sharing that information with the wider sex-work community.

Academic, attorney, and political activist Lawrence Lessig in his book *Code and Other Laws of Cyberspace* argued that there are four main avenues for regulating behavior on the Internet: laws, architecture, norms, and markets. Lessig starts with the argument that laws are the most formal way to regulate behavior—but not necessarily the most effective.

Laws

Attempts by governments to regulate behavior on the Internet often start with laws, but instantly these attempts run into problems, the main one being that the Internet knows no borders. Laws can be passed to regulate what citizens can and cannot do in online spaces in their home states and countries, but governments are unable to pass laws that apply to people in other countries. Charlene pointed out the difficulty of enforcing laws on digital organizations when she noticed that hosting a site in various countries can provide you some level of protection against the laws of each of those individual nations. She noted this in the court case she has been following. "When it comes to Internet laws, when you set up a server overseas and whatnot," she said, "you're pretty much safe. In the past, when [there are] servers over here, in the US, and they come in and shut you down, it's a wrap, and suffer the consequences."

Of course, this has not stopped governments from passing legislation in an attempt to regulate sexual commerce on the Internet. In the United States, the Stop Enabling Sex Traffickers Act (SESTA) and Allow States and Victims to Fight Online Sex Trafficking Act (FOSTA) are suites of acts passed in 2018 to regulate online sexual commerce in an effort to quell sex trafficking.

Timaree Schmit, journalist and doctor of human sexuality, has written extensively about the intersection of sex work and society. I had the opportunity to speak with her about how legislation can impact the lives of providers.

"The issue is, anytime there are laws passed relating to sex work, they're almost always punitive," she said, blowing on her cup of coffee. Legislators have often approached social issues through a lens of policing and punishment, rather than more measured attempts to look for root causes or listen to the voices of people impacted by legislation. Stock responses can be used to justify ineffective or even harmful legislation if the intent is agreeable. "They're going to say that it's a quality-of-life issue or they're going to say that the police need to get involved because that's the way you get those ladies drug treatment." She shook her head. "The police are literally just like the customer service agents of the government." But, she said, a lot of this kind of legislation just reinforces the status quo for the kinds of policy initiatives that receive public support. "Part of this is—if you have a hammer everything's a nail," she said. The problem of dealing with almost any social ill (especially in the United States) is an overreliance on police. "They still treat the police as the only means of doing any sort of social work," she said with a sigh.

She explained that the bills essentially approach the issue from similar angles. "There's two different bills. One was the House, one was the Senate, and what they purport to do is combat human trafficking." However, the tactics for attempting to stop trafficking essentially prohibit any form of sex work. "It holds websites responsible for any sexual services that were sold on their sites. So because the West doesn't distinguish between sex work and sex trafficking, any sexual services that are sold are legally considered." Timaree said that these efforts can have a chilling effect on sites, increasing corporate censorship. "Basically, the websites just like stopped allowing sexual content and sexual communications, and narrowed the images that can be shared and stuff like that, because they did not want to be held liable for sex trafficking."

In the ensuing years since the passage of the bills, there has been evidence that FOSTA/SESTA has actually hindered efforts to stop trafficking. Scholarship by a consortium of researchers from the United States, Europe, and Australia found that the laws had cut two ways. First, they had heightened the vulnerabilities of all workers, by driving sexual commerce underground, more so than before the laws were passed. Second, and more striking, is the failure of these policies to appreciably impact trafficking victimization.[22] Timaree agreed, saying, "It's not just going to affect traffickers. It's going to impact anybody whose services are remotely sexual, including a variety of legal occupations."

Recently, Timaree wrote an article on the wide-ranging impact the bills are having on providers of all stripes, pointing out that often these kinds of policies impact the most vulnerable first. "[Their] insidiousness is in the unintended impact of silencing already marginalized groups: sex workers were affected most severely—as well as queer people, artists, educators and grassroots justice groups that fought for sexual freedom."[23]

Architecture

Another way in which behavior can be impacted in digital spaces is with what Lessig calls "architecture." This tactic uses the digital limitations and user experiences of specific websites and programs to encourage certain behaviors and discourage others. Most people are aware of the various algorithms that calculate what we see on the Internet on the basis of things like search histories and preferences. Examples of this kind of behavior management would be financial sites not allowing users to send money for sexual activity or prohibiting certain words or phrases that could indicate a sexual transaction. In a now-infamous move, a major social media site attempted to comply with FOSTA/SESTA by creating an "automated content moderation algorithm" to identify possible sexual images that flagged everything from raw chicken to vomiting unicorns as sexually explicit material.[24]

Providers spoke frequently about the frustrations of this kind of informal behavior control. They would often find ways to circumvent it by using applications and programs for things they were not intended for. Emma, a twenty-one-year-old escort, laughed as though she had just pulled off a bank heist every time she described one of her tactics. She found a dating app intended to help women who were going out on a first date avoid assault. "You put in [your] emergency contacts and you have the app open and if you feel in danger, you click the button. It allows you to either make a phone call or send a mass text message to your contacts saying, 'I need help, can you come get me here or can you call me to get me out of a situation.' It will actually send GPS coordinates to your contacts if you say, 'Come get me here.'" Providers repurposed technology in a lot of different ways. Applications that cater to privacy were always welcome additions. Janine, a thirty-year-old escort, communicated with clients via an encrypted messaging application. "It's just an app you download on your phone," she said, picking up her phone and pointing the screen at me. "You create a username, and it's just a text messaging service, but it anonymizes you and you can send pictures and video." She flipped past screens full of little square icons. "And it deletes things after a certain volume of messaging has transpired," she said, clicking the sleep button. "So that's what I use for almost all of my clients."

Osu, a twenty-seven-year-old escort, found a hotel application that is marketed to businesspeople who may need a temporary office space for a few hours or just a place to freshen up. "Basically, you could book four-star hotels by the hour," she told me. Of course, to say that these applications are being repurposed may be an exaggeration. Osu pointed out that these developers probably know how their applications are being used, but are swift to act shocked when questions are raised. "I feel like they know what they're doing. I know a couple of other girls from the agency I used to work with that used [it], and all their accounts got shut down. So we can't use [it] anymore," she said, tossing her head back.

One of the pieces of architecture that seems to be changing is the Internet's proclivity for risk taking. Before laws like FOSTA/SESTA and others, the reputation of the Internet was as the new "wild west," an undiscovered frontier. But as both governments and society at large are beginning to ask questions about the liability of activity on the Internet, the norms around what can be considered "safe" content are beginning to trend in a more puritanical direction.

Norms

Most social behaviors are managed through norms. People enter new situations, observe how others in a group or community behave, and then use those others to model their own behavior. One of the most fundamental ideas of social science is that people learn from those around them. No one would deny that the Internet can be at times an openly hostile place, but one of the norms of the Internet, with its semi-anonymity, is to foster rude and antisocial interactions.

Nicole discussed how she was able to combat trolls in her chat rooms by using the very client community they were part of against them. "If a troll comes into the room, like, my room will attack them so hard. Before I even get the chance to! And I just—damn," she said with a chuckle. "Even if somebody comes in and seems a little awkward. Sometimes people that aren't necessarily trolling, come in and say something and my room jumps on them and I have to like, 'Dudes, woah! Back off, we're scaring people away here, we don't wanna do that. Like, he wasn't being shitty, just—cool.'" Providers pointed out that they were able to subtly shape most interactions with community members. And though both the worker and client were often aware that this was happening, some providers saw it as an additional resource to keep in their back pocket. But most, as Nicole suggested, keep a close eye on it.

Mona, a forty-six-year-old escort, who did not want to "get to seventy-five and regret I didn't try something," said that she knew a few clients whom she could ask to step in, but that she would rather handle things on her own. "I mean, I'm sure they wouldn't mind if I called them and said, 'Hey, this person's bothering me. Can you be my knight in shining armor?' But no, I've never felt the need for that. I take care of my own battles."

Markets

Lessig notes that economic markets are the final way to manage behavior in digital spaces. Obviously, providers are trying to maximize profits and minimize both labor and risk. And there are both commercial and noncommercial aspects of the Internet, but it would be hard to argue that even the noncommercial aspects are not affected by economic concerns. Because of this, workers were often cautious when it came to implementing any new website or application as a step in their work process. Any new element could be an intervention point where someone might sap some of their earnings. Providers did not like it when third parties took any of the money from their labor. Charlene saw that money was the key factor in the way the American criminal justice system treated people. She threw her hands up and then covered her face with her palms, incensed that websites that had collected millions, if not billions, of dollars from workers could simply flaunt the laws, whereas the workers have to deal with the consequences. "How are [these sites still] masquerading these sex terms and these ads and they're still posting? And how are they still making money off of these ads? [That site] doesn't want to explain to the government that they set up a mirror site for us to pay for the ads and the payment still goes through to them. And that's still how they're making money with credit cards and things like that."

People's behavior is managed in a variety of formal and informal ways. Your mother teaches you that it is rude to pick your nose; your friends teach you the rules of a new sport; the government passes a new law.

These same formal and informal systems extend to our digital lives. But providers, both as individuals and as a culture, are an adaptive group. They routinely are early adopters and share their information with the broader community.

Workers endure and find ways to insulate themselves from restrictive laws, change and adjust the architecture of technology to better serve their own purposes, tactfully navigate subcultural norms to subversively guide interactions, and diligently guard their resources. Providers echoed time and again that the best way to encourage both good processes and good outcomes with sex work was to keep the choices in their hands.

Conclusion: "I Have Room to Just Play"

Nicole stretched to grab her coffee cup on the end table, then shifted back to sit cross-legged on her bed. "I would say that the weirdest part about my job is this weird split personality. You know, that doesn't really exist but in a way has to exist, like that chicken or the egg thing." She took a sip from her mug and thought for a moment. "Does my personality come from my job, or does my job come from me being this person? There's this real sense of surrealness, you know? Life feels really strange sometimes because you don't really know what person you are."

Providers balanced a lot of precarious concepts when it came to working with digital resources. Additional communication with clients and participation in digital communities meant that workers were spending additional time putting on their work style and persona. Workers used digital spaces and resources in a variety of ways. All of them acknowledged that the Internet served utilitarian purposes, and providers universally praised the increased communication, facilitation of community, and availability of information from other workers.

And this led to the realization by many providers that though their work could be categorically or stylistically different from that of others, they shared the same overarching concerns as workers in other parts of the field. But providers who used digital resources took this access a step further and created a variety of ways to interact with clients and foster community. They could also gather and share information quickly and effectively, which put more agency in the hands of the workers themselves, allowing them to deliver services in the ways they felt were the safest, for both their personal and their financial safety.

"It's a more valuable source of entertainment than they would realize," Nicole said. "There's a girl who's a ventriloquist, I've seen mimes, I've seen aerial artists. Even if you aren't interacting at all, someone is going to tip you a dollar," she said with a laugh.

Nicole reached and put her coffee back on her nightstand. "Some of my best routines have been on cam. Because it's just that night like the energy is right, and I'm feeling it." She felt that camming gave her the opportunity to be creative, because of the freedom it provided. "But really, me on cam is just like—there's so much more that can be done because I have room to just play."

3

Entrance

"The Classiest Shit to Ever Hit This City"

Isabelle strode through her brightly lit kitchen as the summer sun spilled through the windows. Her radiant blonde hair bounced as she grabbed ingredients from cabinets and shelves. Isabelle was one of the first providers I spoke with, another worker having referred me to her. She told me that she had a really full schedule, but could make time to talk while she cooked some dinner. She bustled about preparing her meal and recounted how she had first become interested in sex work.

"I thought my boss was being a total creep, you know? Running around with younger women. I thought he should just get an escort and he'd have less drama and I didn't have any moral restraints against it." She had been working for an in-home medical business caring for disabled clients, but her employer had no compunction about harassing female employees or brazenly cheating on his wife.

A shrill squawk pierced through the room, cutting her off, and she paused from selecting spices and looked up.

I raised an eyebrow and asked, "Is that an African gray parrot?"

Isabelle's hand clutched her chest and her eyes widened. "Yes!" she exclaimed. "You know birds?"

"African grays are pretty vocal. They're hard to miss," I responded.

"He's my life-partner bird, Stewart! How do you know about African grays?"

"Well, in high school I had a friend who had an African gray parrot. It was really smart, could say a ton of phrases. It would recognize me every time I'd come by."

At thirty-four years old, Isabelle has been a fetish model for over a decade, and had begun escorting about four years earlier. She paused and smiled broadly, seemingly pleased with my comprehensive bird knowledge. I left out the part where that damned bird would try to bite me every time I walked past.

She continued with her story, all while shuffling components on the countertop. Isabelle had been living with her boyfriend in the city, but their relationship was already in bad shape when a string of events opened her eyes to her need for a change. Her story, like so many others, was complex. Life does not follow a simple A-to-B narrative structure. But, it is safe to say that it all started when her bird died: "Looking back I could see this guy was isolating me from my parents, isolating me from my friends, isolating me from everybody, he's taking my money. You know and things were escalating and I had gotten another bird at that point. I woke up on Christmas Day and this bird was dead and in retrospect I think that this douchebag killed my bird."

The stress of an abusive relationship and the loss of her bird were coupled with a job where Isabelle was secluded most of the week and spent the majority of her time alone, so she began spending more time chatting on fetish forums on the Internet. She found that she enjoyed fur coat modeling—and that the community of fur enthusiasts aligned with things she found attractive and erotic. "There's just something, mentally, about the luxury of fur coats. I grew up very poor and very white trash, so it's the biggest compliment that people can give me when they think I'm one of their sheltered white chicks. But yeah, furs just have this luxury association with them and so guys started sending me furs, so the fur fetish is my specialty."

The providers I met all had their own unique pathway into sex work. Whether they were escorts, webcam performers, fetish models, or something else, all the people I spoke with told stories about their decision to enter sex work and the circumstances that accompanied it. And each of their tales had three elements in common.

First, providers found themselves in a situation, or "turning point," where sex work became a viable option for them. This could be a move to a new town, a sudden need for money, or a situation that opened the door to a preexisting interest in sex work. Second, they passed through a phase of information gathering. Most explained this in terms of Internet research, an overarching cultural knowledge of the existence of sex work, or information from a friend or acquaintance. Lastly, providers often tacitly acknowledged their own personal privileges. Most of these stemmed from their race, middle-class background, or access to high-quality education.

It is worth noting that the processes described by most of the people I spoke with differed greatly from the processes described in much of the previous scholarship on sex work entrée, in two ways: in their descriptions of a decisive agentic process, and in the lack of negative determinants like drugs or violence.

As Isabelle explained her process of entrance, she was shaking her head and staring intently into the pot she was stirring. But, as with so many other parts of her story, her recounting was fast and nonchalant. I waited for her to take a breath and then asked her to walk me through the way she got started. What was her first session like? How did she figure out how to advertise herself or find clients, for example?

She took a pause and scrunched her mouth into a quizzical pucker, put her hand on her hip, and said, "I put an ad on Nearmart" and gave a thoughtful nod. Then, with a spark of realization, she added, "A guide to Internet escorting [had] just come out! Where [a current worker] was blogging about it." Isabelle's eyes narrowed and she smiled. "I was going to be somebody else. So luxurious, so sultry. I'd be the classiest shit to ever hit this city."

Turning Points: "How I Got into It Is Super, Super Embarrassing"

Vivian loved to laugh her way through a story. She was wrapped in a light gray v-neck sweater, and her bright smile was framed by a proscenium of vivid red hair. She grew up traveling the world and as a twenty-nine-year-old escort, described herself as "the little red-headed girl who speaks Japanese," since she had spent a large part of her childhood in southeast Asia.

Her sentences ran together in long elastic strings with an upward snap at the end of every breath. "It's ridiculous, you can laugh at me," she would say with a wry smile. She was recounting how she had started as a provider and could point to the moment when the door of sex work opened as a possibility. These "turning points" were prominent in the stories of workers I spoke to, and often shed light on how and why they entered the field.

"Turning points" are not a new idea. In the 1980s, the prominent sociologist Glen Elder Jr. began exploring how major life events can change the "trajectory" of the people they affect. His major work, *Children of the Great Depression*, codified the theory of life course as a way to explain how structural, social, and cultural contexts can impact an individual's life. Similarly, two prominent criminologists, Robert Sampson and John Laub, spent years unraveling people's life histories and the way life events and contexts related to different forms of deviance. The research identified that people tend to follow "pathways," which they defined as highways people travel over the course of their "age differentiated life span."[1] However, people can take a turn onto a new path via a "turning point," a transition that changes their life course.[2] These turning points come in a variety of flavors—a new career or relationship, a major life accomplishment like earning a degree, or the birth of a child—but can also be influenced by broader social factors like a person's age, race, or class. For Vivian, her turning point was meeting a friendly dog in the park.

It was Vivian's first time away from home. She had moved to a new town to start college. As she was strolling through the park one day, she saw a familiar face, a dog that looked just like her own family pet. After she played with the dog for a few minutes, its owner introduced himself, and after some polite conversation, he offered to introduce Vivian to his girlfriend. She let out a self-conscious little laugh as she told the story of meeting the girlfriend at her apartment, where she and a few friends ran a provider co-op. Vivian went on to describe a large foyer with adjoining hallways that led to bedrooms. There was a circle of couches around a central steel coffee table, where women were lounging and chatting, taking phone calls. "His girlfriend had a whole bunch of hot friends there that hung out in lingerie. Guys would come and go and they had candy bar cell phones on the table and envelopes with money,[3] but I never really put two and two together, because they weren't wearing big shiny red boots, and they didn't have gold earrings."

Things like changes in social networks can lead to new life experiences and situations,[4] and those changes can often be described as turning points that are part of people's life trajectories. When researchers look at turning points in conjunction with sex work, they most often do so to examine the trajectories of providers who are leaving the industry.[5] But these turning points are a suitable way to describe the entrance processes of workers as well. This is the case because turning points, as a theoretical concept, are adaptive in the same way that the providers I spoke with adapted to new situations and opportunities. Furthermore, this adaptation, according to Sampson and Laub, includes a crucial intermingling of cultural contexts. In essence, when people are presented with a turning point, their response is a complex interplay between the choices they currently have available and their own cultural contexts. For Vivian these contexts included moving to a new town, being on the lookout for new friend groups, and viewing these situational elements through the lens of her age, race, and gender.

When providers discussed their entrance process, many of them described turning points that opened the door for them to consider the option of sex work. The most common turning points described by providers were moving to a new area, a need for money, or a situation that opened the door to pursuing a broader interest in or curiosity about sex work in general.

Vivian let out another laugh. "I really love my job, but yes, how I got into it is super, super embarrassing," she said, and shook her head as she smiled. "I actually hung out [at the apartment] for three months without even knowing what was going on. I bought my own lingerie to fit in with them. I know, I know, it's embarrassing. I was nineteen!"

When Vivian started escorting, it was with this new group of friends, before she set off on her own and developed an independent business model based on a small group of stable clients and monthly allowances. When I asked her about the role finances played both in her entrance and in her business, she mentioned that life changes always require resources and that money is, obviously, an intrinsic part of any exchange, even ones based on relationships. "Money has always been a part of sexual interactions, whether you want to admit it or not, and this comes back to a feminist ideology." She looked at me and cocked an eyebrow while she gave a little shrug. "What's the difference between being a stay-at-home wife and a long-term mistress? I know that's offensive, but whatever."

Obviously, money has benefits; it solves problems. Famously, Robert Merton,[6] the twentieth-century sociologist, developed an entire theory around the strains caused by lack of access to the means of achieving the cultural expectations of wealth and status. Merton also noted that money is a nearly universal symbol of status. So, in short, whether people desire status, security, or stability, money becomes an integral part of this equation. This was reflected in the stories from workers. They would often identify money as necessary to solve an immediate problem, but would also emphasize that other work options were often available but would not realistically provide enough money to sustain them.

Isabelle was struggling to get away from an abusive partner and wanted to make a better life for herself and her birds, and though she had a job assisting disabled people that she found quite rewarding, she was torn because it did not provide a good quality of life. "I made more money in a week [escorting] than I made in a month working with mentally challenged people," she said with a plaintive sigh. A friend then agreed to help her get established after she had spent a few years dabbling in fetish modeling and cam work. "He came up one weekend and he was like, 'Oh I really hate to see you struggling with money, you need to get back on your feet. Why don't you start escorting? I can write a big review and I'll help you with your site.' So that weekend, he paid my rent for that month and for the next month and he got me caught up with like a [stage name] and I made a really sexy website."

Money, social status, and legitimate opportunities were often intermingled in the stories of the people I spoke to. Providers noted that the money they made initially solved problems and was then used to maintain a comfortable lifestyle. Previous research has noted this as a cycle that can trap workers within the world of sex work, unable to leave because they have become accustomed to making large amounts of money.[7]

However, most often previous research has paired these concerns with things like drug abuse or a lavish lifestyle.[8] Though these associations were noted by several workers, Osu, a twenty-seven-year-old escort, described the profitability of sex work as a failing of capitalism and institutional job opportunities, rather than a problem with sex work itself. "This is the only line of work where I feel like the monetary benefit that I get out of it is worth the actual effort that I put in. . . . Every other job, every corporate job, even in school, I've felt like I've been exploited. I feel like this line of work is actually something that I've actually set my price to what I think is worth my effort. This is the only job that I feel I've actually been completely happy with." Osu's description was echoed by other participants, although the way the providers framed the turning points and measured the different costs and benefits of beginning sex work differed for everyone.

These stories were strikingly different from the prevailing cultural narratives on the exploitation and abuses that accompany entrance into sex work. This was most evident when workers discussed quality-of-life issues and the amount of money sex work could provide. They would often compare the option of sex work to other, less profitable and more time-consuming conventional work.

Isabelle eventually began to weigh keeping her conventional job against the money she was making modeling. Vivian, on the other hand, hung out with her new friends for a few months before she began working, getting a feel for how they ran their business and the different terminology they used. At one point, she overheard some of the things clients would ask for over the phone. "There was a frequent abbreviation requested over the phone. But I was too embarrassed to ask. I was shy and super dorky. So, I started googling things on the Internet because they kept using these abbreviations," she said as she rolled her eyes and laughed. "It was BBBJ that really got me, a bare-back blowjob. I went home and I googled it and I found a [provider] forum and then put it together slowly, way, way too slowly. All the random guys coming in and out started to make sense. I finally asked, and [the other workers] told me I could work the phones. Then I asked if I could try working for one day, and I did it and that's the day that I fell in love with it, and I haven't fallen out of love with it since."

Since her early introduction into sex work, Vivian has moved to a different business model than most of the other people I spoke with, resembling more of a classic French courtesan model rather than the independent provider with a schedule of hour-or-more appointments.

> I have these genuine relationships with these guys that I think of as my boyfriends and I fall in love with them. I genuinely care about them. . . . I just ask for monthly support so that I don't have to worry about anything else, and I can be there for [them]. It's between friends. I would never

call them clients; I don't think of them as clients. I think of them as my friends and my boyfriends. I get made fun of by a lot of the other sex workers because they say I'm more of a sugar baby but I'm not because I'll take different clients. I'll entertain your emails and for sure if we click, we click, but I turn away 90 percent of my inquiries.

When Vivian described these "genuine relationships," she noted the importance of new methods of communication in helping her stay in contact with her stable of boyfriends. Technology played a largely tacit but ever-present role in the stories of the entry process people shared with me. Technology, specifically the Internet, was widely referenced but often in passive statements, like "I reached out to someone on Twitter" or "I just looked up articles that girls had written." Providers largely considered the use of technological resources as part of those overarching "cultural contexts." This deep familiarity with—and use of—the Internet and people's accompanying racial and cultural contexts can shape responses when providers are presented with turning points. However, workers who described these turning points did not simply turn to sex work with no preparation. Most often, they took their current circumstance as an opportunity to first gather some knowledge and discover the best path to entrance.

Isabelle grabbed a coffee mug from one of the nearby cabinets. For her, the combination of her background, a growing dissatisfaction with her life situation at the time, and her new discovery of online fetish groups were all brought to the forefront by the turning point of the loss of her bird. "I blamed myself for my bird's death and nobody seemed to understand it. That completely tipped me over," she said.

Isabelle poured herself a cup of tea, set it down, spun on her heels to pull sugar out of a cabinet, then slid over to the refrigerator for cream. She would often start a story, then remember to give a piece of important background information, then forget where she left off. Her excitement was infectious. Stories would change locations, characters, and plots as quickly as she glided around the kitchen. "It was just—my friends thought I was a whore anyway. And you get called a whore so eventually you wanna try it out because you might have something to show for it," she said with a grin.

Gathering Information: "The Whole Gamut"

Mandy, a twenty-nine-year-old escort, was energetic and lighthearted. She had been doing sex work for exactly one year when we spoke. Sitting cross-legged on a bed, draped in a white comforter, she looked as though she was perched on a cloud, looking down at all the busy humans bustling about below. Her raven black hair and smooth, pale skin gave her the appearance of a pin-up photo taken in black and white, and her quick wit and perceptive insights leant an air of learned wisdom. Her interest in sex work was sparked when she saw a news story about an Olympic athlete getting "caught" doing sex work and thought, "This is not the normal narrative of sex workers." After that she decided to do some research on the Internet by visiting a few message boards and blogs created and run by providers.

> Everyone was horrified. "Oh my gosh, why does an Olympian athlete need to do sex work?" or "How could she do this to herself?" My first thought is, "Oh my god, this is not the normal narrative of sex workers." It's not like some poor impoverished lady, like she was doing this for fun on the side. I mean she got a lot of enjoyment out of it. So, I started doing more research into it. I'm very sexually open; I don't think that having sex for money is a problem, or something that should be stigmatized, so that's actually how I got started. After a lot of research, I was like, I think I could enjoy this.

Mandy began to hang out in these digital spaces and said that Internet communities were a welcome place to vent her frustrations or get advice on how to operate her business both safely and profitably. Hers was not an isolated case, either. Most of the providers I spoke with did not enter sex work impulsively. When they recounted their entrance stories, they discussed what their lives looked like just prior to entrance. Then, most often, this was followed by a description of how sex work became a viable option.

Though some providers described "taking the plunge" with no preparation, like placing an ad on a local website and seeing the kinds of responses they got, most often entrance was preceded by a period of information gathering, in which they were simultaneously trying to discover best practices for entrance, but also to see whether sex work would be a good fit. Even if providers skipped the initial step of gathering information, they would usually realize that they needed more information after an initial experience of meeting a client with no plan or arrangements.

When I asked exactly how they gathered this information, the most common response was indistinct phrases like "I looked it up" or "I researched." Tacit knowledge of the Internet has become such a ubiquitous part of our everyday lives that most people do not describe detailed interactions with it—so when workers discussed their information gathering, they frequently did so in this tacit fashion. Mandy, however, was an exception and was more precise in describing how she gathered knowledge and the difficulties of homing in on valuable specifics after her initial interest: "It was mostly online researching, because there's really no other good forums for sex workers to get started. There's not a lot of information out there in the first place. Pretty much going online. [One sex worker] wrote a lot on her blog. That was a really good resource for me to figure out what things I needed to watch out for, how to get started. What type of clients I would be meeting. How to advertise, the whole gamut. So it was all online."

Most providers described instances of using the Internet to clarify incorrect assumptions or stereotypes they had previously held about sex work. Strikingly, when they described their entrance processes, most explained that they were completely new to the work, knew no one previously involved in sex work before they began, and pursued a preexisting interest with only a general cultural knowledge of its existence. This is quite common. Researchers from the Urban Justice Center studied indoor providers in New York and found that several workers only knew an acquaintance or single friend who was involved in sex work.[9] And similarly, a few decades prior, Mimi Silbert and Ayala Pines, researchers with the University of California, found that whereas roughly half of their sample had had some contact with a person familiar with sex work, a large portion did not know any other workers.[10] When a provider identified a turning point in which they had little prior knowledge of sex work, they often described their entrance as a "take the plunge" moment in which, for example, they decided to enter a strip contest or attend an adult club's amateur night.

But few people had an entrance as unique as that of Noreen, a thirty-two-year-old escort with over a decade of experience. She had long, flaming red hair, but it was not visible because it was tucked behind a black hijab. "One of the by-products of being a hijabi is my bright hair doesn't stand out and I don't get recognized nearly as much as I used to, which is so nice. It's a small town—if you've seen my ad, you've seen my ad." She had a wide smile and blue eyes that beamed out excitement with every sentence she spoke. She grew up in a very conservative Christian household but, by her own description, was extremely sexually curious from a young age. She would date but never go as far as "the Holy Grail of 'P in V.'" She laughed as she recounted all of these details because she found such a naive and reserved attitude towards sexuality to be a snapshot of a young, misguided woman.

> I was just very much on the whole virgin track, right? I really was like, "Fuck. I don't want to have sex until I get married, so I guess I can't be a sex worker." I was actually really devastated by this fact. During that time, I started doing topless waitressing. That was where I started, I dipped my toe into the industry. I did topless waitressing while I was studying at [university] in Australia.
>
> Then when I discovered my queer identity, that really made me deconstruct the whole virgin concept and how heteronormative, what they were defining sex as, and how I was actually already quite sexually active and I wasn't a virgin, really. I was just having this P in V holy grail thing or whatever of heteronormativity. Once I deconstructed that, I think I just hooked up with some dude that had wanted to bone me before, and I wasn't into it, and then maybe the next day, I went into a brothel and started being a hoe.

I was curious about how quickly the process played out. She explained, "I had heard one of my friends talk about working in the industry, and I remember still it was maybe the first time I'd seen a real-life sex worker just talking frankly about it, and I remember being quite scandalized, honestly, and also just like mesmerized. . . . I got in contact with her, and we had a lunch, coffee that day, and she told me about the brothel where she worked, and I went into the brothel that night."

One explanation for Noreen's unique entrance could be that she was living in a country where brothel work was fully legal, so both the legal implications and the social stigma of sex work could have been less prevalent. There was no need for her to be secretive about her interest in sex work or hide that she was gaining knowledge on the topic. Though she noted that there was still social stigma around being a provider, there was no need for her to fear legal consequences. Or, more likely, the explanation for her entrance lies in Noreen's fast and fearless attitude, which she approached every aspect of her life with.

Even if providers' initial step was not to do some Internet research, all the providers in the study noted that the Internet was essential to performing their work, and that Internet-based resources had become an essential part of increasing the agency and autonomy of many workers. When Noreen did bring up technology—outside of the context of entrance—she was sure to note its many advantages even in a society without the dangers of legal issues. "I can communicate with my clients and do my own safety and security as well. Online forums and stuff like that that are hooker-focused are really helpful for me. . . . I more heavily rely on online forums and stuff like that for peer support and stuff. And then, yeah, of course placing ads."

Even if workers did not report gaining information for the purpose of entrance, most noted using the Internet during entrance: to post or answer an ad, advertise for themselves, or communicate with clients and other providers. Throughout all my conversations with workers, the use of the Internet was an essential element to their entrance. This is almost certainly the case because the Internet is being used at ever-growing rates to advertise all varieties of sexual services.[11] It helps increase exposure to client bases while decreasing the likelihood of victimization or violence.[12] It also created a network of information sharing that helped workers to improve security, strengthen their market presence, and manage existing personal and professional personas through increased communications with clients, peers, and friends.[13]

Though workers appreciated the Internet's ability to facilitate increases in security, they reported mixed results when it came to their ability to remove information once it had been released and expressed concerns about the proliferation of digital threats and abuses. Prominent race, gender, and sexuality researcher Angela Jones noted that though most researchers focus on the facilitation of sex work via technology, more study is needed to uncover the series of complex relationships between technology and sex work, which involve factors such as "the diversity and complexity of sex work online; the rise of individualized erotic labor; how local contexts shape migration into online sex work; issues related to danger and privacy; the reactions by law enforcement to online sex work; the racialization of erotic labor; and further use of intersectional analysis to study the experiences of people who sell sex online."[14] Isabelle embodied these intersections in her entrance story. When she started, she was experiencing a difficult phase in her life, and the Internet provided her with the information and networks she needed to make changes. Her introduction into sex work started when she began to hang out on a few fetish forums. "In 2003 I discovered porn on the Internet and I was like, "Oh my god this is so awesome." And I got into an argument with a dude in Amsterdam about whether Amsterdam was in Holland or Germany and he sent me my first fur coat. . . . So I just decided to put an ad out and see what happened. And I found some advice on the Internet, so I put an ad up." But while advertising herself online, Isabelle tapped into some of the latent advantages she discovered she had. "I had been raised to think I was the ugliest person on earth. A friend gave me a makeover and I actually looked kinda hot, and I was like, 'Oh my gosh I'm blonde with big boobs.' That's when it went to my head and I was like, 'Wow I'm pretty fricking hot, seriously.'"

After the confidence she received from her makeover, Isabelle was able to recognize that she had qualities others would find attractive and that she could leverage those in her business. The relationship between the success of a provider and their own physical attributes was a complex one. And it was a relationship the people I spoke with often had trouble describing.

Privilege: "I'm Already High on the Ladder"

Edward looked frazzled. His shock of blonde hair shot in every direction. He leaned back in his chair and stuffed his fists into the pockets of his black hooded sweatshirt. "Is there a point where I'm supposed to say how privileged I am? I forgot that," he said abruptly, clearing his throat.

"Am I supposed to say I realize I'm privileged? I'm a white dude. There're some sex workers who sometimes don't have the choice. I'll express that I'm aware of that."

He let out a dry cough and dropped his gaze from behind his horn-rimmed glasses. "It sucks, and it's complicated. . . . I'm white, I'm already high on the ladder outside of the industry. One can assume I'm fairly high-ish on the ladder within the 'whorearchy,' other than I make less money than almost literally everyone."

The way Edward addressed issues of race, class, and privilege mirrored the way the overwhelming majority of providers expressed these concerns. He realized well after describing his entrance that his personal privilege played a role in his decision to become a provider. But these contexts were largely unspoken or unrecognized in his original story.

This jumbled complexity found its way into several of my discussions on race with providers. I would ask workers to describe the personal aspects of their lives that affected their entry process, and many would talk about the experiences that led them to their decision, only later rolling in aspects of their identity, describing their sexuality, education, class, gender, and race. And though these conversations came about organically, like Edward, most had a hard time confronting their own privilege, and especially racial privilege.

Race and class are crucial parts of people's opportunity to utilize resources and make decisions, but the implicit nature of race and class can make those factors difficult to disentangle.[15] Most of the people I spoke to came from white, middle-class backgrounds, and when they noted the role that structural factors played during their work, the acknowledgment was often muted. They did not explicitly compare their own class and race with those of others, as Edward and a few others did; instead, they referenced these differences in more veiled ways.

Research by sociologists VoonChin Phua and Allison Caras looked at how, when advertising themselves, providers used their race and ethnicity not just as descriptors but as a "feature for differentiating their personal brand."[16] To many of the workers I spoke with, their race and class were not merely underlying privileges; they were obvious commodities.

Recently, researchers have been trying to unpack the role that race plays not only in sex work but in the way involvement in a subculture can reflect and change those roles. In her fantastic exploration on the experiences of Black women in sexual commerce, *A Taste for Brown Sugar: Black Women in Pornography*, Mireille Miller-Young noted that porn, like so many other aspects of society, has innate sociopolitical implications. She argues that the production of porn is a reflection of the racialization—described as "the process by which meanings are made and power is structured around racial differences"[17]—of society in two important ways: "in the titillating images themselves and in the behind-the-scenes dynamics where sex workers are hired to perform in the production of those images."[18] These, according to Miller-Young, are racialized depictions that reify the racial, gender, and sexual stereotypes promoted by society.

But the paradox of these issues is that sexual commerce is driven by "market concerns" that push providers and producers to advertise and utilize racialization to cater to consumers. So the question, Why don't these conscientious workers do something about the racist aspects of sex work? is answered with the observation that it can be difficult to address these issues when race and privilege are woven into the very structure of sex work itself. Providers can either profit from privilege, play to racial fetishization, or leave money on the table. It is also important to recognize that, as Miller-Young pointed out, these reifications are ever present in society, and the taboo of sex work, combined with the anonymity and blunt quality of the Internet, simply brings them to the forefront. It is the removal of these buffers of polite propriety that brings the discomfort of that juxtaposition into stark contrast, demanding that something must be done. This is the case even though issues of race and privilege are frankly no different in sex work than in any other line of work.

Research by prominent scholars like Angela Jones and Jennifer Nash has looked at the connection between racialization and the use of race and ethnicity as an advertisement technique for providers,[19] catering to the desires of what Jones calls the "erotic other." Similarly, a group of researchers from Amsterdam also found this to be a troubling trend in sexual commerce and suggest that the business urgently needs to elevate the voices of people of color to help transform the existing "sexual cybertypes" and hopefully help to create a new system where workers can be "creative, dynamic, and unexploited."[20]

Most of the providers who spoke with me were not exactly sure how to broach the subject. So, a common approach was to compare themselves to a hypothetical worker who had not received the same advantages and opportunities that they had received. Charles W. Mills suggested the idea of an unspoken contract that exists among all whites, in his book *The Racial Contract*.[21] In this work he says that this unspoken version of the social contract regulates interactions between both white people and the "others" outside that group. And even these kinds of othering abstractions can be a form of privilege in and of themselves. The ability to elevate problems, struggles, and issues to the level of hypotheticals is often a benefit of sitting in a position of privilege.

Words like "privilege" and "status" are often tossed around in academic research, but when people speak of privileges, things like money and education invariably become a proxy for race and status. Providers would use phrases like being "from a good family" or "well educated" to subtly acknowledge their own privilege. But phrases like these do not fully capture the complexity of race or privilege. For example, when Edward noted that despite making less money than almost all of his counterparts, he enjoys high amounts of privilege, he initially appeared to be describing a contradiction, but his remark suggests that the cultural contexts that accompany privilege in sex work are more than just monetary.

One of the most well-known pieces of scholarship on privilege is an essay by American antiracist and feminist scholar Peggy McIntosh.[22] In it she described privilege, and especially white privilege, as a weightless, invisible backpack of which the wearer is oblivious. She went on to say that most young people are taught that racism is a personal failing, an undesirable trait, and that racism can be easily recognized in overt acts of placing one person above another because of their race. However, once racism is linked to individuals and divorced from innate structural issues, whites can feel confident that racism is not a problem. But racism is not simply a detriment; racism is also present in the advantages of those in the privileged group. Mills called this being a "beneficiary." The racial contract acts as a "differential privileging of whites as a group with respect to nonwhites as a group. . . . All whites are beneficiaries of the Contract, though some whites are not signatories to it."[23]

The main idea in the concepts of both Mills and McIntosh is that white privilege is an invisible construct, both "elusive and fugitive," and "the pressure to avoid it [is] great, for in facing it [one has] to give up the myth of meritocracy."[24] Essentially, when a person confronts the wide-reaching impact of their privilege, they must acknowledge the largely unspoken role social constructs play in their own life course. Privilege increases the choices for those in the promoted group, then beats a hasty retreat, whispering all the while that success is due to hard work and personal fortitude, whereas losses are a defect of an unprincipled individual.

The term that popped up often in conjunction with these discussions on privilege was the word "whorearchy."[25] Gertrude, a forty-year-old, white escort with four years' experience and a broad Australian accent, explained, "The whorearchy is where you have the street-based workers who are seen as the lower rungs, then you've got maybe the brothel, average sort of person, and then the high-class escorts. I kind of had that mindset as well. And it's because there's so much stigma, and discrimination against sex workers, it's almost like even within ourselves we do bring a little of that to work. And so it's like we have to sanitize ourselves to try to be a bit more acceptable, or to try and avoid the criticism and the harm." The whorearchy is a way to describe the stratification of sex work into different levels of power or importance. Obviously, this could be measured in terms of money or fame—or more directly, in terms of who is a "real" provider and who is not. But most often it can be understood as a broad catch-all to describe the paradox of benefiting from membership in a marginalized group.

The complexity of this paradox was not lost on the workers I spoke to. Its wide-reaching effects shaped the decision making of many of them, especially their decision to enter sex work. Petunia, a white, queer, thirty-five-year-old escort who bills herself as "your sexy librarian," became flustered when our discussion turned to issues of race and privilege and told me so: "This is an annoying question. You haven't defined your terms." She spoke in a quick, pointed manner that conveyed both confidence and capability—like listening to a baseball coach give out assignments.

> Okay, if you take the ladder that's the one in terms of, I don't know what else to call it, "the whorearchy" is the term people use, I'm quite close to the top. I'm independent, I charge fairly high rates, I am white, I am privileged, I am educated, I can absolutely dictate the terms of my working, I'm doing this entirely voluntarily, all that stuff. . . . A lot of sex-work

policy is going to be, if it's decently written, will be written to benefit me and my demographic even though I'm a fairly small part of overall sex work.

Being a privileged member of a stigmatized group makes it difficult for workers to take definitive action. Most of the workers I spoke with acknowledged that the whorearchy exists, theoretically, but many of them saw it as a hurtful concept that needlessly harmed workers, shaming some while celebrating others. Overall, providers wanted to encourage equality and respect within the worldwide community of sex workers. Gertrude was quick to add that all workers "have the same importance, they're all human, they all deserve protecting," but most workers pointed out that being higher on the "whorearchy" gave them access to more advantages. It is the access to these advantages—racial, financial, and technological—that aided some workers in viewing entrance differently than the way the prevailing cultural narrative on worker entrance describes it—as a step made out of desperation or manipulation. The risks of entrance would be perceived differently by someone who has other choices afforded to them because of privilege.[26] When the majority of workers say that they would not consider doing their jobs without the Internet, there is a latent story about not doing their jobs without the invisible backpack of the various advantages, resources, and safety measures that their race and class provide, facilitated by new technologies.

The idea of external prejudices and implicit biases being present in marginalized communities is not a new one. Psychologists have examined how prejudices and internal biases can act as affirmations of our own self-esteem and worth;[27] how we assess our own successes in terms of those prejudices and biases;[28] and how biases can play a role in our own mistreatment.[29] But the idea of the whorearchy places these biases and privileges along a spectrum and can reveal just how complex ideas of race, class, and privilege are.

When Edward wanted to broach the subject of privilege, he did so by bluntly identifying the two factors he felt were most closely connected with his privilege. Remarking, "I'm a white dude," he referenced his race and his gender. And when providers talked about entrance, it was clear that their race and class and their accompanying privilege were all factors in the decision to enter sex work. Yet, most often when I spoke to providers about these issues, my questions would be met with sideways glances and rubbed necks. Race and racialization were part of providers' work, and many middle-class white providers acknowledged, after reflection, that their involvement in a traditionally marginalized group meant that they felt far less at risk while receiving far more of a benefit. However, these concerns always came from a genuine place.

Workers would acknowledge their racial privilege, both overtly and tacitly, but wanted providers everywhere to have access to resources and not suffer under the specter of stigma. But everyone carries internal biases, and Gertrude pointed out that these hierarchies are not only imposed by external forces but carried in and maintained by workers in an effort to protect themselves from the heavy stigma of sex work: "It's like we have to sanitize ourselves to try to be a bit more acceptable or to try to avoid the criticism. But the problem with that is, it doesn't matter whether you're doing a high-class service or whether you're doing it because it will get you your next fix of drugs. . . . No one is better than anyone else. And that's something I've always believed in. We all need to be looked after." In essence, Gertrude was saying that workers can often perpetuate stigma in an effort to preserve their own sense of self-preservation. This made talking about inequalities between different groups of sex workers and varieties of people difficult—because though workers ultimately recognized the existence of privilege, many of them felt that there was little they could do about it, essentially making it a nonissue.

Most workers who did discuss privilege used words like "recognize" and "awareness" when describing its effects. They understood that their racial and class privilege had far-reaching implications but were not always sure what to do about it other than acknowledge its existence. So then why broach the subject at all, even tacitly? When workers began to explore online communities, there was a realization that sex work is varied and sex workers are diverse. Entering providers saw that their privilege often acted as an insulator from some of the more serious consequences of this work and wanted to acknowledge that not everyone received these benefits.

Alyson, a thirty-two-year-old escort, for example, discussed how similar circumstances had different outcomes for her compared to her African

American friends, both during and away from work. Alyson spoke quickly and had an easy laugh when recounting stories, but her tone shifted to being more serious when she discussed the outcomes of privilege.

> Obviously, I have a ton of privilege. I'm a white, college-educated, younger woman, of course. . . . I'm definitely aware of the fact that I have privilege that keeps me protected from things like police. I have girlfriends . . . that I work with [who] are both Black. They've both been arrested. They both get treated differently when we're out and about, even if we're not working. They get shouted at. It's things that you don't see when you're just walking around by yourself. I don't like to be an advocate or a spokesperson for anyone, because I just speak for myself. I'm definitely aware that I am speaking from a place of relative privilege, which I can't really do anything about, but I can acknowledge [it] I guess.

Privilege not only had tangible benefits but also shielded the wearer from negative consequences. Alyson affirmed the invisibility of these privileges and spoke to the frustration of receiving individual benefit from a default group membership. This plays into a theme that most workers spoke to at some point during their interviews: the duality of being a member of a group while also acknowledging their individual experience. Alyson expressed the complexity of benefiting from being a member of a privileged group and a marginalized group simultaneously, yet lamented her inability to do anything about it other than acknowledge its existence. The frustrations and benefits of the complexity of privilege were themes that workers spoke to, but they would often discuss privilege in abstract, rather than concrete, terms.

The various ways in which workers defined their terms when describing privilege could make it difficult to draw definitive lines between the various aspects of race and class. Few of the providers I spoke to were workers of color, but when Yvette, a twenty-year-old Asian cammer and escort, described her entrance, she wanted to emphasize the paradox wherein her race played a positive role in her entrance but also threatened to become exploitative and troubling. Yvette explained how her race—both as her personal identity and as a social construct—creates a complex interdependence that needs constant attention to keep it from becoming "problematic."

When I first started out, I was eighteen years old, I was in the middle of college, I didn't have a degree, and I was sitting there pulling in like crazy amounts of money, and it felt really good to be a woman, and a racial minority, and actually like being able to make my own money, and define how I was going to make that money, set my own terms, things like that. . . . [Then] I walk into some porn store and I'd see a DVD and it would say something like "my sweet concubine" on it, and it would be a collection of Asian girls, and it would make me feel really cheap. That began to like draw away from the feeling of empowerment, where I felt like I would be taken advantage of, and I felt like I was being fetishized for my race, but at the same time I feel like having more educated people who care about how their stuff is being sold and how their bodies are being sold, like those people are what the industry needs to be made out of, so that people are able to educate themselves, people are able to realize what types of things are problematic.

Racial and class privileges were overarching themes in the lives of the people I spoke with, and they affected many of the decisions workers made. When describing their entrance processes, most workers did not specifically articulate the racial and class privilege being a causal part of their decision to enter. But they would later reflect that because of their demographic characteristics, they had more options than other workers and felt free to make their decisions from the place of confidence that privilege provides. The situations that most of the providers described during their entrance processes were tacitly shaded by these overarching cultural contexts and played an important part in their entrance stories.

Edward took a swig of coffee and lit a cigarette. "I think there's more than one ladder." He held up his fingers, counting. "You got to think about race, gender, cultural background, ethnicity, language, class, all of these other things in addition to the whorearchy." Holding up the two fingers for race and gender, he nestled the cigarette between them. "I think it's more complicated than some of the rhetoric you see online. I think for the most part, good analysis is obviously rooted in the same things that create inequality in the general population. Race, class, ethnicity, whatever." He nodded his head and repeated, "It sucks, and it's complicated."

Conclusion: "It's the Business of Pleasure"

Isabelle snapped off the burner and slid the contents of the pan onto her plate. I asked what her first in-person appointment was like. "My first experience was with a private pilot and we did it in a Leer jet that was under some hangar." She smiled. "So I was completely spoiled. I mean like, it was surreal."

"And what did you think of him?" I asked.

"He was very cool and I was like, 'Oh this is awesome, I totally would have done that for free,'" she said, laughing.

"So did that first experience affect your 'normie' life?"

"I started to have less patience with my mainstream job."

I expected Isabelle to say that the money was just better, since so many of the providers I spoke with were quick to mention that they felt sex work paid better than most other employment options. But as it turned out, her rationale was more about freeing herself from work situations that were stressful and abusive. "It was just my boss, you know, who I dated briefly. . . . He was like thirty years older than me. I just started seeing his pattern of dating women half his age. . . . This dude had been acting like an asshole and made me cry at work and my last email was like, 'Screw this. If you're gonna come after me like this I quit. Consider this my two weeks' notice.'"

When providers described their entrance, they often highlighted their independence. Most workers described the situations and turning points that led up to their initial interest in sex work. Those situations were positioned within broader cultural, and specifically racial and class, contexts. These contexts envelop every aspect of people's lives, and often workers would tell the story of their entrance in a straightforward fashion, but only later expound on their recognition of their privileged position in society, garnered by their race or class.

Once providers recognized their situation, they would use the Internet to gather some initial information on best practices for business and security. Even though these techniques were common, most workers described them in tacit terms, using phrases like "I did my research" or "I looked it up," rather than explicitly describing the act of using the Internet to gather information. Similar to the cultural contexts that surround the lives of entering workers, technology played a ubiquitous but often unspoken role in their entrance process.

Providers enter sex work in a variety of ways, but the majority of the people I spoke with took opportunities afforded to them as a result of cultural contexts that decreased risks and increased safety. Workers could then respond to situational turning points by using digital resources to gather information on the best ways to enter.

Though these three elements—turning points, information gathering, and recognizing privilege—were frequent themes in providers' narratives, they were not discrete elements in the entrance process. When combined, these elements form the complex social contexts that influenced the decisions of workers to weigh the risks and rewards of entrance into sex work.

Before her first full-service appointment, Isabelle had done some fetish modeling and dominatrixing, but was starting to see sex work as more of a full-time gig rather than a side job for extra cash. So she began to explore how to call it a career. But after she quit her nine-to-five, she started to worry about being able to take care of herself. "You think— 'I'm gonna be homeless. And I have no winter coat,' and this is getting to be like late August, like what the fuck?" She had a concerned look on her face, but then, for the first time in our discussion, she slowed down and took a pause. "You know, if it wasn't for Internet sex, I would have never gotten out of [that town]. I would never have left that abusive dude, or it would have gone on much longer."

4

The Girlfriend Persona

"Then, the Sexy Happens"

Roxy was dressed all in purple, sitting on a black vinyl kitchen chair with one foot tucked under her. Her long sweater flowed over the side like a cape, and the chair creaked when she reached for her coffee cup. "You want a real experience," she said, cradling the mug in both hands and taking a sip. "You try to make it as normal an interaction as anyone would have with someone that they're dating or sexually involved with."

She set down the cup and replaced it with the lit cigarette smoldering in the ashtray, balancing it between her fingers before putting it to her lips. "There's generally foreplay. I like to kiss; I think that's a really important part of making it seem like I'm your girlfriend." She took a drag and tilted her head to peek at my notepad as I sat next to her scratching observations. I asked how she felt about interacting with her clients and she nodded her head, exhaling a long plume of smoke.

> It's incredibly empowering for a [woman]. I feel like I'm getting paid to be myself, or if not complete, a version of myself, at least. There are endless versions of me, or facets of my personality. Depending on the job, I get to utilize all of them. I also feel as though, almost in a way, my entire life has been building up to this point because this is a job that utilizes every single skill set, talent, that I have in my arsenal and I really enjoy that. It's psychologically fascinating. . . . You're doing a constant and varied case study on human sexuality and psychology.

She explained the duality of attempting to give clients what they want while still maintaining a level of distance. "It's flirtatious without being grotesque or over the top. . . . You want to sound girlie, and fun, and cutesy, and professional all at the same time. That you won't broker any shit, you know? . . . It's a lot to balance."

Roxy described how her presentation to clients served a purpose: to fit a role that is necessary for her brand of sex work, or any kind of work. "You change yourself, and your persona, and your voice according to what job interview you're going to. It's just very similar."

She noted that this additional effort to present a specific tailored version of herself to clients was a crucial part of what was being sold. "That's what I'm trying to sell; that's an idea. That brand comes with a certain verbiage, a certain style of language, and communication." Roxy was selling an "authentic" experience, that many of the providers I spoke with also described: the girlfriend experience (GFE).[1] "We really try to set our business apart. It's a luxury, it's a mini-vacation, and we want to have the distinction of remembering details about clients and bringing those up again so that they do feel like we care. Especially because of the GFE, the girlfriend experience, you want to remember those details and pursue them so that they feel like there's a kind of connection."

I was curious how she and her partner managed to remember all the details of her clients' preference, and she nodded while sipping her coffee. "We have a client journal, where we write about every client postsession," she continued. "We try to do it as quickly [as we can] after a session to remember details. We often follow up a session with an email. Saying in general, it was great to meet you, xyz detail was really great."

I asked if this was the case with all her clients. She bobbed her head left and right, thinking it over. "Sometimes the guys lay out a slightly more specific plan than just a GFE," she said, shifting in her seat. "That leaves it pretty much up in the air, although it does set a certain tone. I think that's my job, or a big part of my job, is setting the tone. Especially, because this is a situation where I want to be in control."

The providers described how they presented their personal identity to clients. Some compartmentalized their work into a completely different persona, while others were consistent in their presentation of self but accentuated different aspects of themselves. But consistently, workers noted that the persona they "put on" involved a delicate balance designed to insulate themselves from clients while still conveying a sense of the authenticity that a "meaningful" encounter necessitates.

Sociologist Elizabeth Bernstein coined the term "bounded authenticity" to describe the exchange of intimacy between workers and clients within the limits of the erotic exchange.[2] Most providers described some level of bounded authenticity, and said that connecting with clients in this way took additional work. Some people even described this extra effort as "emotional labor," a term coined by author and sociologist Arlie Russell Hochschild in her 1979 book, *The Managed Heart*. She described emotional labor as "the management of feeling to create a publicly observable facial and bodily display . . . [requiring] one to induce or suppress feeling in order to sustain the outward countenance that produces the proper state of mind in others—in this case, the sense of being cared for in a convivial and safe place. This kind of labor calls for a coordination of mind and feeling, and it sometimes draws on a source of self that we honor as deep and integral to our individuality."[3]

Most providers felt that doing the emotional labor required to convey a caring and invested attitude was a necessary part of providing clients with a unique, authentic experience, but these boundaries were flexible and frequently renegotiated. Social scientists have been paying more attention to the emotional aspect of sex work since the Internet has become the primary tool for independent workers. Criminologists and researchers Tammy Castle and Jenifer Lee looked at the expectations of clients and found that "in addition to the sexual services, escorts were expected to provide 'emotional services' that could include conversation and affectionate touching such as kissing, hugging and nonsexual massages."[4]

This concept of emotional labor as an expected but largely unspoken part of sexual services has found its way into all aspects of sex work, regardless of the type or style. Cam workers, for example, have found that engaging in emotional labor (cultivating friendly relationships, personalizing their work, communicating informally with clients) can help frame their work as more than just sexual services and that new technologies are facilitating these changes.[5] But, this also increases the amount of time workers spend molding and shaping their work persona at times when they may not be compensated. The rise of digital communications means that providers are in contact with both new and long-term clients more often, and this leads to more time spent in this performative exchange. Granted, in-person meetings can be more involved, especially when one considers the heteronormative nature of GFE, but workers who deliver only digital services also have to spend additional time on the performance of their work persona.

Other research has examined how advertisements for male sex workers avoid using language that describes "robotic" or "nonemotional"
services, instead wanting to highlight intellectual or emotional connections.[6] Edward, a twenty-nine-year-old escort, was outfitted in his signature black hoodie and thick horn-rimmed glasses. He rocked back
and forth in his desk chair while describing the parallel version of GFE
for men, which, he explained, is a relational experience. There is an
emotional-labor element involved in a boyfriend experience, and it is
additional to what is expected in a traditional transactional encounter.
"I do what is called the boyfriend experience. That's my primary thing, I
guess, which is the couch, the wine, the talking, the water, whatever, getting to know each other a bit. That's like 90 percent of what I do. Every
now and then, there is more of a 'wham, bam, thank you ma'am' kind of
thing where it's just a quick in and out blow job or something. Those are
easy and nice because I charge the same."

Charging "for time" was the main way that the providers discussed
the exchange of services for money. So, it is no surprise that Edward
would not charge more for a boyfriend experience. But when workers
discussed the emotional labor that goes into GFE, they acknowledged
that it takes more effort than a simple "transaction." Edward told me that
the Internet plays a large part in this and that frequently he would exchange half a dozen messages with clients—learning more about them,
teasing out personal details for security purposes, or discovering their
preferences—before scheduling a meet-up. Prior to websites being the
main form of advertisement and communication, the exchange would
be a much more discrete encounter.

Roxy stubbed out another cigarette and rifled through the pockets
of her sweater for her pack. She fished out a fresh one and lit it with a
snap from her lighter, then dropped the lighter on the table and stared
at it for a moment before adjusting it to be parallel to the ashtray. "The
girlfriend experience is generally an hour. It's creating the fantasy or
illusion that someone is coming over to their girlfriend's house." She
drew one leg up onto the black vinyl chair and rested her cheek on her
knee. She had a far-away look in her eye as she added, "There's, I think,
more of a slightly emotional element to it. There's a personable element
to it. Like I said, remembering details about someone. Listening. A lot
of these guys are lonely and just want to be listened to. Yeah, it's almost

not just fucking. They want to feel like they're having sex or making love with someone." The additional emotional labor involved in a GFE encounter was rarely recognized by clients and was simply an expected part of an exchange. This was echoed by others as well when they described encounters with a client in terms of amount of money for time spent, rather than the amount of labor or effort that goes into a specific meeting.

Tellingly, most providers never drew a distinction between the emotional labor involved in a GFE (or, frankly, even a "standard" appointment) and the "wham, bam, thank you ma'am" of a streetcorner sex worker because this newer mode of sex work is all they have ever known. Very few providers I spoke to had been working pre-Internet.

The addition of emotional labor to what has now become the "standard" appointment would indicate that, as Hochschild describes, emotional labor represents an added value to an encounter, and though workers described not charging for this additional emotional labor, clients overwhelmingly preferred it. When describing her work overall, Francis, a thirty-three-year-old escort with a stylish lip piercing and a decade of experience, noted that "half of my job is just emotional labor." She described "stroking people's egos, listening to their personal problems, which are sometimes incredibly intense emotionally. Having clients who are talking about their wives who have cancer, or other really debilitating illnesses. Or there's someone who, they're thirty-six and they've never slept with a woman before. And how did you get to that point? There's a lot of emotional labor around that and it can take its toll. That is a thing."

Providers noted that emotional labor is simply an expectation in most aspects of their work unless specifically requested otherwise. Building rapport with clients from initial contacts, scheduling appointments, and conducting the sessions themselves all contained emotional labor. The labor was so pervasive that workers frequently made parallels to other service industries such as caretaking, therapy, or counseling, but often providers described feeling frustrated at the additional toll emotional labor took on their well-being.

"So what do these sessions usually look like?" I asked Roxy.

"Well," she said, flicking her ash into the small ceramic dish, "they arrive, you offer them something to drink, coffee, water, if they'd like to use the bathroom real quick. Spend a few minutes chatting, especially if it's a new client. Then, the sexy happens."

The Cost of Emotional Labor: "It's Definitely a Buffed and Polished Persona"

Alyson, a thirty-two-year-old escort, sat cross-legged on her bed. There was a rainbow unicorn poster behind her that gave the room a play-ful atmosphere. She was buffing her purple manicured nails in quick strokes while she told me a story of meeting a prospective client, and how she could sense whether a new person was going to wind up being a challenge.

"This guy messaged me two days ago, and first of all, he didn't fill out my contact form, which annoys me, because it's the first hurdle. Can you follow directions? Can you respect my process? Every girl's process is different." She was describing the specifics of meeting with a new cli-ent and the additional labor that goes into creating a welcoming envi-ronment while still garnering helpful information to move the process forward.

"He emails, 'I'm in town, I want to meet. What do you have available this week?' Which is completely useless to me when you just write to me and say, 'Are you free this week?'" Her voice quickly stutters through her frustration as she describes the exchange.

"Yes, I'm free! I'm a ho, I'm free all the time. You don't call your hair-dresser and be like, 'Are you free at all this week?' You say, 'Hey, I want to meet. I want to get my hair cut on Tuesday at three o'clock. Can you see me then?'" She let out a flustered little laugh and blew on her nails.

"I emailed back. I said, 'I'd like to get together this week, sure. Just let me know when.'" She described the back and forth that followed, slowly repeating her questions to emphasize them. "Again, I said, 'What time were you thinking? When do you want to meet? How long do you want to meet for? Where are you staying?'" She let out an exasperated sigh.

I probably asked him point blank three or four times all those questions and got no response. Then he wrote back, "Okay, I'm thinking tomorrow evening." I was like, "Okay, no. I can't keep doing this with you, this back and forth. That's it. You're clearly not respectful of me or my time. . . . Go find somebody else." . . . I get a lot of that. That's probably happened to me four or five times in the last week. . . . I have tags on everybody [in my email], what city they want to meet in, if they're okay, if they passed screening. This one definitely got an annoying tag. They do not see the tag. . . . That's literally the only information that I need from you is when and where and how long. You'd be surprised at how difficult those basic questions can be. . . . Which, no, I can't. I have a time-waster tag for sure. I also have a "good time" tag, which I do not give out often enough. That's a fun tag. I think maybe 2 percent of my emails have that tag over eight years.

When providers discussed their work, they would note the effort that goes into building their business, staying connected with clients, and fostering community. However, most highlighted the additional labor involved in dealing with clients—the largely invisible work that gives their business the polished look and feel that differentiate them from other providers.

Kavita Nayar, a gender and sexuality researcher at New York University, noticed this trend among workers to separate the "on duty" and "off duty" activities that are necessary to be a successful provider. Answering private messages via various social media accounts, working out, and staying on top of fashion trends are all part of the unseen work that goes into facilitating an authentic experience with clients. But as Nayar reports, sex work has not yet become professionalized enough for workers to account for "the production of emotional intimacy."[7]

Other researchers have found that the Internet has hastened the expectation that emotional labor will be part of a sex-work encounter,[8] and that the inclusion of emotional labor as an additional feature has become one of the staples in advertising sex work online. In turn, providers acknowledge that this impacts the amount of time they feel they need to be "on," answering casual texts and messages from clients or fostering new interactions with prospective customers.

Alyson explained how an interaction with a client can become excessive and yield no benefits, even after a flurry of initial effort. The providers who spoke with me tended to describe this extra emotional labor as occurring in three different areas: (1) dealing with "time wasters," (2) making efforts during provider/client exchanges, and (3) participating in the broader digital community building of the sex-worker subculture.

As Hochschild described it, emotional labor is more than performative; it is evocative. In order for emotional labor to be successful, it must elicit the perception of an authentic emotional connection. However, workers explained that they had to be careful in managing their abilities to create these connections, to save themselves from the damage of emotional burnout or simply to avoid additional work that does not result in income that can rob their business of its profitability. Some people spoke to the cost of getting lost in that emotional labor. Stirring up authentic compassion for utilitarian ends can impact the way they respond in their personal lives and cause them to begin to question the depth of their own authenticity. Also, the Internet, as the main form of communication for most workers, is an artificial social construct that carries with it a fundamental paradox: How can inherently contrived interactions be perceived as authentic? This is not a new concern. Famously, in the eighteenth century, Jean Jacque Rousseau argued throughout his book *The New Heloise* that any attempt to instrumentally master one's affective life could result in the fragmentation of one's own identity.[9]

But more immediately, there is also the concern that workers are putting on a persona that seemingly reinforces patriarchal gender roles and standards. GFE is, by its very nature, a heteronormative exchange. Providers are expected to be deferential to their clients in traditionally gendered ways. Most providers I spoke with described their sexuality as bi or queer, with an accompanying alternative/progressive ethos that would seem to belie the almost Rockwellian picture of sexual encounters they described. But Deana, a twenty-three-year-old escort, pointed out that though these more ideological concerns have merit, workers are doing their best to endure the late-stage capitalism they exist in.

> I feel like the emotional labor that I do as a woman in my personal life anyway for men is something that's—I feel like I should just be able to get paid for because it's part of the reason I went into sex work in the first place because I was like, okay, clearly I have to interact with these communities to make money. I mean we all through some sort of way get paid by rich white men so it's like, it's such a depressing thing to wrap your head around, but you know, I was like, I want to tap that right at the root but I don't want to be super far down on the rung. I was just like, I'll

mingle with these politicians and stuff like that, but I just have to bear them for a couple hours a month versus having to work in other areas.

The providers I spoke with, and especially the women, expressed that emotional labor was part of their day-to-day experience, and having those tacit expectations compensated helped to increase the sense of empowerment of their work. Sure, GFE could be described as obsequious, but at least they are being paid for it.

Emotional labor in sex work manifested in several ways in the stories providers told me, but most pointed out that these efforts are most noticeable at the beginning of an interaction with a prospective client because workers are attempting to walk a thin tightrope assessing the risks of this new situation, accommodating the requests of the client, and conveying that they are affable and fun all at the same time.

Many providers told stories of clients who required additional communication or guidance, and how frustrating that can be because it lowers the value of the worker's time, and this was only exacerbated with the inclusion of digital communications: texts, emails, messaging apps. Any client who is a "time waster" is consuming provider resources without remuneration, thus lowering the value of the work. Providers were concerned with ensuring that the time they put into work was highly valued, and if a prospective client was a time waster, this value must be recovered elsewhere.

Bethany, a twenty-eight-year-old cam and fetish model, took a bite from a vegan cheesesteak that dripped onto a crumpled piece of aluminum foil before she dropped it and wiped her hands on a napkin. She nodded her head as she chewed, and mumbled a "mm-hmm" in agreement when time wasters came up. In addition to doing cam work, Bethany sells her personal underwear online and explained why this was so difficult.

> I get nothing out of it other than aggravation. You get your hopes up that somebody's going to buy from you. . . . Or, like, especially if I go through all the hassle of sending them pictures of my selection and giving them all the information and all that stuff, and they pick out what they want, so I'll even take stuff out, and put it in a bag for them, sometimes I'll even get

it ready. And then, I just don't hear from them, and so then I waste more of my time to follow up, be like, "Are you ready to buy? Are you ready to buy?" And then, nothing. Oh, god. It just aggravates me.

Troublesome or dangerous clients can ideally be screened out early with a nominal amount of effort. Workers routinely described "screening" as a process of gathering information on prospective clients to preemptively avoid problems (more on this in chapter 6).

But, time wasters were problematic because they appear on the surface to be viable prospective clients, only to reveal themselves as time wasters after the labor and effort have already been expended. Bethany smoothed the corners of the aluminum and eyed her lunch as she continued describing why time wasters were such a specific concern for workers.

> If anyone's going to be abusive or something . . . they always reveal themselves in like the first message to me, so I don't even have to reply to it. But time wasters are different. Because a lot of people will send emails back and forth, will ask to see the different underwear I have, and I'll send them pictures, and we can talk for like a week just going back and forth, and then they don't end up buying. But, other times, we'll go back and forth for a week, and they will buy, and sometimes they'll become a regular.

Time wasters are particularly frustrating because of the initial investment of time and effort to identify them among their pool of prospective clients early in their screening process. But the ways in which providers assessed whether a client might be a time waster were different worker to worker. Francis, a thirty-three-year-old escort, described how small details, like one-word texts and abbreviations, in the initial contacts with clients can be used to avoid time wasters. "That's just something I've learned over the years. In all of the cases where I had extra time and I wasn't doing anything, so I actually did engage with some of these people, it never goes anywhere. It's always a waste of time. They don't book. So, I just don't anymore." Francis was even more concerned about time wasters than most of the providers I spoke with. This was the case because Francis is disabled. She kept a very careful metric of well-spent versus misspent energy expended on work.

Francis considered sex work a form of self-care. She told me that when clients hire her for a session, it makes her feel beautiful, especially because her body type is not typically considered sexy by current societal standards. But time wasters can disrupt the gentle balance she has created to get the most benefit out of her work while still caring for herself.

Encountering time wasters was almost exclusively a digital phenomenon that occurs most often during initial contact. In a few rare instances, workers noted clients being time wasters during an in-person appointment, for example, when they would meet a prospective client for coffee or drinks before a session. Several workers noted that clients could leave them waiting or abruptly walk out, leaving them to pay the bill.

Even after clients move from being an unknown prospective to a regular, several providers noted needing to be aware of the extra emotional labor that clients would attempt to elicit through digital communication between appointments. Essentially, clients would attempt to elicit unpaid labor in the form of an authentic connection fostered by providers even when the two were not together. Many workers noted that communicating with clients between sessions can be a complicated issue because though workers did not want to "give away" free labor, they also did not want to alienate reliable clients.

Mona, at the age of forty-six, was one of the older providers I spoke with. She had a punk rock aesthetic with jet-black hair cut in a Bettie Page style. She wore silver rings on her fingers and thick black leather bracelets on each wrist. Other than her punk accessories, she was dressed casually in a pair of boxer shorts and a muscle shirt.

Mona got into sex work late in life and has been doing it for the last few years. She was initially a member of the local fetish and BDSM community in her city. Other members of the community made her aware of a website that was closed off and only accessible to members where she could advertise, and eventually she moved into escorting. She described how good clients do not try to get extra emotional labor through things like "chitchat" or digital exchanges, but said that these relationships require careful navigation. "They'll send me ninety messages back and forth. . . . The ideal client doesn't go back and forth for three hours. I am not going to play this text game with you. My phone when I'm working is for confirming only. It's not for chitchat, although I do play a client in Words with Friends.[10] I make exceptions, what can I say? I have a heavy game going now." Mona's point about making exceptions reinforced the autonomy of providers. Time wasters are a major issue, but it is up to the provider to decide when a line has been crossed and a client is now costing too much. Not only must providers navigate when, how, and how much emotional labor to expend on a client relationship; when emotional labor becomes overwhelming, the onus for management is also on the workers.

Similarly, Mandy, a twenty-nine-year-old escort, was energetic and lighthearted, funny and poignant. She had been doing sex work for exactly one year when we spoke. Most of her clients had been successful business people, and she enjoyed this because she is a business owner herself and appreciates their insights into how to improve her work. She would always meet clients in public first when checking out someone new. She said she was "looking for a connection." And these meetings were designed to assess whether or not the new situation would be a good one, not just for herself but for the client.

Mandy often spoke about this concept of "good situations" because she recognized that clients have a certain amount of entitlement. They believe they can push limits simply because they have paid for her time. This can be a point of friction for her, and other workers. Providers must be on the lookout for boundary-pushing clients because limits cannot be set strictly, specifically, or precisely in advance because communications, especially digital communications, are limited due to matters of legality and discretion.

> It's very emotionally taxing. I used to do multiple appointments in a day, and I just got so tired at the end of the day, and it just wasn't good for me emotionally to do that, because it still is a very intimate process, even if I don't get emotionally attached to my clients. . . . For that time period of a couple of hours, you pretty much are their girlfriend. You try to connect with them, there's intimacy involved, and doing that for me with multiple people, the girlfriend experience, every day was just too much. . . . I told multiple ladies on [message boards] that your emotional safety is the most important part. Don't ever let somebody tell you no, if you're a hooker you can't screen for people based on weight, or ethnicity, or anything. No, no, no, you've got to figure out what you need to do to stay okay. Not what everyone else is telling you to do. Yeah, find out who is

emotionally taxing for you to see, and also find out the amount of people that it takes for you to still be okay at the end of the day.

Mandy's point about screening for preference is an interesting take on emotional labor. Workers wanted to ensure that clients received the benefit of an authentic emotional connection during their sessions, but not at the cost of their own personal mental health or well-being. This also highlighted an additional aspect of emotional labor that workers had very different judgments on: the emotional labor of community support.

Providers insisted that supporting the broader community of sex workers, both in digital spaces and in real life, was never a poor use of time. When they discussed reaching out to other workers, seeking advice, or offering support, they overwhelmingly expressed that this outreach was both a positive aspect of their work and worth the additional effort. Mandy explained how helpful the broader digital sex-worker community has been to her. "All my business is online. I think the most important part technology plays other than that, is connecting with other escorts, and connecting with the broader community. . . . When you're doing this and you can't really talk to anyone about it— my family, I think they kind of know now, but it's not like my friends know, or wider community knows. You can't tell anyone, because there's a stigma. So joining [the message boards] and getting to vent, and getting to talk to other sex workers, that was the biggest benefit for me."

When providers discussed emotional labor, they described the different ways it could be spent or, conversely, wasted. They described the frustrations of unprofitable labor, but felt that using emotional labor to support their fellow workers was a good use of both their time and their efforts. However, they cautioned that emotional risks or burnout should be avoided and would frequently note the different ways they minimize the effect emotional labor can have on them. The "putting on" of the girlfriend persona in "off hours" was roundly seen as additional effort that was ultimately uncompensated. But their persona was not just for advertisement; it could be used to establish a rapport that helps create connection with clients and ultimately keeps them safe. Though few workers experienced "pre-Internet" sex work, they said that this additional emotional labor was simply part of the way their job was constructed now.

The Girlfriend Persona: "You're Just Better That Day, Just More Likable"

Roxy leaned forward and balanced her cigarette on the lip of the ashtray. "What I do day in and day out is not unpleasant enough to have to take my mind away." She grasps the filter between her thumb and index finger, pivoting it on the edge. "I just take myself, the real name of me elsewhere, and keep it safe, wrapped up and tucked away." She rolls the tip into the bowl, slowly extinguishing one side of the ember, then the other. "For the most part, I enjoy the roles that I play on a daily basis."

Most of the providers described the use of a work persona. And nearly universally, they described changing their personality either wholly or in part to aid in their own comfort, making themselves feel safer on both a physical and an emotional level, all while facilitating emotional labor and maintaining an authentic aesthetic. Workers described a variety of ways to interpret and define a change in persona. Some claimed that the person they "put on" is a completely different creation, whereas others accentuated the parts of themselves clients find appealing.[11]

Fiona, a twenty-five-year-old cam worker, had a raspy cough on the morning we talked. She was getting over the flu and made a low groan when her webcam began to stutter and freeze in place. She flicked the lens with her finger and shook her head: "Better or worse?"

Fiona had an interesting journey into sex work. She moved from the production side of the camera, as a photographer, to being a webcam performer. "[It's] the first thing that was drawing me to work in this industry in the first place, that you can pick a fake name and become sort of somebody else, but it's just like a better, more turned-on version of myself I guess." She laughed to herself before lowering her voice to a smoky growl, emulating a bad attitude. "You know, because a lot of the time I'll just be like moody or grumpy or just not really want to talk."

Fiona continued that her work persona is an augmentation of her identity, a common method used by the providers I spoke to.

Of course, with the clients you have to be very smart and engage with them and be funny, I guess. Then, they're of course giving you attention, which is nice. That kind of compels you to continue this particular performance. I guess mostly it's just like a much more energetic, bubbly version. I don't think I can construct a cohesive other self without [some of myself] because clients remember things too, so it would be hard to lie, because I would forget, but they wouldn't, probably. Also, because I'm on camera telling stories about my actual life as well. It's just a lot easier if you tell the truth but you're just better that day, just more likable.

But she was adamant that all sex work included a healthy dose of emotional labor and that revealing true details about herself can be emotionally taxing. Even when wrangling clients during a webcam session, she noted, declining a request from a client had to be done with a certain "sexiness," and "flirtily declining" was a way to keep the peace in a crowded webcam lobby. She argued that if you are only doing this for money it can be "soul destroying," so she likes to acknowledge the things she gets out of her work beyond monetary benefit, like having a unique experience and creating connections with others.

> I'm also getting something out of it too, not just money. I guess I talked to other people who wanted to do it, but they were looking to do it more for the money aspect, which is always just soul destroying. My other friends who did it enjoyed it also because it was a good experience. . . . They're kind of inspired by the people that you're meeting, because a lot of the other models are hyperintelligent, like pursuing multiple degrees, like just running their lives very well, in this particular side of the industry anyways. It was just really nice to kind of see that there was so many smart, powerful, sexy women who were doing this, and it wasn't like degrading, if that makes sense.

When some providers described their work persona, they wanted to note that this persona was not drastically different from their "real" identity, but it simply accentuated certain aspects of their personality and aided workers in being more comfortable during work exchanges. Overwhelmingly, providers used pseudonyms, but the majority of workers I spoke to said that a change in persona was distinctly different from simple anonymity.

Cate, a twenty-two-year-old cammer and pro-dom, had just moved into her new apartment with her two partners. She sat on her bed in a pair of black fleece pajama pants with tiny red hearts. Her long auburn hair was gathered in a ponytail that she fidgeted with as we talked. "People always tell me they're worried about my relationships." She said people expressed this concern because they felt that investing in her webcam clients was taking attention away from her partners. But she replied that people should know "it's not me being invested, it's my persona being invested." Cate's work persona was more than just a stage name; it was a tool she used to moderate work risks and stressors. "I feel a little bit [safer] because I have worked really hard on the persona I use to the point of where if you Google the persona you can't find any real information about me unless you know what my face looks like and you can guess what my proper first name is."

She also noted that her digital persona accentuates different aspects of her personality and that, in reality, she doesn't have the most extroverted of personalities: "I'm a lot more talkative online. Honestly . . . I tell my partner I hate people. This is the best job ever 'cause I don't have to deal with customers. I deal with perverts."

Beyond obscuring their personal identity, accentuating specific personality traits, or increasing security, providers noted that their change in persona aided them with emotional labor. By separating themselves from the various parts of their work persona, as Cate described, providers helped create a divide between their work life and their personal life. The construction of a separate work persona provided emotional or psychological distance from clients that was helpful in reducing the cost of providing effective emotional labor.

Hannah, a tall, thin, eighteen-year-old escort, folded herself into a small wooden deck chair on her porch and rested her forearms on her knees. She was an American living in Australia, where sex work was legal. And she had been a provider for only two weeks when we talked about her experiences. She told me that she enjoyed the work for the most part—that she had a lot of casual sex in her personal life, but now she gets paid for it.

"So how did you get started?" I asked.

"Basically, I hooked up with an escort. I didn't know that she was an escort. And afterwards, she was sort of talking to me about it," she told me. "It was already something I had researched pretty heavily over the past few years. Just like kind of a bit of a fascination with sex work. . . . And she said that she thought I'd be good at it," she said with a playful shrug. "She just said, 'Here's my email. Let me know if you're interested.' So I thought about it for a few days, and then I emailed her . . . and I was working two days later."

Hannah had moved to Australia with a dream of racing horses, but found that the time and effort she was putting into her racing career was not paying her enough to live on. Even with only two weeks of experience, Hannah recognized that she needed a way to separate her private life and work life. "I definitely tend to be more outgoing, sweet, caring [while working]. I don't know, just trying to be this very sweet, bubbly, awesome girl. And I think I'm a bit more cynical, in general. I mean, I'm still nice, but yeah. After work, I just make fun of clients with my partner. . . . I sort of take a deep a breath and you're like, 'I am this person when I walk in the door.' And then, I always heave a big sigh, every time someone walks out. Like, 'Okay. And we're done.'"

The notion of presenting separate personas in different social situations is not a new concept. Researchers have observed the differences between public and private personas for decades.[12] This even led to the creation of specific methods used to observe workplace culture to better understand how people perform identity, live, and interact in work spaces.[13] But the introduction of digital communications has led to different ways to convey providers' work personas to clients.

Hannah's work with a more experienced provider helped her not only set up her business but also construct a persona to improve advertisement and attract her preferred type of client: "She sort of got this persona for me. 'Oh, like, cute, innocent, American country girl.' And I was just like, 'Okay.'" Hannah described how her persona was presented to prospective clients on social media using hashtags and lifestyle posts.

Here's a hashtag, bare back blowjob, BBBJ. Hashtag, fuck toy. Hashtag, threesome. Hashtag, strap on. That was from a double. Hashtag, skills. Let me see. Oh, hashtag, GFE, which is girlfriend experience, and PSE, which is porn star experience. . . . I have my nipples pierced, so there's hashtag, pierced nipples. . . . But I actually send [my partner] a lot of the stuff she puts up [on social media]. . . . It's not all just like pictures. Some of it's lifestyle stuff. Like, "Oh, at the gym." There's a picture of my shoes and some weights. Or, I don't know, food that I cook, or whatever. . . . I do show my face in pictures, and she gave me the option of not. She said she does as well. And it's because she believes that if you show your face in pictures, a lot of the time, you attract more people who are less abusive, versus, if you don't show your face, sometimes, she said they can be more abusive. Because they don't think of you as a human being, just a body.

Being "just a body" shows the flip side to constructing a work persona. The authentic persona workers project can give clients an experience they are looking for. It can also serve as an emotional barrier for workers that separates work and private life. But if clients perceive a worker's persona to be authentic, that perception can foster a relationship that can be seen as an additional layer of security.

Arden, a twenty-six-year-old escort, had wide green eyes and a gold nose ring that matched the gold hardware of her pristine white leather jacket. Her tight black jeans gave her whole outfit a late '70s vibe, but every part was presented in crisp and immaculate fashion, which matched her professional and detailed-oriented personality. She explained that her authentic work persona with clients can provide her with additional benefits, like resources or security, but these interactions need to be very carefully navigated.

> I choose to communicate with [clients] on a personal level. But that's my job, and I take my job very seriously, and I know for a fact it also goes both ways. These people, I help them with certain things, and they help me with certain things. I do consider some of my clients to be like good friends of mine. If I'm in trouble, and I need money, they'll send me money. If I need a favor done, they'll do me a favor. I have clients that will literally chauffeur for me. Especially the fetish clients. They do my laundry. They clean my house. They pay to get my hair done. They send me gifts. They'll buy me clothes. . . . And it's those little things, it's those little texts that you send out that is the difference between just getting three hundred dollars in an hour or getting three hundred dollars and then also getting, you know, A, B, C, and D. But you have to be really selective, and you have to be really aware of who you're dealing with because you could very easily send the wrong message to someone. Some people don't understand that there's a line that's actually drawn in the sand. That there's a place where the fantasy ends and reality begins. That we're not actually in a relationship, but we are at the same point in time. It's a balancing act. . . .

I mean you have to keep some things personal. Otherwise you lose your fucking mind.

Authentic personas lead to authentic experiences; and authentic experiences lead to authentic relationships. But workers wanted to be clear that this authenticity is a construction that requires effort, even if the resulting relationships blur the lines between "real" and fabrication.

Workers walk a duplicitous edge when balancing the real world and the fantasy world Arden describes. Tapping into the authenticity of her true self with her clients gives her material benefits, but she is also concerned both that she maintains her own safety and that her clients are receiving the quality of experience she wants to provide. Arden's "balancing act" was described by many of the workers I talked to, including putting on no persona whatsoever or being subversive enough to be a completely different person.

Deborah was a twenty-five-year-old cammer who punctuated nearly every sentence with three low, rhythmic laughs. She had begun working about seven years earlier and said that she prefers cam work to other jobs because "when you're camming no one can follow you home," then laughed.

She described herself as "low energy" and looked for ways to increase her income without adding extra effort. I asked her if she put on a particular work persona, and she laughed three times and said, "I used to really try and play out different personas and stuff, and it just never really worked for me." She shrugged. "It was really exhausting. I would feel like I would end my shift and not really know how to come back to reality. I'd have to watch [television] for eight hours."

Constructing and presenting a work persona for Deborah was not an option, and she laughed when she told me how her customers responded to her actual authentic persona. "I just act like myself. Some people think I'm annoying, and some people think I'm a bitch, and that's fine, 'cause that's what people thought before, too." Even though she does not put on a work persona, the projection of authenticity still played a big role in her work life—just not in the way most workers described it. Deborah found a way to become two workers at once.

"So, I have a texting site that I work with, that I put it on the back burner, 'cause I was trying to do more camming than texting," she said.

"And [my boyfriend] does Uber and had two flat tires on Thanksgiving. So he wasn't able to work for a minute."

"Oh? Oh!" I laughed three times, seeing what was coming.

"And I was like, 'Well, you can just log on to the texting site, right?' Like, 'Why not?' So he's actually been texting and learning about all the wonderful fetishes. So he's made like three hundred dollars a week!"

Her boyfriend took up the mantle of Deborah's work persona so they could earn extra money, and she laughed when she told me that clients preferred sext interactions with him more than interactions with her.[14]

> We were over at a friend's house, . . . and he was just texting trying to make money. I'm sure he wanted them to ask, they're like, "What are you doing on your phone? You're normally on your phone, but not like this." So he starts explaining it, and everybody's like, "That is amazing." All the dudes are like, "How can I get in on that?" "Send pictures of my girlfriend? Sounds great!" What we discovered is, he's actually better at it than I am! First of all, there's a slight amount of resentment that always comes out when I'm talking to men. . . . But for him, he's like, "This is great! I'm making money! This is fun!" He's way nicer, and there are reviews and stuff, that people can give, and my reviews just got way better when he started doing it. He's such a nice girl!

The Internet played a very obvious dual role in the stories of providers. The "digital version" of the provider combined with more frequent communication fosters these bounded relationships. This is not dissimilar to the sociological concept of a "para-social relationship." Two researchers in the 1950s, Donald Horton and Richard Wohl, observed that when "real people play out the roles of fictional characters . . . for a brief interval, the fictional takes precedence over the actual,"[15] and audiences feel a sense of genuine connection with the character being portrayed. Yet, these types of interactions become even more nebulous with the inclusion of digital communications. Yes, the person on the other side of the screen is "real," indicating an authentic exchange, but this mixture of reality and fantasy is a difficult line to walk.

The construction of an authentic experience combined with the consistent digital management of workplace personas begs the question, Why not limit the emotional labor of "fake" authenticity by simply replacing it with actual intimacy? Vivian, the twenty-nine-year-old escort, was a rare case. Most workers who talked to me either saw novel clients on a regular basis or had a semi-stable group of regular clients. Vivian, by contrast, had between five and seven regular clients whom she had been seeing for nearly a decade and whom she described as her boyfriends. She explained that her particular kind of sex work is almost completely comprised of emotional labor and that both her work persona and her relationships with clients are not constructed but instead are very real. "I would say I have sex maybe once every three or four times that I meet up with someone, and if I do, it's 5 or 6 percent of the time that we're together. It's not sex; it's selling love and companionship and a relationship. If you come to it at a truly honest point in your life, I really think that there's complete freedom to keep being, whatever you want to do, explored. It's like a therapist but better with bigger tits, depending on who it is." For Vivian, being "truly honest" seems to lessen the amount of effort associated with the emotional labor she was describing. However, most workers said that they preferred their relationships with clients to be separate and that the creation of authenticity was a byproduct indicating that their emotional labor was effective.

Providers largely took pride in their work, and though more often than not, they used their work persona to insulate them from intimacy with clients, they still wanted their clients to perceive an authentic connection and had a variety of techniques to achieve this.

Authenticity: "It's like a Hyperfocused Truth"

Jordan's light blue hair was swept behind her ear, held in place by haute square librarian glasses. "I've learned over the years that the client base that I want to attract are the ones that go for ads that offer a connection or authenticity or things that more appeal to an emotional connection, plus a physical connection, not necessarily like, 'I'm gonna rock your world.'" She tugged at her gray cardigan before continuing. "There's some authenticity to it. But at the same time, it's also kind of creating that image of the ideal me. . . . And that's it, that's who my work identity is, it's like this ideal version of me where I'm always ready for someone to make out with me even though women get headaches and have periods and may not always be into sex." She took a pull on her vaporizer.

"But . . . there's a certain limit to that authenticity. My work room is away from everything else in my life. So when I'm done working, I can close that door and have that closure in that compartmentalization where, 'That's it. I'm done.' And I don't have to open that door again until I have to work again."

Constructing authenticity is a difficult process, and it takes a toll on workers. Jordan went on to describe how a client whom she has not seen in months can still require time and effort that can go unpaid or even unappreciated.

> It was a lot of emotional labor. It was constant emails when I may not see him for three months at a time. It was this expectation that I would reply to his emails or his texts or whatever. And it just became. . . . It wasn't a good input versus output sort of relationship. Thankfully, I haven't had too many of those. And I think I've gotten better over the years at managing the expectations of clients that might become emotionally attached. That was definitely a big one. Apparently, I'm really good at faking an emotional connection.

When providers discussed their work personas, authenticity was the most prominent theme. Bernstein notes in her book *Temporarily Yours* that as indoor sex work began to emerge as a cultural phenomenon bolstered by the Internet, the nature of the exchange was refocused to be less transactional and more relational. In short, workers were providing intimacy to clients within the bounds of a commercial erotic exchange, with the authenticity of that intimacy desired by clients and a goal for providers. The construction of authenticity is a process, and many of the workers I spoke to had steps that they took to produce the kinds of interactions they were looking for, both for themselves and for clients.

Hope, a twenty-eight-year-old escort, described her job as educating people on how to "bring fantasy safely into reality." The role of an educator fit her well, and as we talked, she recounted several stories in a narrator cadence, as if she were reading a fairy tale.

> My partner actually describes me as a chameleon. We talk about how one of [my] strengths . . . is that I'm able to shift with the dynamic of whatever person I'm with. But, also in my personal life, what I've been working on is

being less of a performer and more authentic. Even when that means not necessarily doing the most beautiful or sexy thing or what have you. . . . Part of what I'm working towards with clients is ultimately the kind of experiences that they want to have and the kind of experiences that I want to have are not that different, like, when I think about what makes a good work encounter it's being present, it's being alert and enjoying your body.

Authenticity was a desirable trait that both the clients and the workers wanted. However, when workers discussed authenticity as an aspect of an encounter, the majority noted that the process of producing authenticity was achieved at the same time that they adopted the performative persona that best fit that interaction.

Bernstein calls this concept "bounded authenticity." Workers are attempting to provide an authentic experience for clients, but within the contexts that surround an erotic exchange, such as their personal security procedures and their performative work persona. But how does this process change with the variety of digital interactions providers and clients have at their disposal?

In recent years, several researchers have examined the process of creating bounded authenticity, and have found that workers have a variety of techniques to evoke authenticity with clients. A team of researchers from City University of New York found that workers begin to convey authenticity before they even meet prospective clients, by "presenting [their] authentic personality in the advertisement in order to connect with clients they would 'click' with on a personal level."[16] Similarly, researchers have found that online interactions also benefit from the construction of authenticity. Kavita Nayar from the University of Massachusetts researched the intersection of "professional" and "amateur" webcam performers and found that providers often attempt to let their natural personality shine through in an effort to create an authentic performance.[17] Sociologist, activist, and writer Dr. Angela Jones has even posited that these digital interactions constitute a different kind of "authentic" presentation to customers. She coined the term "embodied authenticity" because although the "body work" providers are doing is digital in nature, "the model uses a highly stylized bodily performance to present an 'authentic' presentation to customers, which is highly valuable in the world of erotic labor."[18]

Early labor scholars often focused on the body of the worker, but rarely on how a worker can interact with the body of clients in their work.[19] Obviously, digital sex work has the mediation of a computer screen that separates workers and clients, but Jones sees this as an advantage: "It is precisely in the absence of the ability to physically touch—and the absence of the many risks associated with physical encounters—that this new online sex market has flourished, and that has made it so pleasurable for workers and clients."[20]

Several providers I spoke with noted that the creation of authenticity in less-than-ideal circumstances was a crucial part of their job, not because of the quality of client/provider interactions per se but because accepting enough clients is the only way to maintain a business.

Gertrude, a forty-year-old escort, said she perpetually felt as though she was twenty-nine. She had an Australian brogue that made her instantly affable. "You need to be very nonjudgmental and accepting and understanding of people, and most people nowadays aren't." People would approach her about becoming a sex worker, but she explained that the ability to connect with anyone is not a skill most people have.

> I kind of give them a little test. . . . I tend to say, "Okay, so what if some big, fat, ugly, hairy, smelly, like the worst-case scenario or some like old, decrepit, woman." You know, just build the most disgusting picture I can in their brain if someone comes in and wants to see you, what are you gonna do? And they're like, "Oh, well I'll just say no. You know, it's my right." I'm like, . . . "They're everyday people. If you say no to all of them, you're not going to have any business. So you can't say no to everyone." Or they'd be like, "Oh, well I'll just take the attractive one." I'm like, "There's not that many attractive [clients], it's what's attractive to you." So that's not gonna work either. And then they start actually thinking about what it is that they'd have to do and then they're like, "Oh, no, maybe not."

Constructing authenticity by its very nature is a challenge. If clients perceive that a provider is distancing themselves, the authenticity would be negated. Yet, providers overwhelmingly voiced the need to preserve both physical and emotional barriers from clients. Arden described this duality as well when she discussed both trying to prevent her true feelings and identity from being revealed and also maintaining a core of authenticity. To combat this, she uses a technique she calls "hyper-focused truth," which describes a method that workers use to achieve Bernstein's bounded authenticity within a fundamentally contradictory setting. Essentially, hyperfocused truth is used to construct the authenticity of intimacy between both parties within the confines that the interaction allows.

> I try to keep it all loosely based on the truth because the best lies are based in truth, and it's just a really great way for me to express different sides of my personality. . . . I genuinely believe that there's good in all people, and I try, even if I'm with, like, a super-repulsive overweight man or someone that I'm just really not attracted to, I really try to focus on that one thing that I am attracted to and exploit that to my favor so that I can provide them with the experience that they're looking for. So, I do try to base the experience in truth, but it's like a hyperfocused truth. . . . I'm able to be a lot more like my real self because that's what they're looking for, something more authentic.

When workers discussed having an authentic connection with clients, authenticity was not unidirectional. Though workers noted more frequently that authenticity was an aspect of the exchange that aided in advertisement and client satisfaction, they also described a desire for authenticity for themselves.

Noreen, a thirty-two-year-old escort, shared every story with exuberance. Her big, bright smile was framed by a black hijab while she described using the same method of hyperfocused truth to achieve a feeling of authentic desire with a client she initially was uninterested in.

> I get to liberate people to a degree, like let people embrace aspects of themselves, let people feel authentic desire and feel desired, authentically desired. I used to be a terribly judgmental person, very, very superficial, judgmental person, and had all these stipulations of like, "Ew. Ew. Ew." And then this guy really liked me, and just was really quite persistent, and I found him physically repulsive, but he was just so lovely that I just couldn't help but totally fall in love with him, and by the end of it, all the things that physically repulsed me about him, I thought were like the hottest things ever, so that really challenged me, and after that, whenever

I get physically repulsed by something, I'd always be like, "Look. Look at that. What's going on there? Why are you repulsed, miss? What's wrong with you?"

She continued to describe hyperfocused truth as a technique that has been around for a while and can be applicable to a multitude of situations for a variety of workers. "And so I feel like one of my very early brothel tricks was if I saw a client, and there was something about them that I could see that in some point in their life, they've probably received some sort of flak about, and struggled with or anything like that, I just look at that thing, and I love that thing so fucking hard, like so hard, like it's the most beautiful thing in the world, whether it be problem acne, or alopecia, or the various things that human bodies do."

By limiting their focus to specific aspects of either the client or the confines of the interaction, workers are able to cultivate a form of bounded authenticity. And many discussed focusing on specific aspects of the client/provider interactions to generate the authenticity, but were not as explicit as Noreen about the limitations of their focus.

When some providers explained the specifics of authenticity, they were frustrated that sex work is stigmatized as an inherently inauthentic exchange between provider and client, and wanted to emphasize the validity of their work relationships. Suzy, a twenty-seven-year-old escort, had a lot of experience with camming, not only because she herself cammed in addition to escorting but also because she studied camming as part of her master's thesis. But she admitted that she had a difficult time "faking" authenticity. "I have a really hard time with that. I think that in doing sex work, my authentic personality comes out a lot more than it does in my day-to-day life."

She described a conflict when a client covertly found her "real" online identity and accused her of being inauthentic. The situation she described represents what many workers told me when discussing authenticity: that there is a delicate balance of creating an authentic experience with clients, while still delineating between fantasy and reality.

I think he was definitely in love with me. He wanted to come . . . live here, or he wanted me to go where he was and live there. . . . I let him have that. I was pretty up-front about this is a fantasy, but to some point I was pretty invested in that dream. I think we were both getting something out of it, but also I think it couldn't happen. . . . He found my [social media] account one day and got super mad, and was like, "I don't understand, you're pretending to be a different person, and you said all these things, and blah blah," and I was just like, "Cool, I don't think there's that much discrepancy in my comments on [social media] and what I say to you. I'm a complex person with a lot of different ideas and not a static person in your brain. You need to chill."

Suzy explained that because so much of the relationship was based on communication via the Internet, she expected from the outset that they would eventually simply stop talking. "He had asked me, 'How do you think this is going to end?' and I was like, 'You know, we'll figure it out, and there's not going to be any kind of big blowup; we're just eventually going to stop talking,' and that's eventually what happened after years."

This conflict between authenticity and identity can reach an impasse wherein, a few providers explained, even though they can create a situation conducive to an authentic experience, it will never be "truly authentic," and because of this there will be a limit to the connection they can have with a client. But some workers found the concept of constructed authenticity and a performative work persona to be completely incompatible. Liz, a thirty-two-year-old escort, was finishing her PhD and started escorting to help pay for school. She was soft-spoken and referred to her work as a necessary service that was her calling. She explained that a separate work persona is not something she can bring herself to perform because she would be robbing herself, along with her clients, of "real" authenticity.

> I saw this client just a couple months ago. He was actually a quadriplegic. Yeah, that was definitely like my hardest experience since I've been doing this, like I cried all the way home and for the rest of the day and it was really difficult. But at one point he said, "If I had to describe you in one word, it would be 'genuine.'" And like, I hear that kind of thing a lot. . . . Of course, I'm sure that I do act a little bit different, you know, than I do in real life. I'm more accommodating; I'm not as bitchy to my client as I would be to my boyfriend, you know? I try to be very accommodating but without being fake. So, I try very hard to present myself honestly

and to not put on a persona. I know a lot of other girls do kind of put on a persona, but I just don't. I don't like that, you know? I wouldn't feel good about doing that, I guess. I don't know, I don't even know if that's valid or not but that's how I feel. To me, it feels important that I'm doing something authentic.

Liz felt that combining a performative work persona and authenticity was fundamentally conflicting. She explained that her genuineness was a desirable quality for some clients, but her inability to artificially create authenticity limited her business. However, whereas providers who discussed authenticity as an aspect of their work persona considered it part of the appeal for clients, workers who discussed authenticity in lieu of a performative persona wanted to highlight that it was important to them.

Conclusion: "The Über Roxy"

Roxy held the flame of her lighter to the tip of a fresh cigarette, inhaled, and snapped it shut. "It clears my mind and gets me ready to set up for whatever I'm doing." She took a long drag and nodded her head as she exhaled. "I think in the same respect that a professional athlete would have when getting ready for a game. Or somebody before a big presentation at work. You just want to clear that space to be able to work and do your job."

She held the lit cylinder in front of her face and squinted at it, then looked at me. "You have a stage persona," she said, pointing the glowing ember at me.

I nodded, "Yeah, I do."[21]

She grinned and spread her hands. "So you set yourself apart to do that?"

I nodded again.

I guess we can smell our own.

The girlfriend experience was the most common type of service provided, regardless of the type of work being delivered. It required additional emotional labor than a traditional "transactional" sex-worker interaction, and workers described this additional emotional labor at every level of their work and interactions with clients.

But the interplay between the personas that workers present in real and in digital spaces brings with it new concerns. When workers described their work personas, they often noted the "taking off" process which occurred when they were not in a session—how they had to reconnect with their authentic self after catering to the desires of others for work. But, with the proliferation of Internet communication, many providers spoke of the constant management of the relationships among their personal identity, their work persona, and their clients.

"It's an enhanced version of yourself—like the über Roxy, I guess. The über self. But that goes along with setting a tone, too," she said, drawing on her cigarette again.

But when this work persona is presented, people talked about how essential authenticity was as a commodity workers attempted to cultivate and monetize. Workers used overlapping in-person and digital personas to provide clients with that "authentic" girlfriend experience. And then they used digital communication to produce authenticity (both bounded and embodied) during and away from sessions with clients.

Providers described constructing work personas for a variety of reasons, though ensuring anonymity and increasing their comfort and safety at work were frequently noted. Some explained that they used these work personas to foster a "bounded authenticity" during their sessions by using what they called "hyperfocused truth." In essence, they centered on an aspect of their client they could find appealing and exploited that feature to nurture authentic intimacy.

The creation of this authenticity takes a certain amount of emotional labor, and when all the elements are balanced, workers said that it can be demanding but that the production of authenticity, either for the clients or for themselves, was the sign of quality work. Ultimately, these tactics shift the power dynamic during a social exchange in favor of providers. When a client and provider interact for the first time, it is almost always in a digital reality the provider has constructed. The person the client is seeing is the person workers want them to see, and the client has a certain level of vulnerability that benefits the providers.

Roxy twisted her cigarette into the ashtray and concluded that "those are the initial terms for power, as well. We have the information, and the knowledge and the power automatically. And, the vaginas."

5

Risks

"Guess Who Has a Gun Pointed in Their Face"

Charlene lived in a second-floor walk-up at the end of a quiet street. The cul-de-sac was off a main road through town that hummed with cars, but few ever made the turn onto the small block of squat houses.

It was a working-class neighborhood, with empty driveways waiting dry-mouthed for happy hour to bring tired residents in tired cars back from the bar.

The only driveway occupied at the moment held a black BMW sedan—not out of place in this setting, but certainly a point of pride for someone. The chrome and onyx shone like a piece of jewelry against the slab of angled concrete.

It sat in front of a gray stucco house. Two red doors adorned the face of the building, one leading to the first-floor apartment and the other, up a set of stairs. A pair of glass sliding doors opened to a small balcony on the second floor and a cacophony of sound spilled out onto the street below.

Charlene bustled around her living room, a bottle of cleaner in one hand and a rag in the other. Her heavy gold bracelets jangled as she sprayed cleaner on each empty surface and rhythmically swiped at it with a yellow cloth. She was tidying up for an expected appointment later that day.

Blades of golden sunlight cut through venetian blinds that struggled against the West Coast afternoon. She hurried past our open Zoom meeting on her computer, talking over her shoulder.

"I have zero tolerance for bullshit and that explains why I have my call blocker. . . . I'm block-happy; I don't have time for their shit."

She stopped cleaning the coffee table, a gold and glass affair that sparkled in the late afternoon sun. She stood up, put her hand on her hip, and shook her head.

"Being online is like high school," she said, pointing a red manicured nail at me. "Too much drama!"

Charlene was in her midthirties, but she had the youthful face and energy of someone a decade younger. She was dressed in a tight pair of blue jeans and a white undershirt that contrasted her dark skin. Charlene had a long history as a provider and was one of the few people I spoke with who moved from street-level work to independent escorting.

This fact gave her strong opinions on the dangers of sex work, and she felt that there was more to the risks than client/provider interactions— that part of what makes sex work dangerous is its connection to the broader culture. "Society has made it bad. Society has fucked it. Every time something happens, they put it on the news and it becomes kitchen table talk and that brings out more weirdos, creeps, pranksters. And then you got these pimps and these young girls and it's very dangerous. You've got girls out here fucking for fifty dollars completely unprotected. You know? Shit like that. And that creates a health hazard and a safety hazard because you think that just because the bitch over here do it, that I'm going to do that shit, and it's not going."

Charlene sprayed some cleaner on the table and scrubbed it vigorously with a rag, shaking her head and "mm-mm"-ing in disapproval, attacking the corners with brisk strokes. The frustration she expressed around the risks and dangers of sex work was a common theme with the workers I spoke to.

The cultural fascination with sex work focuses on the most extreme risks and paints the work with a broad, homogenous brush: if one worker is threatened with violence from a client, this must be true for all workers and all clients. Charlene's description runs the gamut, from creepy clients to abusive pimps to sexually transmitted diseases. When these examples become "kitchen table talk," it affects the lives of workers.

Stigma can increase and is persistent, access to traditional social resources can be difficult, and workers are left to deal with a variety of risks on their own. Because this is the overarching cultural narrative, when providers described the risks of sex work, they echoed these anxieties. However, when providers described the reality of their personal experiences and daily concerns, they often noted that risks were present, but not overwhelming. Charlene explained.

I think I have the same dangers as anybody else, like a police officer, a fireman or a bank teller. It's a job just like anything else that has its risks because at any time you can be working a regular job, obviously, and anything can happen. I can work at [a bank] right now and let's say you decide you're having a bad day and you decided, "These hoes," and you come in and rob it. Well, you know, guess who has a gun pointed in their face and got to try to give up some money or lose their job regardless? Me.

The perceived danger of sex work has been a long-standing concern both in the majority of sex-work research and in the culture at large. Lack of access to conventional social resources leaves sex workers vulnerable, and victimization is a common focus in research,[1] with violence, drug abuse, robbery, and other forms of victimization being the most recurring themes.

The providers I spoke with had very different concerns than those emphasized in the traditional literature. Most wanted to draw a distinction between the general risks associated with sex work and their own management of personal risks. This is not to say that they wanted to minimize the plight of other workers; quite the opposite. But their lack of personal experience with some risks meant that they often had difficulty contrasting their own experiences with those of the broader subculture of sex workers.

Ultimately, providers did speak about their personal concerns, but most often these were born not from broader, homogenous, culturally perceived risks, like violence from clients, but from issues that stem from their position in society and the specific situations that accompany their specific type of work. Concerns around stigma, lack of access to traditional social resources, and digital or emotional abuse were intermingled with the conceit that these risks are associated with the independence and commoditization of sex work. Yet, most providers said that there was a fundamental misunderstanding about how dangerous their work is.

Charlene brushed the hair from her eyes. "I just take it with a grain of salt," she said, speaking of the risks others point out to her. "I just have that information in the back of my head. I'm just pretty cautious. I'm not paranoid about it, but I do keep it in mind; I keep it in consideration."

Risk Perceptions: "Everyone's Seen That Bad Episode of
Law & Order"

Izzy, a nineteen-year-old cammer, had an unsure quiver in her voice,
and she was wrapped in an impossibly fuzzy pink robe that made it look
as though she was being devoured by a Muppet.

"Who else would threaten me in my job but clients? I don't know.
It's hard to put into words." She hesitated between phrases; though she
admitted that there were risks in her job, she did not believe they were
very plausible.

"I guess what I'm saying is, if I had a client that was a stalker and
wanted to find out where I live and come and break into my house, that
would be a threat to my physical safety, and I can't think of any reason
that—I don't think." She cut herself off and began again, vehemently: "I
guess what I'm saying is, a lot of people will say sex work is dangerous,
but I don't think that sex work itself is dangerous. I think having clients
that are dangerous is what's dangerous."

When providers discussed the risks associated with their work, most
often they would list the various risks highlighted by Western, and specifically American, culture that are presumed to be associated with sex
work. As Izzy put it, "A lot of people will say sex work is dangerous."

It is this overarching cultural narrative that workers often spoke to
when deconstructing the various risks associated with their jobs. However, it is important to note that Izzy wanted to make a subtle but important distinction as to exactly what is dangerous: dangerous clients—not
the work itself, or even just clients in general.

Similarly, Mona, a forty-six-year-old escort with a punk ethos, agreed
when she gave a sardonic explanation. "That [risk] factor is always there.
Come on. Everyone's seen that bad episode of *Law & Order*." She tags
her statement with a sarcastic "it must be true" before waving off the
remainder of her answer: "I've never ever—I'm not picking anyone up
off the street." But she ended with a dismissive, "Sure, it could happen."

Both Mona and Izzy waver between addressing the overarching cultural perceptions of the dangers involved in sex work and qualifying that
they have never personally felt particularly endangered. This interplay
between the broader cultural assumptions and the lived experiences of
providers made talking about risks difficult. Often providers would note

these broad perceived risks, but then reevaluate on the basis of their own experiences. But no one ever wanted to undermine the concerns of workers who were not in a similarly advantageous position.

The insight that risks are present but not a concern "for me" speaks to people's ability to accurately assess risk. This framing of risks as an acknowledgment of cultural perception followed by a personal assessment and response is a process that risk researchers have a long history of examining.

In the 1980s, Peter Sandman became somewhat of a guru on the way people and society at large recognize and respond to risks. He found that often the reality of a risk is not its driving force; rather, the driving force is the indignation felt by the public, which ranges according to a series of "outrage factors."[2] These include voluntariness, control, fairness, familiarity, and a spate of others. Sandman found that people do not so much assess whether behavior is risky; instead, they decide whether the behavior contains certain elements that heighten a sense of injustice and a removal of agency. For example, being afraid to fly is a fairly common phobia, yet car accidents are a far more routine and a far more statistically likely way for someone to be hurt or killed. But the combination of lack of agency (we place ourselves in the care of a pilot while flying, rather than driving a car ourselves), an unfamiliar circumstance (most people drive a car more frequently than they fly), and a "cataclysmic" outcome (most people survive car accidents, whereas plane crashes are more deadly) increases the perception that the act of flying is far riskier than driving a car, even though science and statistics tell us that flying is the safest way to travel.

Another aspect of Sandman's risk assessment is that people weigh risks differently if the risks are inherently unfair. If a risk touches everyone the same—as with natural disasters, for example—we see the risk as more acceptable, but if the risk targets a specific group, it is less acceptable and therefore a cause for outrage.

Researchers have often paired people of color, the LGBTQ+ community, and sex workers because they all represent a "risk group." And the unfair distribution of risks to these groups helps transmit the cultural idea that sex work *must be* dangerous. Research by a group of Australian scholars observed this in the rise of the AIDS/HIV epidemic in the '80s, which placed additional focus on marginalized groups, and found that the new attention fueled the perception that sex work is dangerous.[3] But how are the perceptions of workers different from those of the general public? And how does the fact that the subculture of sex workers is comprised of the "general public" impact those perceptions?

Paula had a lot invested in the virtual community of sex workers. She called herself an Internet native, since she had migrated to online message boards in the late '90s and spent most of her adult life in digital spaces. Now a forty-year-old escort and the moderator of one of the largest virtual sex-worker communities on the Internet, she was always careful not to minimize the concerns and risks of others. She wanted to be sure to explain that she was in a situation with very low risk, one that she had designed and sustained for a long time. "I've never felt unsafe. I mean I'm sure there are [risks], but in my five clients a month times twelve months ratio, I've never felt physically uncomfortable."

She added a quick, matter-of-fact, "I know it happens, but I've never felt that way," before she transitioned into talking about how she handles safer-sex practices. "I always use condoms. I don't let their crotch anywhere near mine, even when we're making out. That's a no. It's too easy to get pregnant these days and STDs, so I don't let them near me until they have a cover on, as we call it. I get tested every three months. I usually go into my doctor, my regular doctor, once a year and then I'll go to rapid testing, where the porn stars go, about every three months." These types of qualifying statements ("I know it happens") and slight changes in topic (from violence to safer-sex practices) were a very common way for providers to try to convey their complex feelings on risk perceptions. They would both confirm and refute the broad cultural perception that sex work is dangerous by acknowledging that sex work can be dangerous and that others are affected by victimization, but then asserting that the risks are both more minimal and more manageable for themselves.

But as the Internet has become more ubiquitous, workers use it to reduce their own personal risks. Additionally, research has found that the Internet has played a major role in another way as well: workers not only reduce their risk of violence, but as safety in one area grows, providers want to replicate that safety in other areas.[4] For example, a group of researchers from the City University of New York found that as providers moderated risk through using the Internet, they also were less willing to partake in risky activities that could increase their chances of STI infection.[5] And concerns about risk extended to digital-only sex work, where cam workers were able to assess their work satisfaction without excessive worry around physical violence.[6]

But when people think of the risks of sex work, the most common form would be danger from clients. Francis, a thirty-three-year-old escort, addressed this when she explained where the risks in her work come from, and the ways in which her social position insulated her from many of them.

Francis had an edgy-looking lip piercing and shiny silver nails that poked out of the sleeves of her baggy black hoodie. She said she did not feel that her job was particularly risky, but bluntly stated that it is contextual factors that play into her not being at risk for client violence specifically. "Yeah, clients don't scare me. What's so scary about a thirty-six-year-old virgin who's never kissed a woman before? That's fucking harmless. That was literally my Wednesday night. I'm actually not complaining about it. . . . Just because, I'm white, I work indoors, I charge a relatively large amount. I'm still low/midrange, but it's still a decent chunk of change. So, I feel like, in terms of client safety, I'm pretty okay."

The risks in sex work are contextual—not just with respect to the specific situation ("What's so scary about a thirty-six-year-old virgin?") but also with respect to the context of the worker themselves ("I'm white, I work indoors, I charge a relatively large amount"). It is these personal contexts that mediate the risks, reducing them before they become a danger.

Making a distinction between a "risk" and "danger," providers would admit that their work contained risks, but most noted that they personally felt those risks did not extend into the realm of "danger," specifically for them. Petunia, a thirty-five-year-old escort, hesitated as she explained the risks of sex work, trying to convey that the kind of work she participated in does not contain the elements that would turn risks into danger.

> I think people overestimate the danger. It's not as safe as some other jobs, but it's nowhere near—especially the end of it that I am, the danger is nowhere near what it would be. . . . Every single client I've ever had has been fairly respectful. They're not there just to fuck a piece of meat. I don't deny

that I'm sure somewhere in the industry that exists, but it's just really not my part of it. I know a lot of agency girls, I know down to midrange personally. Nobody has said that's really the case. Yeah, the whole seediness and the—the other thing is the demographics of it, like the idea of sex work as being streetcorner.

Petunia's position as an independent escort, and her racial and class status, meant that she could acknowledge the risks of her work but feel somewhat insulated by her position. These same contexts were often echoed in the decision-making process upon entrance. Hope, a twenty-eight-year-old escort, discussed this when she spoke about her entrance into sex work. "Having the education that I do and having the access to healthcare that I do, and the physical, like, you know, genetics that I do. Like, being a conventionally attractive, white, young, cis, fem, woman. . . . Like, there's just certain—I'm able to charge certain rates and do certain things, like insist on safety precautions and still have clients." Both Francis and Petunia were explaining that the perception of danger was part of the overarching homogenous cultural view of sex work. But Hope's description reveals the fundamental contradiction that the majority of workers noted during our discussions.

Sex work contains risks, but those risks are different depending on the type of work, the privilege, characteristics, and status of the worker, and the effectiveness of their security measures. When providers viewed their work through these contextual lenses, they could then categorize the risks of their work according to their ability to manage them.

Managing Risks: "Likely Partly Super Privileged"

Laura, a twenty-nine-year-old escort, sat in her kitchen tapping the side of her computer screen every few moments because her Internet connection was glitchy. Laura did not spend too much time on the Internet; she admitted that she used the available resources, but stays off the message boards because she likes to "avoid the drama."

She was explaining the physical risks associated with her work but noted that she was mostly concerned about active steps she could take to reduce the risk of sexually transmitted infections (STI), believing that these concerns were more manageable. Like many of the other providers I spoke with, she started her discussion by talking about the broad cultural perceptions of danger: "I could get assaulted. I could be raped. I could get an STD. It's highly unlikely I will get pregnant, but I could get pregnant. I could have some kind of mental trauma that could happen. That's a huge risk and something that does happen."

This was the most common way workers discussed the risks of their job. They started with a broad assertion about general risks. Most often, this would be followed by a specific example of a risk, and what could be done to reduce it to a manageable level. Routinely, the first and most common risk they noted was STIs.

These discussions tended to follow the same process: first confirmation, then refutation; first, vague references to risk, then descriptions of specific risks; and finally, explanations about a method of management. Laura spoke to her own experience, acknowledging the risks that most people presume about her job, denying that they are a real concern for her, and concluding that she had effective ways of dealing with them. "The physical part of being assaulted or raped, I'm not terribly worried about that, partly because I'm more likely to have that happen from a boyfriend or husband than from some client, because that has happened to me from somebody I love. It's already happened. I've already been through that. It's not a big deal. STDs, I take PrEP for HIV prevention. Then, everything else, other STDs, I'm not very worried about. I get tested about every six weeks for STDs. Nothing. Haven't gotten anything. Pregnancy? I'm on birth control."

Laura's description of broad risks ("I could get assaulted"), followed by a repudiation ("I'm not terribly worried about that"), was typical of the way providers contextualized violence. Then, frequently they would follow this by refocusing on a specific issue ("STDs") that can be mitigated ("I get tested"). Laura did say that she is not particularly worried about STIs, but these risks are minimized because of the specific steps she is taking, whereas she rejected the risk of violence by stating that she has been a victim of violence in the past and it is "not a big deal." Also, many were well versed in the current state of research and could speak to both likelihood ("it's more likely to happen from a boyfriend") and the scientific advancements the community uses to keep themselves safe ("I take PrEP/birth control").

—

Many of the workers discussed the use of PrEP, which stands for "pre-exposure prophylaxis." It is a drug that helps prevent the transmission and infection of HIV. And it can reduce the risk of infection by up to 92 percent when taken consistently.[7] This gave providers an affirmative way to combat risks preemptively, which was the ideal way to address risks, according to the majority of workers. The times when providers could enact a prevention strategy to abate a risk were when they felt their most empowered.

Providers' confidence around managing the risk of STIs and pregnancy has slowly been making its way into sex-work scholarship. Contemporary research has found that the relationship between sex work and higher rates of STIs is complicated at best, with some studies showing the rate of STIs among sex-worker populations to be the same as among the general population. Others have shown lower rates than among the general population when high-risk variables like drug abuse and poverty are controlled for.[8]

White, middle-class workers would speak to STI transmission as an existing but manageable risk that could be applied across most, if not all, workers. Definitive safer-sex protocols were so effective that they, in turn, became the principal measure taken to prevent all risks faced by workers. And it was this interplay between risk and privilege that made these discussions so interesting.

Being a "conventionally attractive, white, young, cis, fem woman," as Hope noted of herself, are all statuses that cannot be transmitted to other workers, and those nontransferable statuses are accompanied by privilege. Everyone wanted workers to be safe, as safe as the most privileged providers. But the insulation afforded by that privilege cannot, unfortunately, be shared.

This is not to say that workers dismissed the more serious risks faced by less privileged providers; indeed, the discussions were always accompanied by a wistful yearning for a more just world where their inherent statuses did not play such a large and unspoken role in their personal safety. So they wanted to focus on things that could be shared. But this theme of "if you're not privileged, use a condom" always gave the conversations on risks and safety the same vague, tepid feel—especially when the subject was something as serious as violence.

Though the risk of violence from clients was a frequent theme, workers commonly did not give specific detail on how to minimize these risks. This was especially common when they discussed ways to manage violence risks during appointments. Edward, the twenty-nine-year-old escort and my doppelganger, had a scholarly look while explaining why he is not very concerned about violence.

> There's always this theoretical fear of violence that you see in the media or you see in movies, but it's never literally happened or come close to happening to me, so that's maybe super-privileged, likely partly super-privileged, likely also less common than we assume or than many people think. Otherwise, I practice safe sex or safer sex as best I can. . . . I use condoms for fucking all the time. As a dude, I have either an inflated sense of how I can defend myself, but also I think most of the time, my clients are more afraid of me than I would be afraid of them, and I talk to my friends who are women who are in the industry, and they're like that's literally never happened. That's never been a thing I felt. That's a big difference. As a dude, I have a certain amount of A: misplaced confidence, but then B: a cultural-social sort of position that they're fearful, usually, more of me.

He noted that his lack of concern was a by-product of his social privileges. Like others, he mentioned the interplay between the presumed violence in sex work and the broader culture and its media representations. Edward was not only white and middle-class but also a man; he felt that this minimized his risks even more, compared to women. He called his risk of violence "theoretical" before, like many other workers, only discussing specifics concerning safer-sex practices.

Edward's sense of security stemmed from his perception that clients were more afraid of him than he was of them. He even doubted whether this observation was accurate, but the perception, paired with his race, gender, social status, and a lack of violent incidents in his work, was enough to keep him from being concerned. Instead, he focused on the positive steps he took to decrease his risks of STIs. Furthermore, Edward's perception that he would be able to handle any situation that arose was a common theme among many of the providers, suggesting that it was not just his gender privilege but other facets of social status and the organization of digital sex work that shaped exposure to risk and risk-management strategies.

The ability to manage risks is part of the complex relationship between sex work and broader social constructs. Independent providers noted that part of the appeal of independent work was being in control of their own safety, not in the sense of completely eliminating risk but in the sense of being able to assess what risks were manageable versus ones that could become dangerous. But this balancing of independence and risk reduction also gave workers a sense of pride in being able to "handle what comes my way."

Charlene finally sat down for a moment, but even as we continued our conversation, she was shuffling magazines and adjusting knick-knacks on her coffee table. "Oh, I've had all types of stupid ass shit happen," she said as she slid a candle to the middle of the table, nodded at it thoughtfully, and then moved it again.

She said that sex work can have risks simply because something unexpected might happen, and if it does there is no accessing traditional social resources like police or ambulances. This has the potential of placing workers in a delicate position with choices that carry real consequences. I asked for an example and Charlene smiled. She loved to recount the unusual anecdotes that happened during her work, and she took a lot of pride in her ability to take charge of these—unique—situations.

I went over to see one couple one time and the guy was a severe diabetic. I told these stupid motherfuckers, "When I come over, don't drink, don't do any fucking drugs." Both of these motherfuckers [were] fucking wasted as hell. So, I get there, and the wife is talking to me. She throws up all over the kitchen. He sees it, then he throws up all over the kitchen. And guess what? I have to act like I'm Wolf from fucking *Pulp Fiction* and shit, like, "All this is perfectly fine. We're going to clean this up, we're going to clean you up, you're going to get in the shower and clean up." . . . You know? 'Cause I need my money. It's like, that's what I came out here for. Shit. So, I had to clean them up, get them in the shower, and kind of get them sobered up. And they're just drunk as hell. It was just a nightmare. But then they called me over a second time during one of their birthdays and shit. [So], he wants to fist her. And he's fisting her in the ass and it's gross and now you have anal leakage coming out and it was just gross . . . and you're just like, "You know what? Fuck this. This is my line. I'm not about to deal with this shit. I didn't sign up for this."

Charlene's reference to Mr. Wolf is to a character from the movie *Pulp Fiction* who works best in stressful, dangerous, or, "explosive" situations. Also, Mr. Wolf's presence in the film is strikingly similar to that of a sex worker. He arrives with little prior introduction and is there for a singular purpose at which he excels. He arrives promptly when needed, presents himself in a very blunt but professional manner, and acknowledges risks but remains calm. Similarly to Charlene, Mr. Wolf also describes his limits in these risky situations: "I'm here to help. If my help's not appreciated, lots of luck."[9] Finally, the other characters in the scene recognize that part of what makes Mr. Wolf so good at his job is his ability to handle these situations while remaining in control. Samuel L. Jackson's character, Jules, explains, "[He's] totally fucking cool, in control, [doesn't] even really get pissed when you're fuckin' with him."[10]

Charlene likening herself to Mr. Wolf was meant to highlight that though her job could be "messy," she was adept at navigating these conditions, and it was a point of pride that she was able to take control of absurd situations. The fact that she returned for another appointment with the couple was the culmination of the story. "But then they called me over a second time," she said, her voice rising at the end of the sentence to accentuate just how outlandish the request was. Yet, she went back to give the couple another chance and see if she would be able to handle them a second time. In this case, it was only to find that she had reached her limit and could choose not to participate. This shows the duality of independent sex work. Though Charlene was able to handle messy situations, she could not rely on conventional social resources to help manage the risks of her work. Charlene was describing situations in which, because what she does is both illegal and socially stigmatized, whatever situations arose during her appointments were ultimately her problem. This also meant that limits and levels of involvement were decided by the workers themselves.

The trade of risk for independence was a common theme and transcended the type of work providers participated in. Sometimes providers had to deal with stressful or upsetting situations that, though they are not illegal, they still found problematic. Deborah, a twenty-five-year-old cammer with fiery red hair and wide green eyes, recounted such a scenario. She said that while camming, she has been asked by clients to utter racially charged insults that she was uncomfortable with.

> A lot of times the dude's user name will be the N word in all capital let-ters, or the N word three times in all capital letters, and he wants you to say horrible things, and things that I [am] like, "Sorry, but that's not going to be me. That's not going to be my mouth" kind of thing. So that's really common. . . . The first time I had someone ask me to do that was when I was eighteen. . . . This guy was like . . . "Can you call me the N word?" And I was like, "No. I'm not. Sorry." He was like, "Really? I'm paying you five dollars a minute. You can't say that?" And I'm like, "Look, it doesn't matter. The only reason I'm doing this job is so that I can do it on my fucking terms. I'm not going to do that." And he was like, "I guess I kind of like that. I haven't had a girl outright refuse." And he offered to tip me money and I was like, "No, this is a deal breaker. I don't care."

Deborah had a serious look on her face. She was adamant that she was doing this job on her own terms and that if she found a request from a client to be inappropriate or offensive, it was within her power to deny that request.

The risks that could be definitively reduced were noted, but risks that were more difficult to manage were described as part of the cost of being an independent worker. To accentuate their capability and in-dependence, providers would then focus on the parts they could man-age. Though many workers found risks to be overestimated, providers admitted that there were specific elements about sex work that tangibly increased the amount of risk involved.

One of the factors that providers said aggravated the risks in their work was the secrecy of sex work, which resulted from its stigmatization and resulted in a lack of access to conventional social resources. These problems can play a large part in not only generating risks for providers but aggravating existing risks. Providers lack access to the traditional so-cial resources that help reduce risk for "vanilla" citizens.[11] When work-ers assessed the amount of risk involved in their jobs, questions of STIs or client violence were measured alongside social risks, such as stigma and law enforcement.

Stigma and Structural Risks: "It's a Dirty, Seedy Thing"

Penny, a twenty-one-year-old escort, sat in a dark room in front of a blank wall. The glow from her laptop and the camera's oblique angle made it look as though she was calling from a dystopian future. "There are some [risks], in terms of feeling self-doubt about what you are doing or willing to do, but I still think that the majority of that all just comes from stigma rather than anything that actually transpires with clients."

She pulled the sleeves of her long gray sweater over her knuckles. "It's more because of the societal attitude or misconceptions about sex work than something about getting too attached to someone or even a relationship being affected by someone knowing that I've done it." She reached up and tucked some of her lavender hair behind her ear. "I wouldn't have a relationship with someone that had a strong stigma against it; that would feel emotionally harmful for me."

Penny also noted that decriminalizing sex work would have beneficial effects for safety but that stigma cannot be regulated through legislation. "[Decriminalization] doesn't mean that the social role or stigma will be taken away. . . . That's not really as important as actual safety or not being treated as either a victim or a criminal. . . . But there's still the social side that wouldn't necessarily be changed that much from it, I think."

Penny viewed stigma as an external influence that forced its way into both her life and the wider sex-worker community. Stigma represents another way that sex work interacts with broader culture. The famous sociologist Erving Goffman defined stigma as "an attribute, behavior, or reputation which is socially discrediting in a particular way: it causes an individual to be mentally classified by others in an undesirable, rejected stereotype rather than in an accepted, normal one."[12] This definition encapsulates the way many workers described trying to negotiate risks in their work. Not only was stigma a negative result of sex work; it also augmented the existing risks.[13] As noted above, workers would concede that the broader culture views sex work as dangerous, but they emphasized that danger is increased because of stigma.

Stigma played the same dual role as risk of being both a broad concern for the subculture and a more complex concern for individuals. Penny went on to explain that though she does not feel particularly stigmatized, she avoids specific activities—not because she does not want to try them but because she is concerned about being recorded on video and having it live on in perpetuity. "There's a valid range of things that I would try but I'm not sure exactly how I would feel about doing them because camming and porn and other video things. . . . There are things that I would be very open to doing personally but in terms of the social stigma don't seem worthwhile for the money, so I guess those. Yeah, because of the documentation. But the thing is, it becomes hypothetical—the social reaction—where it's not really my own personal feelings at all about the morality or my own comfort or something."

Stigma, by definition, is the unseen disapproval of the broader culture, yet any society is made of a collection of individuals. Just as with the assessments of other risks, stigma was ever present in broad discussions, but workers had contradicting ideas when applying stigma to their own personal situations. Two providers, Noreen and Alyson, both nervously admitted that there were even some scenarios where the stigma of sex work actually worked in their favor.

Noreen, a thirty-two-year-old nonbinary escort, quieted their normally exuberant voice to convey the seriousness of their explanation. She did not want to diminish its negative impacts, but she saw sex work's relationship with broader society as more complex than simply wishing there could be less stigma around her job. "[Reduce] the stigma of being a sex worker but, at the same time, that's where I feel a lot of the power comes from and a lot of the money comes from because it's a dirty, seedy thing. Like people will spend more money because it's dirty and like that kinda helps it. . . . It's a double-edged sword, you know? You want it to not be a big deal, but at the same time if it wasn't, we wouldn't be making as much money."

Alyson, a thirty-two-year-old escort, agreed with this sentiment. She described stigma in a similar fashion but believed that since it has a complicated relationship to broader society, the fact that the work is stigmatized, and also illegal, delivers benefits. The perceived scarcity of workers ensures fewer women in sex work overall and an increase in monetary value. "There's two devils on my shoulder. The social-justice-warrior part of me is very much in favor of criminal [justice] reform, but the other part of me knows that there are advantages to a black market. . . . Honestly, I don't think it makes a huge difference either way. There's always going to be stigma attached to it. As long as there's that stigma, that will keep a lot of women out of the industry. I don't know if that's better for the industry as a whole or if it's worse."

Both Noreen and Alyson saw that though sex work is broadly stigmatized, that stigma also made the forbidden nature of the work more valuable. The fact that the Internet could be simultaneously used to expose them to abuses while also protecting them through the use of anonymity was a contrast not lost on workers. And though stigma has been a serious issue for workers for a few centuries,[14] the ability to bifurcate one's identity on the Internet was a way that they said could be used to help with that stigma, both as an outlet for frustrations and as a conduit for community. "I'm friends with a lot of girls who have the marketing, client-facing profile, and then they have their anonymous, bitchy, complain-y profile. Those are the only ones I can follow," Alyson said with a laugh. "I can't follow the ones that are, 'Oh, so excited to see my clients!' I can't. It's just, I can't do it."

Many of the providers I spoke to noted that stigma could have far-reaching effects but that their fear of stigma could often be more harmful than the actual results of people discovering their work. And they said that finding ways, both digitally and in real life, to connect with other workers and sympathetic groups was a good way to mitigate those stigmatized feelings.

Jordan, a thirty-five-year-old escort, had a low growl in her voice as a result of only having slept three hours the night before. She fumbled around her desk looking for her vape pen. "I discovered the joys of quitting smoking. So now I'm one of those assholes who vapes." She shuffled papers around and raised the pen in victory after finding it. "There we go!" Jordan noted the difference between stigma as a far-reaching cultural indictment and the reactions of her friends to being told of her work: "I didn't tell anyone about sex work for years because I was terrified as to what their reactions would be. . . . But the friends that I have come out to have been really fucking cool about it."

Though Jordan described a situation in which her friends were accepting of her work, the reality of living with stigma is that it can be internalized, impacting the lives of providers whether or not it is objectively "true." A team of researchers from Johns Hopkins studied providers from a major East Coast city in the United States and found increases in shame and guilt associated with internalized stigma.[15] They also found that the majority of these negative feelings were based on the workers' perception of being stigmatized, rather than external sources.

Jordan also acknowledged that though a lot of the negative impacts of stigma can originate internally, there are still risks associated with the level of independence a worker has and their ability to make their own decisions about their work. She specifically noted the relationship between stigma and lack of access to social resources like the police, including how the interplay between lack of independence and lack of access to resources affected her ability to manage the risks of her job. "I've had a client assault me. Unfortunately, that was when I worked for a third party in a massage parlor. That's when I had no control over screening or who walked through the door. So that was like, 'Get the fuck out.' But even that, if somebody assaulted me in regular life, it would be like, 'I'm calling 911 right now.' But as a sex worker, you don't have the same abilities to do that because of the stigma that's involved. Because it's like the fear of being outed because of A, B, C, and D."

When most providers discussed stigma in broad cultural terms, it was to describe losing a job, being ostracized from friends or family, or being publicly shamed. But in this instance stigma precluded access to conventional social resources, which in turn resulted in a dangerous situation. Similarly, Arden, a twenty-six-year-old escort, noted that working for a third party reduced her independence. An agency sent her a client who was dangerous, and the agency was unapologetic for exposing her to greater risk. "They had no good reason for that other than, 'Oops, shit happens.' So that was like a huge turning point for me. Fortunately, it's just a bad story that I remind myself of. Nothing bad actually happened. I didn't get raped, but there are plenty of girls out there that do, and horrible things happen to them and you know it's really a shame, I think, that there isn't a way for women to have protection because you can't call the police." As Arden explained, social risks came in a variety of forms besides stigma, such as both lack of access to and fear of police. When the providers spoke of police specifically, they most frequently noted that they were looking to avoid them at all costs, and a major concern was to ensure that any new or prospective client was not a police officer in disguise.

Not having access to police protections was all but universal for the providers I talked to. Though workers came from different countries with varying degrees of legality, they felt that the risks of interacting with the police far outweighed the benefits. The police represent a volatile risk that has both extreme and sweeping consequences. Hope, a twenty-eight-year-old escort, explained why this is the case: "I don't know of a single woman who's an escort who feels comfortable going to the police if anything happened to her. And in fact the police are one of the biggest threats, because there are consequences for your future employment in any other industry. . . . The police have power and their word counts as more than a sex worker's. I'm more afraid of the police, of corrupt police, than of corrupt clients." Overall, workers described a complicated relationship with this specific social resource. Sex-work laws were different for many of the providers I spoke to, as some came from countries with full or partial legalization whereas others came from countries where sex work was fully outlawed. The police, as the enforcement hand of the government, were the introduction to the criminal justice system, and providers had carefully designed their work process to completely avoid intersecting with either police officers or the law.

None more so than Emma.

Emma was the only provider who admitted to doing sex work before she was eighteen years old. Now, at twenty-one, she had been a worker for five years. She was sitting in front of a low-hanging lamp that bathed her in shadow, like a silhouette in witness protection. I asked her if she took steps to hide her work from either friends or the police, and she said that she had to since she still lived at home with her parents, both of whom were police officers. "When I was younger I would pretend to be somebody's daughter to avoid being detected by [police]. . . . I have law enforcement parents. So, I don't talk to them! I'd sort of throw questions at them like, 'How often do police officers actually have busts on prostitution and things like that?' And just kind of throw hypotheticals at them." She admitted that early in her career she was a bit too careless and ended up being lucky, never having run into any serious trouble. But as she got older, she needed to incorporate better security measures, not only to keep herself safe but to keep the information away from her family. "I wasn't paying attention to the risks of being a teenage girl," she said. "I felt like I was invincible—then once I got older, I realized that I'm not really invincible. . . . I actually have to protect myself."

I asked what she thought could be done to improve the relationship between sex workers and the police. She paused for a moment and looked at the floor. "[We need to] educate police officers to be more compassionate toward people who are in this line of work, because there are people who were forced into it. There are some who are desperate, like I was, to pay bills, and we need as much compassion as somebody with an actual job, because this is a real job." The legitimacy of sex work seemed to be a bit of a panacea for the providers I spoke to. Acknowledging sex work as work would decrease stigma, lead to better legislation, and increase their safety, but figuring out how to get there was always the difficult part.

For my part, I was just amazed that Emma had managed to work for five years while living literally under the nose of the police. I laughed that what I had heard from providers rarely shocked me, but "then you come out with, 'by the way, my parents are cops.' My mind is blown!"

We both laughed, and she grinned a little. "Well, so is my sister."

New Dangers: "It Preys on Your Insecurities"

Laura did not spend much time on the Internet, and she had a frustrated look on her face while she tried to get her webcam to work right. She was sitting at her kitchen table while a breeze was rustling a set of sheer curtains behind her, an ethereal hand that would reach out before floating back down to stand at attention.

Despite her difficulty, this was all part of a strategy to avoid online harassment and keep her personal information secure. She only ventured online when she needed a specific service or information, like advertising and date-check sites.[16] She was telling me about her interactions with potential clients, and how these could be one of the riskier aspects of her work because there was no familiarity or trust built up yet in these early communications.

> You can have potential clients that text you rude things when you won't meet with them, and that makes me feel sad. I don't like people saying mean things to me. There was this one person, . . . he set up an appointment, and I gave him the general area I was in. Then, he guessed what apartment complex I was in, and then he said, "Oh, I'm a cop with the LA

Sheriff's Vice Department." . . . I was like, "Yeah, I wasn't born yesterday. Shut up. That's not how it works." . . . He left me alone pretty quickly, but it really messed with my head that day.

The Internet has created new ways for workers and clients to communicate, but these connections come with unique risks that workers have learned to navigate. For example, disrespectful and judgmental clients can lead to negative mental health consequences.

These types of concerns were often discussed in a very different fashion than in discussions of the broader culturally associated risks of sex work. The emotional labor of sex work does not have the corresponding cultural equivalent that the risks of violence or STIs have.[17]

Providers said that emotional risks were pervasive and difficult to both anticipate and prevent. When Charlene finally slowed down, she nodded thoughtfully when discussing the emotional impact of her work, and said that the Internet, specifically, created new kinds of interactions with clients that could be frustrating and require additional effort. "You kind of see the personality through the posts and you can see that they're dramatic or ratchet or however they're displayed and whatnot. So it'd be like, Do I really want to deal with this? Do I really have a capacity to want to deal with this person?"

Digital communication and its abuses were mentioned often by the providers, but with far fewer definitive strategies to manage them. Digital harassment is a relatively new phenomenon, and thus far the criminal justice system has been slow to respond with formal intervention strategies.[18]

The risk of exhaustion from the emotional connection that clients requested (see chapter 4) was a risk that workers felt was part of the job that bridged the gap between digital and real-life interactions. These interactions were not reserved for only in-person meetings, but were actually enhanced by the digital facets of their work.

Liz, a thirty-two-year-old escort, sat in an antique wooden chair in front of a wall covered floor to ceiling in books. Her chestnut hair was pulled back into a bun, and she was wearing a pair of thin, framed glasses. She looked like a librarian who could demand silence by furrowing her brow and squinting in your general direction. Her voice matched her demeanor, as our entire conversation was conducted in hushed tones. Liz was finishing her doctorate in English literature, but started escorting because she needed to sustain herself during her studies. She discovered that she loved the work and was one of the most emphatic people I talked to during my interviews.

She told me that she adores her job—that she helps people and could not imagine another job that gives her that kind of fulfillment while also paying her a lot of money, but the job requires that she connect with her clients in an authentic way, and that can leave providers vulnerable to a different kind of risk. "I'd say there are definitely emotional risks, I mean one is that . . . if you end up with a client who is disrespectful or doesn't treat you well, I mean, it can be really devastating just because you're in such an intimate and vulnerable position. If you get the sense that you are like used or looked down upon, it really hurts." Liz explained that the relationship between her job and her social anxiety is complicated. Being a provider can be beneficial for her social anxiety because she is in control and does not have to deal with a lot of the ancillary issues that come with having a conventional job. But the unique aspects of sex work can aggravate those issues as well.

She described how even experiences during the menial business tasks of sex work could have emotional effects. Many workers, for example, were members of review boards that "rate" the quality of the providers and their services.

> The whole like review system is really hard, you know, it preys on your insecurities, like really bad. And even without reviews, just the fact that you know that this guy is coming in, he's going to be judging you on how you look and he's going to be seeing every inch of you, I've found that that's one of the most difficult parts of what I'm doing. Just the insecurity feeling like I'm always going to be judged and rated and ranked, and all of that . . . I think that it's really easy to feel depressed, like I find especially if I'm working a lot.

Liz's work put her in an emotionally vulnerable position. When the providers discussed the broader culturally perceived risks of sex work, they described relying on increased independence to either manage the risks or accept their presence. But personal emotional risks were generally interpreted in a much more individual way than more general concerns, like violence or STIs. Emotional risks also tended to be expansive and could include almost any aspect of their work.

Osu, a twenty-seven-year-old escort, had been doing sex work on and off since college, but had decided to go full-time about six months earlier. She had short black hair cut jagged like an anime character, and she sat on her bed as the morning sun spilled into the room. Osu did not like lying about what she did for a living. She was concerned over the stigma associated with sex work and wanted to protect herself, but did not anticipate the additional emotional toll of having to frequently mislead people.

> I used to think, "I lie to everyone to protect them because I'm not ashamed of what I do. But I don't want to burden them with—" Then I'm think-ing about it. I'm like, "Who the fuck am I kidding? No. I lie to people to protect myself," because I don't want to be that one friend who does the taboo thing, the questionable one. I don't want to be the one who like—something's missing or something happens, I'm the one who's thrown un-der the bus just because of what I do. So, it's constantly lying, and I think now it kind of makes me want to. . . . I don't have as many friends, and I don't know if it's the result of me getting older and just being like, "I'm tired of everyone's bullshit," or if it's because I don't want to deal with having to make up these back stories and keep up with this lie. But that being said, it's not like awful. It's not bad, but it does get kind of lonely sometimes.

Osu's observation that attempting to avoid stigmatization has left her lonely was similar to workers' discussions of other risks. Often, they acknowledged that in their work they were trading risks for indepen-dence, and if they were able to work "on their own terms," certain risks were acceptable. But even when a risk was deemed acceptable, there could be unforeseen consequences. If stigma is "the unseen disapproval of the broader culture," what happens when that disapproval is no longer hidden, instead coming into full view?

Shaming women for their private choices is a theme many workers were familiar with. And the silence that accompanies shaming is a con-cept well known in feminist theory. The seminal work *Women's Ways of Knowing* even lists silence as the first epistemological stage wherein women are disconnected from both knowledge and their sense of self.[19]

Shame is not simply a state of disapproval, a clucked tongue over an indiscretion; it is a tool to impose silent conformity.

With the repeal of *Roe v. Wade* in the summer of 2022, access to abortion services became increasingly limited in the United States. Though my discussions with providers predated the Supreme Court decision, Isabelle pointed out that the stigma that surrounds sex work is not dissimilar from the pressure many women feel to hide the fact that they have had an abortion. "How can we, with abortion being stigmatized so much?" she asked in a somber tone. "If you can't say, 'Hey I had an abortion,' how can you say, 'Hey ten years ago, I used to be an escort.'"

Kelly, a thirty-three-year-old escort, knew what it was like to be pressured into silence. She squared her shoulders and tucked her chin to her chest, her eyes narrowed, giving her a serious look. She lowered her voice to a whisper and emphasized, "I'm not paranoid." She was telling me about an incident when a client refused to pay her and she was tempted to call the police. But she knew that though calling on police might diffuse this specific situation, it could jeopardize her career, her overall reputation, and especially her safety.

> There would be other [workers] that would be like, "Oh, did you hear that, you know, Kelly is outing people?" I'd be like, "No, I'm not outing people. I just want to get paid for what—" I can't call the cops. I can't take him to Judge Judy. Now because of the way things are set up, and it's so client-centric, because people are just trying to get the client's money, I don't really have a way—even though I have his information, because it wasn't violent, I feel like it's not [something I could go to the police for]. . . . Because it's just a monetary thing basically that I got ripped off, I feel like it's bad for business if I was to make a big deal about it.

Kelly explained that she would call the police if violence were involved, but in situations that involve arguments over payment, she had little to no recourse. Moreover, if she were to contact the police, she would almost certainly be accused of "outing," which was enough of a threat to induce her silence. Kelly's description of "outing," revealing the identity of providers or clients either accidentally or, more concerningly, maliciously, was a major concern when it came to accessing any social resources. A worker who calls the police risks being outed to their family, friends, and community. This can ruin relationships, affect their ability to find work, and lead to jail time.

Hope, a twenty-eight-year-old escort, described a similar situation in which she was outed. She was an enigma by design and was the only provider I spoke to whose interview was neither in-person nor on webcam. She felt that participating in the research was important, but her own safety protocols prohibited her from showing her face. Instead, she talked to me via videoconferencing software with her camera disconnected. She explained that her precautions were a direct result of an outing incident.

> Unfortunately, I had a stalker, which decimated my business, and it was really awful. And, you know, [I] lost most of my clients and [it] scared the shit out of me, too. So, it was really—really terrible. My email was anonymously hacked. I actually don't know who it was to this day. [They] used it to find out all the names of my clients and my friends and my lovers. [They] spent the next six months sending awful, threatening emails. They got my vanilla name [and] used the power of the Internet to look up my family members and were emailing private pictures from my email account to my family members. It was really awful.

Talking to friends and family about her work seemed daunting, but Hope laughed when she recounted that she was pleased that both her family and her vanilla job were supportive.

> It was a very difficult time with my family. Ultimately, we're stronger for it because, this way, you know, my family knows the work that I do. I would have rather preferred that they find out in a different way, you know. Well actually, I would have preferred they find out never. But it happened. And professionally, my [job] was actually extremely supportive. Luckily, I was [at a progressive institution], so they're not exactly close-minded. [But] to be living in constant fear and also having to navigate opening a case with the police. . . . Although it's actually been positive. This is because I had really amazing resources and privilege. Cis privilege and fem privilege. . . . I also had a close friend who's a feminist blogger [and] a very powerful lawyer. And this person, pro bono, wrote to the [police] for me. [They] helped me draft a cease-and-desist letter to the stalker. And, if we had found who

the stalker was, [they were] gonna help me sue the fuck out of him in civil court. So, I had resources that most sex workers don't have.

Hope noted the same social privileges others specified when discussing risks and risk management. However, her example was an extreme case of specific risks for workers being drastically different than the overarching cultural expectations. When workers described outing, it was one of the most extreme possible outcomes, yet Hope and others managed to weather the storm and maintain their business.

The Internet is often credited for making sex work safer, especially for independent workers, but there are also new dangers associated with the digital landscape. Hope was never able to discover who outed her because of the anonymity the Internet provides, and many workers described new risks that accompany digital interactions that this new venue of sex work necessitate. Also, once a worker is outed, it is difficult to know the extent of the damage until it happens. The Internet is notorious for its arbitrary and capricious application of "justice."

In 2015, Jon Ronson tracked down a series of unfortunate individuals for his book *So You've Been Publicly Shamed* and discovered just how ruthless the Internet can be when it latches onto a public (or even semipublic) statement by someone. The book is both a cautionary tale and a condemnation of the Internet's penchant for turning public shaming into an orgy of cruelty.

For providers, outing was a roll of the dice. A few workers told stories of malicious friends, partners, or clients who attempted to hurt them by revealing their secrets. Most managed to endure the ordeal and then lent encouragement to others by sharing their stories. But as Hope noted, you never know when you will have to worry about the reaction of more than friends and family.

"There's a risk of social safety when being outed. I think the most terrifying to me is the social safety one."

Conclusion: "No One's Job Is Easy"

Charlene sprayed some Windex on her glass-topped coffee table and wiped it with a paper towel. Her gaze shifted back and forth as if she were watching a tennis match, trying to see if she had left any streaks.

"When I'm online I'm mostly marketing my clip sites and my cam sites and things like that," she said, swiping the rag. "Or when I'm online it's more business, not really personal. In general, I like to have my work, go in my corner, do what I got to do, and keep it moving."

The assertion that most workers made—that sex work is dangerous but not for them personally—speaks to the duality of a new digital model of sex work.

There are clearly risks in sex work, as Olivia noted. "At the end of the day you're in a room alone with somebody. So, it's always a risk." But overwhelmingly providers discussed the personal ways in which the majority of risks could be reduced. And if a risk could not be adequately addressed, it had to be accepted as part of the cost of doing business.

Most providers felt a sense of attachment with the broader sex-work community and wanted to acknowledge the dangers other workers might face. But when workers examined their own personal risks, they found far less to fear. Most discussed the overarching cultural narrative of the dangers of sex work, and would make a broad proclamation that echoed those sentiments, then slowly reduce those sentiments until they eventually landed on the fact that, due to a variety of protective and privilege factors, they faced minimal risks.

The danger that most workers identified with specific detail was the threat of STIs, and most pointed to this danger both as proof of positive change in the sex-worker community (via the predominant culture of safer-sex practices) and as a risk that can successfully be prevented (via the lowered rates of STIs among certain sex-worker subpopulations).

The social risks associated with stigmatization were a far more relevant concern for the providers I spoke with. But, similarly to the discussions of race and privilege, workers noted that the dual role of stigma as a structural issue should be reduced, but on a personal level some felt that stigma could aid in the empowerment of sex work, either by defying patriarchal norms or simply by making the work more valuable due to its illegality and consequent lack of supply. Again, the duality of being both a member of a marginalized community and a privileged individual made confronting the risk of stigmatization difficult for providers to articulate.

The role of the Internet often complicated this duality further by simultaneously providing resources in the form of knowledge and support, while also creating new risks due to increased connectivity with clients, other workers, and society at large.

When workers were affected by emotional risks, they had far fewer responses than they had to more tangible physical or social-structural risks. Emotional concerns weighed heaviest on the providers I spoke with, but these new risks were part of the cost of doing business in the new digital era of sex work. Charlene and others pointed out that every job contains a risk, and it is up to the individual to decide whether a risk is one worth taking, given their own personal judgment.

"I could be a policeman or a fireman and say, 'Hey, there's a fire over here, I'm going to go put it out,' and the roof falls in and I fall into it." She said, decisively, "It's the same risk. You're still dealing with people with mental issues and crap like that, too. Their job ain't easy. No one's job is easy."

6

Security

"No One Is Gonna Be as Invested in My Safety as I Am"

Arden drove down the street to the house at the end of a long block of row homes. Across the alley was a blacktop basketball court that substituted as a schoolyard, and the paint peeling off the mural on the side of the school's brick façade mirrored that of the homes on the opposite side.

The neighborhood once proudly housed the local Polish immigrant community, but years of hard living had taken its toll, and the windows that faced the alley were sporting crow's feet and their white-irised panes had jaundiced.

Students milled about, dressed in uniforms of drab gray, white, and beige, waiting for the mechanical clank of the school bell to start the day. Most of the young men played basketball or darted from one friend group to another, while the young women lined the fence, chatting, laughing, and showing each other pictures on their phones.

Arden parked her sporty white coupe by the faded yellow curb between the "no parking during school hours" signs. She got out and strode past the schoolyard, shoulders back, chin up, and made her way towards my front door.

There was coffee brewing in the kitchen when I heard three firm knocks. I opened the front door and a hand thrust through the entryway as Arden smiled widely and announced, "I'm Arden. You must be Kurt." I shook her hand and commented that she had quite the firm handshake.

"I like to be professional," she responded. She certainly exuded an air of professionalism that fit her overall look. She stood in the center of the porch, her five-foot-four frame at rigid attention, shiny patent leather heeled ankle boots and tight black jeans contrasting a spotless white leather racer jacket. The jacket's gold appointments matched a small nose ring just below a pair of intense green eyes framed by blonde bangs.

Her outfit, and overall demeanor, were presented without a single wrinkle or crease, like a '70s punk fresh from military school. I motioned for her to come in, and she breezed past me and stood at the edge of the entryway. I spread my hands and asked if she would prefer to talk in the living room or sit at the kitchen table. She replied that the kitchen table would be more professional.

I agreed.

She sat at the old gray Formica table, an overhead lamp bathing her in a ring of white light as she described her first experience working for an escort agency.

"I ended up leaving [the agency], because I had a really bad experience with a client that [the manager] did not screen. And he came into my home and actually attacked me." She sat with her back straight against the kitchen chair. "I realized that no one is gonna be as invested in my safety as I am. I'm always going to screen a client better than someone who is just exclusively doing it for the money."

Taking control of her own safety was important to Arden, but like many of the providers I spoke with, she recognized that it was her own responsibility. As discussed in chapter 5, when workers talked about the risks they faced, they noted how their own specific risks differed from the culturally perceived risks associated with sex work, and how those risks could be diminished when placed in the hands of workers themselves.

Arden was very clear that her personal autonomy played a central role in her own safety: "I work for myself. I employ myself. I screen clients myself. I'm obviously doing this of my own volition. There's nobody pulling the strings behind me," she said firmly.

Independence was a recurring theme when providers talked about their security concerns, and the Internet's role in personal independence was nearly universally referenced in all the discussions I had with workers. Providers tied the use of the Internet directly to personal autonomy, as Arden did when she explained how her screening measures were superior to those in her previous work for an agency: "I use my personal prostitute black book, if you will, to reference these guys. If they haven't seen a girl that I know personally, I make them send me contact information for two women that they've seen that I don't know. . . . I'll run his phone number through a date-check service or something like that. . . . It's a website that runs background checks and builds profiles for gentlemen that are interested in seeing providers. It makes my life a lot easier." Arden described how Internet resources can lead to better security measures. However, both risks and security are contextual. Like many providers, Arden was vocal and detailed about her screening and security measures but noted that these measures changed frequently to address contextual concerns.

She only used screening techniques she trusted to produce valid and reliable information about prospective clients. In the quotation above, she described the security measures she used for meeting a new client who had references from workers she trusted. However, she had different protocols for meeting clients without references, those who had profiles on sex-work review websites, or clients for whom she needed to gather information directly.

Similarly, the majority of providers who spoke to me described a variety of security procedures, both digital and in-person, that they used according to the contexts involved. Workers could produce trusted information a variety of ways, but at the cost of varying levels of effort.

Arden flicked the cigarette between her pink painted nails, and an unbroken thread of smoke crawled out of the ashtray in front of her. "Even though [the agency] might have a financial incentive to keep me safe and working for them, it's still not their safety in jeopardy. I'm not sure what she did to screen properly." Arden took a drag and stabbed her spent cigarette into the ashtray. "But I think it was a crock of shit."

Screening as Work: "You Can't Vouch for Yourself"

"I couldn't do this job without the Internet. I couldn't do it," Paula said as she adjusted the microphone on her headset and shifted in her gaming chair. Most of the workers I spoke to used smart phones or laptops when they were working, but Paula told me, "I need a command station! I sit at my computer all the time. I'm still that old school '90s thing. I need a desk, a computer, a keyboard, a printer. I'm not into the laptop on my lap on the couch type of thing."

Paula was a forty-year-old escort and cammer who had always felt comfortable in digital spaces and was the moderator of a large, online sex-worker forum that answered providers' questions, discussed timely topics, and built community. Her long blonde ponytail and bright blue eyes gave her a Rockwellian "girl next door" vibe, as she discussed how technology has changed sex work in the last decade.

"I wouldn't have been comfortable doing it ten years ago with just NearMart. These websites, they've been around for seventeen years, but you couldn't find them as easily." Paula was open and casual in her discussion of her work, and she acknowledged that this was the case because she so rarely got to let her guard down and speak candidly about it with anyone who was not a provider.

"There were actually girls that I know, actually one girl in particular, she tells these horror stories about ten years ago when screening wasn't the norm. She was robbed and beaten and all this stuff." As the morning crept on and the temperature rose in her dining room, she fanned herself with an envelope she picked up from the table. "Without Google and Blackout and MateRate,[1] where you can verify guys, and without being able to check their [social media] presence, without all that, we wouldn't be able to do this safely, I don't think."

The Internet has provided several benefits for providers. First, it aids in their advertisement, helping them reach a large number of potential clients and helping them present their particular work brand or services. Second, it helps workers maintain a reputation for high-quality work, regardless of type. And, third, it provides information on prospective clients and their level of risk.[2] Specifically, the Internet is a place for workers to form community and trade useful information and best practices. Providers have access to specific client-screening websites and can set up profiles online to communicate and advertise to new customers.[3]

Often the public is surprised to learn that providers have elaborate security tactics. In 2005, the Urban Justice Center interviewed a variety of "indoor" workers and found that 92 percent had some form of safety protocols they used while working, including "trusting his or her gut/instinct; screening customers; being aware of surroundings; ensuring that a friend or co-worker knows of their location; seeing only regulars; keeping a weapon or mace on hand; relying on the house or agency to maintain safety."[4] But, 79 percent exercised precautions beyond "gut feelings."

Though it is clear that workers are concerned for their safety, when asked if they would approach police for help, only 16 percent had ever had an experience where they found police to be helpful, only 43 percent would even consider talking to police, and most thought that police would not be trustworthy or even helpful.[5]

Paula was acutely aware of the contribution the Internet has made to the world of sex work for those with access to such technology. Sex and the Internet have been bedfellows for her since the late 1990s, when she was spending her leisure time finding dates in dial-up chat rooms. She was technologically savvy and was aware of the digital resources for workers during their formation. But the marriage of sex and technology is not a new phenomenon.

Technology journalist Patchen Barss's book *The Erotic Engine* looked at the parallel tracks of technology and sexuality and saw that "there was never a time when sexuality was not a driving force in communication."[6] Pornography is one of the forms of sex work that easily and directly mirrors advancements in technology, and new technologies adopted in society consistently have an early erotic counterpart.

When the providers I spoke to discussed risk, the overwhelming majority explained that they perceived themselves to be safer than the average sex worker. But most attributed their reduced risks to effective security protocols facilitated by the Internet. There are a lot of ways in which technology helps workers communicate and stay safe, but screening was what most people pointed to as an improvement that accompanied the movement of business online.

Screening is the process of preemptively gathering information on prospective clients via the Internet to judge their safety and suitability. Roxy gave a straightforward definition of how she and her partner screen prospective clients.

> Screening is actually a pretty simple process. We require a lot of personal information from the client. Their full real name and email address. A work email, place of employment, home address if we feel as though they're a little sketchy or we need to have more leverage. A social media profile at times. That is often to be able to match a face, a picture, with who they say they are when they show up. Then, especially important is how we verify through other girls that they've seen, other providers. So we'll ask for the names and contact info of other providers that they've seen. Get in touch with those girls and verify through them.

Though screening was routine, workers described a variety of strategies that made up their screening procedures. Some providers required in-depth information to the extent of home addresses or bank account numbers, whereas others needed a minimal amount of information such as a full name and a place of employment. Screening serves an important dual purpose. First, it confirms that a potential client is safe and reliable to deal with, and not a danger. And second, it keeps workers who are in danger of arrest from crossing paths with the police in the form of a sting or vice patrol.

Screening is not a new tactic. Prior to the Internet, communities of providers would pass along information about safe or dangerous clients via word of mouth. The information they shared came either from previous experience with other workers or via investigative work like phone calls to a client's place of business.[7] Screening is so pervasive in the sex-worker community that I was screened without my knowledge so my identity could be verified for the providers I spoke to. Lydia, a twenty-three-year-old escort with a hint of a southern accent, spoke often about her concerns for other workers, so it came as no surprise when she revealed she had surreptitiously called to verify my status with the university.

One gray spring morning I walked down the hallway of the Center for Law and Justice on my university's campus. I took a left turn and continued past a series of brown doors with nonconsecutive numbers on tiny black placards: 504, 511, 512a, 515. I opened the door to my office, dropped my bag on my desk, and sat down at my computer. There was a yellow post-it note in the center of the screen: "Please come to the front office." Was I being called to see the principal?

I poked my head through the door of the front office and smiled at the department admin, who responded with a sing-songy "Morning!" and raised her eyebrows. I responded by holding up the yellow sticky note. "Oh! Someone called for you," she exclaimed, while patting the top of her desk with both hands to find a different yellow sticky note. "Someone named Lydia called to confirm your employment and asked if you worked with Dr. Miller. I told her that I was pretty sure you did, but that I'd need to doublecheck, but then she just said that was okay and hung up." I blinked a few times and responded with an "oh, thanks." and pulled my head back through the doorway.

When Lydia and I met up for our talk, we both laughed that she had used the same screening measures to verify me that she would use on a prospective client. For me, it was an odd little rite of passage, but for Lydia it was a way to confirm that it was safe not only for her but for the rest of the sex-worker community to speak with me.

> LYDIA: Well, I did do your intensive screening (laughing).
> KURT: I know I cannot thank you enough for that. . . . It showed ev-
> erybody that I am who I say I am, which is fantastic. . . . I obviously
> cannot—
> LYDIA: Yeah, you can't vouch for yourself.

Lydia's screening method was a common way for workers to gather information about prospective clients. But more importantly, the result of the screening was that Lydia could confidently recommend me to other workers interested in speaking with me.

Both personal and digital references were a common form of screening, as well as gathering vital information via the Internet to verify employment status, confirm relationships, and test the overall honesty of prospective clients. The screening process was a way for providers to shift the power dynamic in their favor early in the provider/client relationship. A prospective client must show enough vulnerability to make the provider feel comfortable in considering them. But this process did not come without a price. Ensuring security required providers to put in extra work. Workers said that the public is largely unaware of all the additional labor that goes into being a provider. There is a presumption that workers simply make appointments, meet clients, and get paid. But, when providers described their daily work routines, the majority of their time was spent online with administrative tasks.

Alyson, a thirty-two-year-old escort, was someone who took a lot of pride in her work. With eight years' experience escorting, she described her job by saying, "We're basically just naked therapists. You have to be able to make people feel at ease, make people feel comfortable." She told me that most people assume that interacting with clients is the most tiring part of her job, but she considered all the initial advertising and screening to be the most demanding part of her work. "Eighty percent of the job is just sitting in front of the computer, tick tacking away trying to set things up, hoping they don't flake, which is, oh my god, that's the worst part of the whole job. People say, 'Oh, you must meet all kinds of gross weirdos and psychos and guys that do weird things to you.' I mean, no. The worst part is just trying to figure out a specific time, a specific place, and where to meet. If you get through that hurdle, the rest of it is pretty easy and nondescript."

Alyson laughed when she said that she was hopeful because the cultural script about sex work did seem to be changing. People seemed to be slowly coming around to the fact that sex work has changed from what they presumed it was like. "A friend said this to me, she said, 'I think the girls who live in the condo above me are hookers.' I said, 'Why do you think that?' She said, 'Well, they wear pajama pants all day and they're on their laptops all day.' That's basically the picture of the modern sex worker, is just hanging out at home with their dogs in pajama pants staring at their computer all day."

When most workers talked about their work process, they began by describing administrative work that included advertisement, communicating with clients and fellow workers, and screening. For the providers I spoke to, using the Internet was an important part of their work that kept them safer. But the reliance on new technologies was an attempt to solve an existing problem. Providers lacked access to traditional social resources due to the stigma and illegality of their work. So, the independence offered by technology was more than a perk; it was a way to wrestle back some of the agency sapped by the illegality of sex work. But illegality and stigma are persistent.

Mona, a forty-six-year-old escort, sported a classic Bettie Page haircut and leather wristbands. She summed up her thoughts on technology by lamenting that while its ability to increase her safety makes it vital to her job, it can also be seen as another intervention point for those looking to eliminate sex work, who might blame the advances in choice and agency enabled by technology for the proliferation of sex work: "It is indispensable. Watch, all the [abolitionists] are going to blame it on the technology, because 'she wouldn't be doing this if it wasn't for technology.' I wouldn't be, because it wouldn't be safe. I mean, it wouldn't be as safe as it is now." Though Mona stressed that the Internet was a big help in keeping her and her clients safe, mostly she was interested in finding a balance to minimize the amount of work she had to do while still having the freedom to make her own choices.

> I'm at that age that I just don't give a shit. I'm just kind of like, "You know what? If you want to come and stalk me, I dare you. I will make it the worst decision of your lifetime." I almost invite it. Really, I'm that confident. You talk about safety and stuff like that, I'm never, ever worried. I played roller derby. I worked with fifteen-hundred-pound horses. I can handle a dude. You have some feminists who think that prostitution is an affront to feminism, and me, I'm the last one to deal with any form of misogyny or any form of chauvinist behavior, and I actually think it empowers me. Do I have a pimp now? Do I have an appointment setter? Yeah, I do have that, but they're not a manager. They're not a pimp. I never see them. I go and deposit money, and I do pay my taxes, by the way. It empowers me to do what the hell I want to, and I think that's something that is overlooked. It's always portrayed as you've got this old hag madame, or this really greasy pimp that's controlling these women. You rarely hear about us; we're basically running our own business for all practical purposes. And everyone thinks that you're making a lot of money, there's a lot of overhead as well. You have to get your nails done. It's very high maintenance being a hooker. I'm like, "Jesus. I'm so tired of getting my nails done." I'm like, "What do you mean, I got to shave again!?"

There is a fundamental dichotomy that workers recognized in the use of technology. Though it presents opportunities to create a safer working environment, any new way of performing their work will be placed within the existing sex-work paradigms. Proponents will tout the benefits for autonomy and detractors will point out new dangers. However, these simplistic frames starkly reveal why workers felt that their security was solely their own responsibility. Regardless of differing opinions, both positions highlight that workers cannot access traditional social resources, and these new security tactics have to ensure some level of safety in order for providers to enter and then continue in sex work.

This reveals why screening is such an important part of their work: because workers must quickly and discreetly decide whether a new client is safe, and part of this calculation is the acknowledgment that if they are wrong, they cannot call for help.

The Problem of Police: "Well, What Did You Expect?"

The isolation from social resources is so prevalent that most workers viewed the police as a hazard (as discussed in chapter 5). But previous research has found that these views are pretty common when workers report their concerns around social resources like police. Three researchers from British Columbia, Canada, analyzed the lived experiences of workers and found that a variety of physical, social, and policy features impact their overall health and safety, but among them, reducing negative interactions with police helps increase their agency and security.[8]

Other research has shown that this lack of confidence in police can lead to reluctance to report victimization or unlawful behavior by clients.[9] The Internet has helped to reduce some of these negative interactions with police,[10] and it can also foster a sense of community among workers that can promote collective action.[11] The lack of access to traditional social resources and the realization that security is in the hands of workers meant that when providers talked about how they stay safe, their relationship with police and current laws was complicated, to say the least.

Arden started by explaining that workers have a variety of ways they stay safe. Most of them rely on access to resources like friends and technology, but the current state of the laws (especially in the United States) aggravates the vulnerable position that workers find themselves in. After Arden recounted her experience of being attacked by a client whom her agency did not screen well enough, she lamented that other workers might not have fared as well as she did, and she is sure that situations like this happen often and impact workers who do not have the same advantages she does.

> I didn't get raped, but there are plenty of girls out there that do and horrible things happen to them and it's really a shame. I think that there isn't a way for women to have protection because you can't call the police. That's what's so fucked up about this industry, is that the demand for what I do

is never going to go away, but the laws could change to protect women who are put in these vulnerable situations, who don't have a voice, who can't stand up for themselves, who can't screen themselves, who don't have someone to call to say, "Hey, I'm okay," "Hey, I got paid."

The fact that many workers noted their personal privilege when they entered sex work also played a role in how they described their security procedures. Janine, a thirty-year-old escort, was a naturally curious person. Even before becoming a provider, she kept a record of her sexual partners because she wanted to sleep with as many people from around the world as possible.

During our interview she pulled up a spreadsheet and rattled off the countries of the people she had been with. "Let's see. Turkey, the Dominican Republic, Mexico, India. Oh, Algeria, that was horrible. Horrible lover," she said.

"Algeria was horrible? Why?"

"Oh my God. He bit me during oral sex."

"Ow. Okay, yeah, that makes sense."

"Let's see. Canada, Chile, Ukraine, Morocco, Italy, Iran, Colombia, more India." She hummed as she scanned the sheet. "Pakistan, more Turkey. I had a Turkish phase. Guatemala, Venezuela, Romania, Israel, South Africa, Belgium, the United Arab Emirates, that was a good one. And then of course, a bunch of American dudes," she laughed. "So, I moved into a new apartment, and after so many horrible roommate experiences, I said, 'I absolutely must live by myself, unequivocally.' . . . Yeah, so in addition to really needing money, I had been dating for quite a long time, and I'd just been monumentally frustrated with the quality of my sex life, and I thought, 'You know what? If I'm going to have lots of bad sex, I want to get paid for it.' So that's what happened." But when Janine described her screening metrics, she acknowledged that though she tried to be careful about whom she was seeing, she had certain resources and advantages, like a full-time vanilla job and health insurance, that she could use to legitimize herself to police if need be. "I am prepared for either bodily injury or some kind of damage to my apartment. I mean, thankfully with my full-time job, I have superb health insurance, and I also have apartment insurance, so if I pick a client up, and he punches me in the face and knocks me out and steals all my stuff, fine. I call the police and I say my apartment was burglarized, and I file a report."

The threat of police can make early communications with prospective clients difficult. If a provider needs to worry that a message may be from a police officer, they have to be less forthcoming with details, unable to ask specific questions, or limited in discussions of preferences. Mandy, a twenty-nine-year-old escort who had just celebrated her one-year anniversary as a provider, explained that this creates situations where workers make decisions in the moment, rather than with more time and information. "There's always the risk that whoever I'm meeting is a police officer. So I can't have a very open discussion of what things do you like? What's on the table, what's not on the table. . . . It's more an in the moment type, which it shouldn't be. It shouldn't have to be like that." Mandy's frustration was born from the fact that the existing laws were creating additional dangers, rather than alleviating them.

The providers I spoke to from Australia had very different experiences, especially from those in North America. In 1986, the Australian government enacted the Prostitution Regulation Act, essentially making brothel and escort services legal in some territories.[12] While criminal penalties still existed for street prostitution, many of the Australian providers I spoke to only knew a culture that normalized decriminalization.

Gertrude, a forty-year-old escort, said that she perpetually feels twenty-nine and that sex work is her chosen career that she takes a lot of pride in. "It's such a bubble here. It's now second-generation decrim, which also means that everyone in the industry now has grown up only knowing decrim. So I thought the whole world was sort of like this. And then, I looked overseas, and I went, 'Oh my god, what the hell is going on here?' And then that's when I actually started getting into activism and stuff. It's sort of like part of that empowered me to start loving my job." Gertrude differentiated between Australian and American culture when it came to accessing social resources and the agency of workers. Providers at her brothel were able to address problem clients directly and did not have to worry about placating them lest the police get involved. "You don't want to mess with women who are pissed off. You'd be dealing with about four or five girls all in your face going, 'Get the fuck out of here or we're calling the cops.' You're not going to want that."

She identified that it was the combination of access to social resources and the cultural understanding that sex work was legitimate labor that empowers her, and others, to feel more secure in their work. "Because we can call the cops and they're only like maybe two blocks away as well, it's kind of known. I don't even know how to explain it. It's just that society thinking that there's no sort of thoughts of, 'Sex workers, you can get away with doing stuff,' where in other states it is possible. It doesn't mean that people don't try, but it's much more toned down." The contrast between the two cultures was best illustrated when she told the story of an American client coming into her brothel and attempting to break the rules, trying to push the limits by taking pictures of the providers.

> [We] had an American guy who was obnoxious and was like, "It's my right." He was trying to take photos or record the girl in the room. The girl said he wasn't allowed to leave until we saw it and anything we saw was deleted. He was like, "my rights, rah, rah, rah" and those usual things. I think on his way out, because he got kicked out, he was still sort of trying to be as loud as he can, like "this place has violated my rights" and all this kind of crap. It's like, "No one's paying attention to you, just get the fuck out." He still had to leave because if the police came, he's the one that's going to be arrested, not us.

The fact that Australian providers could freely call the police meant that the workers I spoke with all had a slightly different take on the concept of security. Though they acknowledged that safety was extremely important, they felt less personally responsible for it and passed off some of that responsibility to more traditional social resources like employers and police. This state of affairs contrasts with the way others spoke about security being completely a matter of self-reliance.

Hope, a twenty-eight-year-old escort, was the only provider I spoke to who never showed her face or revealed any details about her identity. This was the case because Hope took her personal security very seriously. Hope was outed by an anonymous Internet stalker, which she said was one of her biggest fears. When it happened, she was helped by members of her community, her family and, oddly, the police.

In chapter 5, Hope was quoted discussing the police in her description of possible risks for workers and said, "I don't know of a single woman who's an escort who feels comfortable going to the police if anything happened to her." But when she was outed, she felt that there was enough nuance to the situation that she could enlist the aid of law enforcement.

"I guess I have had an interaction with the police, although it's actually been positive," she said.

> I had a close friend who's a feminist blogger and also a very powerful lawyer. And this person, pro bono, worked with the [police] for me. And helped me draft a cease-and-desist letter to the stalker. . . . I spoke on the phone with a detective a couple of times. The detective was very respectful, actually. I mean I got a little bit of, like, "Well, what did you expect putting yourself out there as a kinky person." And I was like, "Well actually, all these, like, kinky images are from my private email. These aren't from my website. My website doesn't show my face." And he was like, "Oh, okay. That's different." I mean, at that point I was a dominatrix. So, it wasn't like I was an escort. I might've gotten a very different reaction if I was an escort.

Hope was skirting the line of legality by admitting to being a dominatrix, though she moved to escorting after this experience. "The way my lawyer presented it, and the way it was, you know, was like, I was a student who was trying to pick up a little bit of extra money by doing these fetish sessions. I think that played a part in it as well."

Though the police were unable to catch Hope's stalker, in the aftermath she was left to try to salvage the remainder of her business, and hired a consultant to keep something like that from happening again. "I lost all but two of my clients. I had to completely redo my branding. I had to completely rethink my ways of maintaining client safety and security and my personal safety and security. Before I went into escorting, I hired a safety consultant who specifically works with sex workers. And she helped me set up ways to keep things as separate as possible and to show my client information in very secure ways. To maintain my safety as much as possible. Which is part of why I'm only willing to talk with you on the phone."

I asked what these new safety protocols entailed, and Hope told me that part of the security procedures was not revealing them to anyone. But despite the new protocols and the instance of law enforcement helping her, she said that she still feared police intervention more than the prospect of dangerous clients, simply because police wield so much more power than the average citizen. "I'm actually more afraid of police than I am of crazy clients because of the power dynamic there. I've heard horror stories from sex workers who've been raped by police more often than I hear stories of people who've been raped by clients. If the client rapes you that sucks, really, it's awful. But if a policeman rapes you, they rape you and then they arrest you." Even workers who feel that they enjoy a certain level of privilege still roundly rejected interacting with police. Likewise, workers from countries where sex work is legal were still reluctant to involve police in their security plans. Instead, most providers preferred to handle security independently. And security measures had to be effective enough to replace access to "traditional" social resources like police.

Since workers avoided police at all costs, their only option was to create a system that decreased their risks preemptively. Most often, this occurred in the form of screening. Screening is a process with an end result: the trust that a prospective client will be safe and suitable. This result can happen in a few different ways, but as screening measures became more labor intensive, they sapped workers' time and value.

Most workers expressed a desire to minimize labor, which can maximize their income. Gertrude quipped, "I'm lazy! I'm happy to do minimal effort, if I'm making the money that I need. If I make enough money, it's all good, safe, whatever!" She emphasized that there is a minimum level of effort required to ensure safety, and the different security measures take different amounts of work.

Screening Styles: "Nothing in Life Is Foolproof"

Paula, the forty-year-old tech-savvy escort, started working after a friend recommended that she give it a try. The friend gave her advice on which websites she could trust and how to get a good rating quickly. She told me, "I was really lucky that I didn't have to start at the bottom on the really skeevy, seedy websites." Instead, she said, "I started right at the top, which makes my story a little different than most girls." She went on to explain that she had different levels of screening she preferred, from the most trustworthy, quick, and convenient to the most time consuming and problematic.

> Basically, there's three ways I'll do it. This is the really common [procedure], at least at my price range. I'll take one or two references from a well-known, well-reviewed provider. It's gotta be someone that I've heard of that's current on the message boards and has a decent website. Not some fly-by-night threw-my-shit-together website. I have to email them, and you have to give me their contact information. Don't just say I saw Lucy in New Mexico. Tell me their contact information, their website. I'm not going to run around doing the work for you. Then I'll email the girls and I'll say John Smith, this is his number, this is his email address, this is what he looks like, this is where he said he saw you, can you vouch for him? Nine out of ten times they'll get back to me and say, "Yes." I've never had someone say, "No, he was a jerk. I didn't see him; he lied to you." Never happened.

Paula noted that one of her goals with screening processes was that it not be onerous. The most effective screening measure was the one in which Paula did not have to "run around doing the work for you."

Previous research has found that there is no definitive method for screening. But one common trend is that agencies collect less information than independent workers do. But whether a provider works for an agency or as an independent, they have to be knowledgeable enough to know when the information they have collected will inform them if a client is a police officer, if they are dangerous, or even just how good of a fit the client will be for the provider.[13]

Balancing the amount of work it took to screen a client with their own safety was a common theme. Providers often spoke about the different thresholds of trust they had for screening measures.

Liz, the soft-spoken thirty-two-year-old escort, agreed with Paula's take on personal references and noted her additional concerns if they were unavailable: "I would never see someone without references, I mean, or employment." She paused and sighed: "Even employment verification, I get a little nervous because it's still possible either the person, you know, got caught and now he's a narc, or it's a fabricated identity. That's why I much prefer references from girls that I actually know."

As Liz explained, the quality of references matters, and inadequate references will ultimately lead to more work with less certain results. But not all workers implicitly trusted personal references; some viewed them with a certain level of skepticism. Charlene, a thirty-five-year-old escort, wagged a bright red painted nail at the screen and noted that since the client provides the references, it would be fairly simple to mislead a provider. "References can be like fifty-fifty because you can rip a girl off but be nice to another girl. [Then] tell the nice girl to give you a good reference, not knowing that you ripped off another girl."

Often, if references were unreliable or missing, providers would find other ways to screen clients. Paula went on to say that the second way workers can screen clients is by using other digital resources like blacklist sites and review sites. "If they don't have references, then I'll take Blackout or MateRate because I know they verify them already. Usually on those websites, the girls will click 'okay' or 'I approve of him' or 'I recommend' but they've gotta have at least one or two."

Mandy, a twenty-nine-year-old escort, sat in her living room with her legs crossed on an overstuffed beige leather sofa, nodding in time as she counted off the ways digital resources are helpful as a supplement for screening clients, but noting that references are preferred. "Obviously references, number one. Number two, Blackout is very important. I go on that sometimes and I'll cross-reference names and screen names and phone numbers with people. Then usually, in my area there's about five ladies that are in my price range, and we always end up getting the same customers at the end of the day, so we share a lot of information with each other too." Review sites attempt to serve the same purpose as personal references, but often with less trustworthy results. New digital forms of communication often bring new difficulties, like fake provider references from fabricated clients or workers' identities. Digital resources are ostensibly easy for workers to access, but an unknown user base means that it takes additional work to ensure that the information provided is trustworthy and increases the risks of problem clients.

Mona blew her black bangs out of her eyes as she echoed a lot of these same themes. The review site she used for her screening worked well if the information provided was valid. The site provided clients with a profile, providers ranked the quality of their experiences and vice versa, then users were assigned a level. The higher the level, the better the quality of user, supposedly. She said there was no way she could be sure of the accuracy of the information since a client profile could be compromised and the recommendations were coming from community members she did not know personally. So, she had to go through additional steps to confirm the accuracy of the information.

> It's not foolproof. Nothing in life is foolproof. Walking across the street and not getting hit by a bus, I can't say it won't happen, but for the most part, you know. If someone's been around, if they're a level, even a level two, they've seen at least fifteen girls on there. Those fifteen girls have rated them in five separate categories, and if they have any reds, one red you can sometimes overlook. Okay. They didn't get along. Misunderstandings, and you have to consider the source as well. Where did the rating come from? Although I don't really hang out with any of these girls . . . they have blogs as well. You can see who's flakey and who pretty much has their feet on the ground, and their head is in the clouds. . . . Everything's there for me. If they are a new level zero, and they may have two or three people that they've only seen, I won't see them if they haven't seen anyone, or I won't see them if that screen name hasn't seen anyone for let's say a year, and now they're coming back after a year, that handle could belong to anyone. They could have traded it. They could have gotten busted for doing NearMart and said, "Hey, you want an in on this site? Here, let me give you my name." So yeah, I'm more paranoid. My general rule is stay more paranoid than you think you have to be.

Mona's paranoia compelled her to take additional steps to screen her clients. Though workers found references, both personal and digital, to be an effective screening measure, many took extra care to ensure that the information gathered was reliable. But being wary of screening measures and their reliability was not unique to Mona. Many of the providers I spoke to had doubts that the information they were acquiring was trustworthy.

Kelly, a thirty-four-year-old escort, described herself as "quirky and voluptuous," but she paused for a moment and added, "I hate to use flowery language because I think that sort of stuff is really cheesy." Kelly was suspicious of most aspects of sex work and was one of the few providers I spoke with who believed that being a sex worker was a less than ideal career path. She told me that many of the message boards she frequents to screen prospective clients were rampant with misogynistic members who talked down to providers and piled on low-grade grief and abuse. "The girls are all providers and they're operating a business; their hands are basically tied. They can't really say a whole lot in response because it's going to look like they have a bad attitude," she said with a sigh.

This is troubling because many of the workers turned to online message boards for support, resources, or encouragement. Furthermore, clients, according to Kelly, can go in two different directions. First, some clients can band together to create false profiles of providers, then rate themselves as good clients with the intention of either abusing, hurting, or ripping off providers. But Kelly said that within that same community, the "good" clients can use their influence as veteran hobbyists to at least attempt to quell bad behavior among those elements of the community.

> They got a platform and sort of a credibility as hobbyists that providers don't have. Some of the violent hobbyists that would rip girls off are more likely to listen to one of their peers than a girl saying, "Hey, don't do this or don't do that." Especially if they look down on the girl and see her as "oh, she's just a whore." . . . I've seen guys bragging about different ways to trick girls and to having the condom off without them knowing, like sneaking the condom off. Sometimes you'll see guys and they approach it in a really smart way. They're like, "Oh, you know, if you had real game you would be able to talk her out of it. Like you'd be able to be so smooth that she wouldn't wear it in the first place." Which is still bad, but it's the kind of bad that they can relate to and it'll still stop the behavior a little bit.

Review sites and blacklists are only as good as the reports they receive. Most of the issues around screening and digital repositories concerned potentially violent clients, but most providers said that part of screening was about finding clients that not only were not violent but also respected workers' rules and boundaries. Review sites could be used to check for STI safety, if a client is actively spreading an infection to workers, or if they have ever tried "stealthing" a provider.[14] Workers emphasized that it was best to take reports of bad clients at face value and good-client reports with a grain of salt. After all, a false negative would mean a loss of income for the day, but a false positive could mean serious danger.

Some providers said they were not able to trust the information they got from a review site because the validity and reliability of the site's profiles take a back seat to the financial incentive to increase traffic to the site. Kelly was a rare case of a provider who migrated from street-level work to independent escorting by using the Internet. She was staunchly self-reliant and valued being in control of her business and her screening measures. She wryly quipped, "It's not hard to lie online," while she rolled her eyes. She explained her lack of trust for online resources.

> One of the biggest issues I have with trust of MateRate is a lot of people lie and a lot of people misdirect things and there are a lot of shady people and pimps and ne'er-do-wells that really do get involved and they—it's not hard to lie online. If a company sets itself up and tries to get itself a little bit of credibility by saying, "Oh, I'm run by a provider and here's a picture of the provider," you don't really know if that's true unless you meet the girl and you've worked with her and you see things. I know for a fact that BetterDate is legitimately run by a provider who is still working to this day.[15]

Most providers I spoke to had mixed reactions to rating sites. Regardless of their opinions, workers who used digital references attempted to verify the information they were getting by checking either the social media or web presence of the client or provider. However, Kelly continued by noting that she would rather expend the effort to screen clients on her own, because she knew she was capable and could gather trustworthy information. "I would be relying then on other people to do that for me. You never know if you can trust them because they have a financial incentive to get people in your door. I'd rather do those things myself, and with the Internet and the different platforms that are set up, it allows me to do that."

Trust was a prominent theme when workers discussed screening, and ultimately was the motivating force behind the third screening style that Paula described: direct screening, that is, gathering vital information on clients firsthand. This method required the most effort, but some providers felt this was the only way to be sure the information could be trusted. Paula explained that she resorted to collecting data on her own only when a client could not provide any kind of reference.

> If they have none of that, and I hate doing this, it's my least favorite and I don't do it very often, I'll have to verify who they really are and check their employment. Guys don't like to do that. The lower-end guys who want to pay cheap and be in and out quick, they don't want to do it at all. The higher-end guys who are more executive type, they trust the system a little more. They trust the girls. They're seeing high-quality girls. They trust them a little bit more. They're willing to give you that information.

Direct screening was most often concerned with verifying crucial pieces of information about prospective clients—at minimum, just determining that the prospective client was not a police officer and was currently employed. But Paula's observation that clients "trust the system" is an interesting aspect of how emotional labor could play a part in the safety of providers.

Workers felt that the more personal knowledge they had of their clients, the safer they would be. Trusting the "system" that Paula described meant that clients must acquiesce to the requests of workers in order to be seen as viable clients, and clients understood that the more thoroughly they were vetted, the more willing workers would be to see them. "The system" has more elements than just screening employment verification and extends beyond initial provider-client interactions and can include additional labor spent on security measures like "safe calls" and "code words."[16]

As discussed in chapter 4, most of the workers engaged in emotional labor with their clients,[17] creating an atmosphere of intimacy that was authentic up to a point.[18] Within this framework, workers were privy to increasingly sensitive information about the clients, creating a safer work environment. In essence, the better workers were at manufacturing intimacy, the safer they became. From this perspective, "direct screening" can produce more information than just employment information. Often, the more "personal" the information, the safer providers felt.

Mona referred to the precarious position both provider and client were in as "mutual destruction," and noted this concept when referencing a recent client. "It would be mutual destruction if I ever decided to out him, which I wouldn't, obviously. But he trusts me so much that I know where he works. . . . He plays in a band, as well. He works in a very banking atmosphere." Similarly, Vivian, the twenty-nine-year-old escort and redhead who could speak Japanese, noted, "I feel like if I know your kid's name, you're probably not going to hurt me." Vivian's more intense screening procedure also connected the themes of security and emotional labor—so much so that the concept of protecting herself within the confines of a client-provider interaction was an opportunity to make a joke: she reported that she carried a gun for safety before she burst out laughing at the idea.

KURT: Are there other ways you keep yourself safe?
VIVIAN: Oh yeah, I carry a gun.
KURT: Really?
VIVIAN: No, it's Canada (laughing). What?!
KURT: Now you're just fucking with me because I'm American. I was like "Oh, of course, you carry a gun just like everybody else, it's fun!"
VIVIAN: You can't carry a gun here, what the fuck!? (More laughter).
KURT: You're all hunters up there! I thought everyone had a rifle in their magic bag of holding.
VIVIAN: You're not allowed to carry a gun here. No. I make precautions in my screenings. I make sure that I know who I'm talking to. I do have people that I trust that if something went wrong, I could easily call, but I have some lovely clients.

As Vivian's reference to her "lovely clients" suggests, many of the study participants discussed their security being connected with building trust with clients. As Paula noted, trust was placed in "the system" or "the girls."

Higher-end clients were aware of the possibility of "mutual destruction" and saw that screening protocols were meant to exchange trust between providers and extend to clients. However, not all of the providers wanted to engage in that level of additional labor.

Trustworthy sources aided in the reduction of work, and though providers had varying levels of preference and trust, the more they trusted a style of screening, the less effort they felt it took to meet their needs. Gathering information on clients directly was often a litmus test for the suitability of the client, but the more workers increased in their abilities or desire to manufacture intimacy, the more access they had to sensitive information about clients.

Though these themes were discussed frequently by providers, many workers noted that their efforts were also bolstered by individual screening tactics and their personal social, racial, and gender privilege.

Individual Contexts: "I'm the One with All the Power"

Francis, a thirty-three-year-old escort, had a shaved head and several piercings that matched her silver metallic painted nails. She took a swig of coffee and brusquely listed her screening procedures while holding up two fingers: "Phone number and intuition, basically."

Francis had far fewer metrics than the other providers, but said that judging prospective clients on their ability to follow instructions was enough to determine whether they would be a suitable client. "I've set out how you should contact me. And so basically, if you can't follow those instructions . . . then I won't see you," she said as she spread her hands and shrugged. "Because if you're not gonna listen to my instructions online, you're not gonna listen to them in real life." Francis gauged these early interactions very strictly, and other providers also noted the various details they found to be important for their security.

Workers often called these individual approaches "intuition" or "gut feelings," but also were able to precisely identify indicators that led to "feeling off" about a prospective client. Small details like poor grammar or not following instructions were pointed out as warning signs. Regardless of how workers described their perceptions, most were able to articulate why these feelings arose and that they were a reflection of the complexity of the vulnerable position providers were in.

This is illustrated by Paula's final hurdle for screening clients. Though it seemed counterintuitive, she preferred that her clients be somewhat reluctant to divulge their personal information.

Actually, for me, other girls don't feel this way, but for me it's a red flag when they give that information too easily. Yeah. I don't know why. Like they'll message me and say, "Hi, I don't have any references, but I'd like to spend time with you, tell me what you need from me. I'm happy to give it to you," and I'll say, "Name, address, blah blah blah," and they'll just type it all up and give it to me. But for some reason, I don't know why, that seems too good to be true. The guys who hem and haw about it . . . that usually ends up working out well because you can tell they're cautious, which is kind of good. I'd rather someone be cautious than just giving every girl all their information.

Judging the initial exchanges with prospective clients was one of the subtler way providers screened. Even within the relatively banal context of "small talk" with clients, workers were gathering information that could predict a problem.

Osu, a twenty-seven-year-old escort, had been doing sex work on and off since college. Her black anime bangs gave her a striking comic-book vibe, which included her workout outfit that resembled a superhero suit and a huge smile that lit up her face. When I asked her to describe her screening metrics, she explained that she required new clients to provide her with some form of identification but noted that even if the client complied, they could still disqualify themselves by making inappropriate requests. "I require at least two provider references or work identification . . . like a picture of your work badge from your work email. There's been one instance where I took someone's student verification. He went to [college], and he emailed me a picture of his school ID from his school email account. . . . People have inquired, 'Do you do student discounts?' Honestly, that is like the best way for me to never talk to you again. I always say on my profile, 'I don't negotiate.' We're not a flea market."

This ability to be more discerning in client selection was one of the benefits of using the Internet. Most workers noted that screening takes a few days, and rarely did workers describe seeing new same-day clients. This gave them time to reflect on the interaction and make a decision.

Traditionally, scholars and others have presumed that workers have very little choice in client selection. But the majority of workers who spoke with me noted that while several factors went into deciding to see a client, the choice was ultimately theirs. Francis continued her thoughts on the consequences of prospective clients following or failing to follow directions: "I always looked at it like they're applying for a job. Right? Like, clients like to think that they have all this control and they're picking me. But in reality, I'm the one with all the power. So, it's like a job application. And I will pick and choose, and if you fail the job application, see ya!" A test of honesty and rule following was often a clandestine aspect of screening. Assessing the quality of a client involved more than ensuring physical safety and prompt payment. Some workers used their screening measures to make sure that the experience with the client would be a positive one, and attempted to avoid clients who might be "time wasters" (see chapter 4) or just an overall bad match.

Time wasters were a specific issue during screening because they threatened the indirect benefits of the work while not providing any return on the workers' efforts. Though time wasters were not as big a concern as personal safety, they were a frequent nuisance that workers attempted to minimize at every opportunity. Francis explained the subtle ways she judged whether a client would be suitable; poor initial communication was a prime indicator of a time waster. "I don't answer one-word texts. So if they just say like, 'BBBJ question mark,' I don't respond to that. Like, you couldn't even put [it] into a sentence? 'Do you offer [bareback blowjobs]?' No, I don't answer, 'Hey,' or, 'Hi,' or 'Hey babe,' none of that shit. Unless it says something like, 'Hi, I'm so-and-so, are you available at x time?' I'm probably not gonna reply. So, I just don't anymore. There're probably a bazillion dudes in my phone labeled 'WOT.' Waste of time." Clients who were too flippant in early communications were often ruled out immediately. The potential problem with a time waster was that workers might put in additional efforts for less value, decreasing the profitability of their overall labor, which workers guarded fiercely.

A few providers would weigh their current workload with whether they would "take a chance" on a new client, but when most recounted incidents of trying to gain a new client with poor communication, the result was often a time waster.

Janine's natural curiosity often comes in handy when she is screening clients. She has found that she can screen potential clients according to how well they communicate, and has determined that a prospect who is well spoken and respectful can often make a good regular client.

> I ruled out seeing a client because he used so many abbreviations and acronyms and text speak that I could not understand what he was saying, and I was like, "This is just not working for me." So if I see that a client uses full sentences, has good grammar, responds in an intelligent way, if there's any kind of witty banter or if there's any type of substance to the conversation, then that usually is enough for me to agree to see them as a client, and so far, it's worked out very, very well for me, and I know that this is a really unorthodox way of doing things, and like I said, it's pretty risky, but I mean, I am expecting that the longer I do this, the more likely it will be that something bad will happen.

The prediction that Janine would eventually be victimized is another reference to the interplay between the broader cultural perceptions of sex work and the individual contexts of providers. Different kinds of worker privilege extended to the amount of effort they had to expend and, ultimately, their overall security.

Janine explained why the risk that "something bad will happen" was an acceptable level for her. "Thankfully, with my full-time job I have superb health insurance." Janine was in a privileged position where access to healthcare was not as much of a concern as it would be for a worker who did not have an additional job that provided good health insurance. And as with the discussions on both identity and risk, she tacitly acknowledged this position and its benefits. "I know that's a very casual way of looking at things, but it seems to work well for me, and I have never once felt like I was in danger or that I was being threatened or that I was unsafe, ever." The different worker contexts had direct impact on the amount of work providers had to do in order to stay safe.

Personal contexts often remained largely unspoken by the providers I spoke to, but a few workers wanted to note the specific differences between their own personal contexts and those of other workers concerning security. One of the most apparent personal contexts was gender, and the male providers I spoke to often had a different approach to security compared to women. But Walter, a twenty-six-year-old escort who started working after his student loans came due, lived and worked in Germany. He felt that there was a different culture for screening in his country as compared to both Australia and the United States. "Screening is difficult in Germany. There is not a screening culture. . . . I have heard of all these screening techniques that are used in the Americas or Australia or something like that, but there is nothing like screening that I do to others. . . . I'm trying to get better, like I'm trying to find technologies to screen. . . . Maybe I just don't know shit, but that's my impression."

A broad culture of screening could influence workers to take more or less stringent measures when interacting with prospective clients. However, broad cultural contexts can also be perceived at the individual level. Walter, as a male sex worker, perceived and responded to risks very differently than his female counterparts, and his particular lack of screening included those personal frameworks. Edward, the twenty-nine-year-old escort with horn-rimmed glasses and perpetual bedhead, spoke about the contexts of both gender and other facets of privilege, emphasizing what he perceived as the difference between men and women, and straight and gay cultural expectations around sex work.

> I don't [screen] in any sort of traditional way. I know a lot of the women will get references through other women or get workplace information. I shouldn't say a lot of women, a lot of privileged female sex workers tend to be able to do that. I don't. I've never done that. I don't even know how any of my clients would respond to that. . . . I think with the stigma attached to queer gay sex, especially for straight dudes, there would be no way they'd give me their personal information. There are some dudes whose names I don't even know, to this day, and I've seen them for years. I don't really screen them. I read their texts . . . read between the lines, how well are they presenting themselves in an email? Are they saying, "Hello, how are you, this is who I am, this is what I'm looking for," versus "I want to fuck," you know?

In chapter 5, I quoted Edward's description of the way male workers perceived risk from a privileged male position, even as he recognized that his perceptions of safety were likely inflated. But the culture of secrecy and stigma around the gay community made screening through gathering personal information difficult for these workers. This point is crucial, since it highlights how personal contexts interact with broader social frameworks, like using the Internet for security. Though both Edward and Walter had access to the same technology as women providers and shared many of the same social and racial privileges, the singular difference between heterosexual and gay sex work was enough to make the utilization of technology for security purposes completely different.

Edward said that his screening had to be more intuitive, relying on "read[ing] between the lines" to look for clues. This was similar to Janine's description quoted above, but her primary reliance on the subtleties of communication made her an outlier among the women I spoke to. Regardless, potential clients who communicated well were perceived to be better clients, and both Edward and Janine were measuring their relative level of risk on the basis of their privileged positions. This meant that they could make their assessment of safety based on less information than that required by some of the other workers who shared their stories.

Greg, a twenty-five-year-old escort, ran his fingers through his long blonde hair. He had a summery surfer-boy vibe and was wearing a loose white tank top that contrasted his bronze suntan. Greg was the third male provider who spoke to me, and he always wanted to emphasize his "professionalism." To Greg, "professional" meant a level of distance with clients. Even his speech was dry and monotone, which gave our interaction a sterile feel. Greg described how he found covert ways to gather limited information on his clients. He also admitted that his screening timeline was shorter than that of other workers, happening just before he saw a client. He was most concerned with ensuring that they were a "serious" client and not a potential time waster by requiring that clients provide him with a car to meet. "I require a car because I can't run around [the city] and have them cancel on me or some BS like that. So, they get the car, also a security thing because they're using their money, their name. So, if something happens to me, their name is there, somewhere."

The men I spoke to shared a distinctly different experience with screening and security than the women. Broadly, Edward and Walter acknowledged that screening as a security measure was "cultural" and "traditional," speaking to how widespread it was as a practice among providers. As workers, they had an expectation that they should engage in screening, even though they believed that it would be more difficult given their situations as male workers with a male clientele. They tied the use of screening to the context of "privileged female sex workers."

Walter described himself as privileged because he was white, a citizen of his home country, and young. "At least I need to tell myself that." He smiled at the fact that he had recently turned twenty-nine years old, and was maybe not as young as he wished. However, being a man and a gay worker placed him in a different framework for security and screening protocols.

English was Walter's second language, so he spoke slowly and often paused to convey his ideas. He believed that in this specific context, women have an advantage. The demand was higher for women, and privileged workers had an easier time accessing those markets due to their position. Moreover, he believed that clients were less likely to simply walk away from a woman provider when screening was either requested or required, because the market demands for men and women are so different. "I've kind of lately wondered, what are the limits to gay male escorting? Because I just have the impression that they are much more high-profile lines—who are females of course. If you are female and you're going into high-profile escorting, like being independent and having all kind of nice privileges that allow you to go into this upper part of the ladder to climb up that career. So as a woman you will get much more chances I think with clients. Like there's just a much bigger market. I just kind of lately wonder, What are the limits of the market for male escorts, you know?"

The individual contexts of the workers provided different lenses from which to view their own security. Though the majority of workers specifically noted screening as an effective measure to increase their own safety, the practice worked best for workers who shared privileged positions and a subcultural expectation for security, which enabled them to refuse work if their screening requirements were not met. Gender dynamics made for different responses by workers when it came to utilizing that privilege, but some workers were at an increased risk of danger simply because of who they are.

Trans workers have a higher chance of being victimized than any other demographic. A survey by the National Center for Transgender Equality found that one in five transgender adults participate in some form of sex work, with those rates being even higher for minority women.[19] Nearly half have been physically attacked and one-third had been sexually assaulted within the previous year. So, when I asked Kaley, an eighteen-year-old escort and trans woman with long blue hair and pink nails that matched her pink cardigan, about her security procedures, I was not surprised to find that though she participated in many of the same screening routines as other providers, she had a bevy of additional steps she took to keep herself safe.

Kaley leaned back on the wooden headboard of her bed, surrounded by a herd of stuffed animals in every size and shape. She clutched a rainbow-colored pony to her chest as she walked me through her screening process. "I need to know their first name and have them send me a current photo of themselves," she said before adding, "and then I'll look up their email, or their phone number, on national [blacklist] databases." She listed each step as if she had just remembered she needed to pick something up at the store. "Oh! Then I need them to either send me a [social media] page, like a full filled-out and verified [social media] page, or verify their employment, so like show me their company's website that has their name on the directory, and then give me a call from the number next to their name or something like that." She nodded while grooming the mane of her tiny plush horse. But, even if screening information was provided, Kaley said that she was adamant about listening to her intuition. "If anything doesn't check out on the screening, or if like I get a bad vibe, I just stop responding. If he has a mark on his blacklist, but it's like not something super-specific, but it's still something that like makes me nervous, or if there is something—if his paper trail looks shady or something, . . . like that makes me nervous. Or, if I can't find anything at all about him, that makes me more nervous."

However, even with Kaley's heightened caution, she still had additional protections for her sessions that went beyond those of other workers. Most providers laughed off the idea of having weapons, or if they did carry a weapon, it was a small tube of pepper spray they kept on a keychain and never used. But Kaley was always sure to keep a few weapons nearby. "I'm never somewhere in the room not within arm's reach of a weapon, and yeah, that's pretty much all I do. I have pepper spray that's disguised to look like lipstick, so I can just like keep that out on the counter, and then I have a little key chain stabby thing, and I have just full-on mace. And yeah. I kind of distribute those throughout the hotel room. That's why I like to do in-calls. It feels like I have a lot more control, and it's a lot less scary to me." But Kaley felt that all this security would not be necessary if the culture would simply stop dehumanizing workers, and trans workers specifically. She placed her small stuffed pony among her menagerie of felt friends and brushed the hair from the front of her cardigan. "You know, there's a person. The person doing sex work is also a person with parents, and friends, and experiences, and they have a childhood, too. It's not just like they're just someone who is immediately cast aside the second they've done sex work. You know?"

All workers preached the importance of security measures, even the few who did not take many. But in a strange way, the *general* discussion of security said something about the workers *individually*. Workers wanted to be safe, but more than that, they wanted others to be safe. And workers with privilege wanted to find ways to extend their advantages to others. Mandy, a twenty-nine-year-old escort who acknowledged that she was placed high on the ladder of privilege, noted the complexity of this when describing how she, a highly educated, in-demand woman, could take chances that other workers could not, and those chances could be used to benefit others.

> I think it's different for me, because if this line of work somehow didn't give me any returns, I have my other jobs that I can go back to. So, I'm not reliant on this income at the end of the day. I use the money here to help pay for grad school, help finance my businesses, things like that. Where some ladies, they don't have that other option. If something happens to them, if they get a bad review, word gets spread about them, then that's not good. [I talked to a woman on a forum yesterday]. . . . She told me about this really terrible client, he got super-drunk during their session together, and he started getting really verbally abusive and calling her a whore and saying . . . just awful things. I reported him [to a blacklist site] for her. Yeah, I report everybody, but I know a lot of people don't have the luxury to do that.

Mandy used her privileged position to help other workers. Often providers with privileged positions could afford to take more security risks and gathered less information than others. After all, social privilege, by its very nature, provides more deference to its beneficiaries. But though providers often acknowledged how the combination of security protocols and privilege keep them safe, they wanted the same for all workers, especially those providers who might not be as fortunate as they are.

Conclusion: "They're People"

"My screening measures today are a lot more sophisticated than they were then," Arden said with a raised eyebrow. "About a year or two ago, I implemented some new screening practices that have really taken things to the next level." She flipped open the pack of cigarettes and drew one out with her pinky extended, as if she were drinking tea from a fancy cup. "But back then I just ran someone's name and number. I also had a driver who doubled as security for me at the time, and I would pay him depending upon how long the call was, whether he had to drive me somewhere, what have you," she said while waving the unlit cigarette in front of her face.

When providers use existing Internet resources, security is in the hands of the workers. Most providers described security as merely a part of their work. Preventative security measures were the most common way to ensure the safety of workers.

There was a duality between the broader cultural concerns over safety and what this specific subpopulation of workers was most concerned about. Providers said that screening was an effective security measure, but in conjunction with ensuring that clients were safe on both a physical and emotional level, workers screened for suitability. In essence, screening metrics for this group of workers were so effective that they were also used for connecting providers with the clients they desired to see.

Similarly to their concerns over work personas and risks of sex work, providers also acknowledged emotional labor as a screening tactic. If workers felt they could establish bounded intimacy with a client, they perceived that client to be safer. This is the case because a client who is seeking an authentic connection with a worker would more than likely also provide more personal information that gives workers a distinct advantage.

If this new digitally centered way of being a provider is a lens through which all sex work can be viewed, we would find similar concerns among strictly digital sex workers. Cammers described that screening and security were a concern for them and often used the same technique, slightly modified, that in-person workers use. Digital workers screen for suitable digital platforms to host their work, and they can screen client information in real time during chat and video sessions.

Ultimately, what helped Arden the most was seeing her clients as people with whom she could forge a relationship. A good client should be just as interested in safety as a good provider; and Arden felt as though she had found a stable group of clients who would not pose a threat to either her physical or her emotional safety. "Most of my clients that I see now are regulars. They're people. I have clients that I've known for four-plus years," she said as she gently tapped the rim of the ashtray with her cigarette. "Hell, I have clients that I have been seeing longer than I've seen some boyfriends."

7

A New Model

"At Least for Me, It's Empowering"

Roxy needed a change. So she moved to the West Coast. Her apartment was a few blocks up from the train station and a ten-minute stroll from the bay. It was a small, gray, two-story affair across from a bodega that advertised beer, wine, and money orders. There was a stone stairway with a white painted iron railing that led to her new place on the second floor.

She cracked open the fridge and pulled out a beer, squinted an eye, and twisted off the cap.

"Everything's very expensive out here." She tossed the cap into the kitchen sink. "Oh my god, I hate it, but it's real pretty. I'm here and it never gets hot and it pisses me off."

"Is that a problem?" I asked.

She slipped on a pair of oversized sunglasses and took a pull from the bottle. "It's my own weird version of hell because it's the same every day."

Roxy has always thrived on variety. She had moved to the West Coast two years earlier and seemed to be fitting in alright. She had gotten a new job and met a new guy. She wanted to see where the relationship would go and decided to stop escorting.

"So much transition in such little time—the loss of self and sense of identity that came along with that," she said, shaking her head. "My decision to drop the work was very fast and that kind of happened when I first moved out here and got a job."

I asked what kind of job she landed.

"I am back in the restaurant industry," she said, holding up her beer. "I'm servicing motherfuckers, I'm bending over backwards, giving them everything I possibly have and I'm making—" she glanced at the ceiling and tallied it up in her head. "Fifteen something an hour?" she said with a pained look, then shrugged and added, "Plus tips, but like—it's a tough adjustment."

She gave a thoughtful nod and compared her new job to the previous one. "I could work an hour every day, four days a week, and be fine and get to do my own thing. Take care of myself. Read and pursue the things that made me feel whole and happy. I miss that."

"Now that you've settled in and had some time to reflect on it, how do you feel about escorting?" I asked.

"Well," she said. "I've been trying to think about it and I'm kind of almost drawing a blank. No negative connotations; it's just so neutral."

"Neutral?" I echoed.

"I feel like it's still a very viable way to work. I think I was well suited towards it," she said. "I think the only negative feelings I have about it is that I was suited for it because of negative behavior patterns that I already had, in some ways, and it only emphasized them."

"What patterns do you think it emphasized?"

She looked down and twisted the beer bottle in her hands.

"I did focus on the aesthetics of it all and the curation of the experience," she said with a pause. "Because of the ways I have sex—like valuing performance and the way it would look or feel to him over my own experience. Those are things that made me a better sex worker," she said, looking up. "And then, coming around to a more holistic view that that's not a healthy way to have sex in your own life."

I nodded, and she continued.

"It's just like the restaurant industry putting other people's needs first and all that. Catering to other people's needs and not so much your own," she said. "Or, like the detachment—that ability, realizing that I was so detached from my own body and experiences with sex, it allowed me to do that work and then, trying to come back from that has been hard. But it was gratifying to remember all these little details about everyone's lives and like turn it on for the outings." She smiled and gestured in front of her face like a magician. "They take me out to dinner or a show I wanted to see. It was like flexing a set of muscles you don't have to use every day, but it feels really good when you do."

Whether providers described their work as something they fell into or as their chosen calling, the most important message they wanted people to know was that their work was legitimate. I asked workers what message they would like the world to know about them, and the overwhelming majority said that people need to know that this job is work.

"All of the reasons that I did it and believed in it, and still believe in sex work hold true," Roxy said, twisting the cap off a new bottle. "And I think they're actually a little bit more true now than when I was in it."

"Oh?"

"At the time, they kind of seemed like catch phrases, like—sometimes it's hard to describe a thing that you're in the middle of. Great, I'm a catch phrase, yeah. And now it's like, okay, that wasn't just the catch phrase, that's something that I genuinely believe. Sex work is work."

Complicated Choices: "A Battle in a Couple of Different Directions"

When Yvette, a twenty-year-old escort, moved to the city two years previously, she started out as an aerial burlesquer, a performer who climbs long strands of silk fabric high above an audience. But she was interested in other forms of sex work, so she decided to move into acting in pornography and then escorting. The day we talked she was decked out in a mashup of fifties office style and alternative rocker. Her purple hair was swept to the side and cascaded down the shoulders of a cream-colored blouse with a high neckline and lacy collar. A tight black pencil skirt gave her entire outfit a contrasting vibe of business and punk.

"I have a lot of really, really good things to say about sex work, and I have a lot of not so good things to say about sex work. I've benefited immensely and been hurt in a completely different capacity—more than I was able to ever comprehend before starting," she said with a stern look.

Providers expressed that their work was a delicate balance and that it could not be described in simple dichotomies like positive and negative. For Yvette, this manifested itself in the relationship between sex work and her race, and she acknowledged that there were both good and bad aspects. Yvette was Asian, and she used her race to advertise herself. But when companies and agencies focused on her race as her sole characteristic, she found it hurtful.

She held out both palms, moving them up and down like the two sides of a scale. "Being able to make decisions for myself," she said, lifting one hand, and then added, lifting the other, "having to deal with the negative consequences. Feeling increasingly insecure about my race, and my race's relationship to my sexuality, and being objectified in that way.

Like constantly being seen as 'that Asian chick' was very dehumanizing for me. I didn't feel like I was being taken as seriously as everyone else. I wasn't anything to them but my race," she said. "I deal with that in my everyday life, just because that's how the world works. But it's different when those comments are directed not just at your race but at the relationship between your race and your sexuality."

She did not want to perpetuate harmful racial stereotypes, but for Yvette, the issue was not her race or even the advertisement of it. The liability of stigma can become a commodity in the right circumstance. Instead, Yvette said that the state of the industry was "problematic," but she felt that as providers got more knowledge and education, they were best suited to make the choice about the future direction of sex work. "I feel like having more educated people who care about how their stuff is being sold and how their bodies are being sold is what—like the entire industry is problematic, but there are companies that I've worked for, who make an effort to be a completely inclusive and diverse group of people."

Yvette was not the only provider to point out the complexity of their choice to be a sex worker. Penny, a twenty-one-year-old escort, was tired of the lack of nuance in sex-work debates, pointing out that because the work happens out of the public eye, the culture tends to group all workers into the same exploited category.

She tugged at the sleeves of her long gray cardigan, then tucked her lavender hair behind one ear. "If you're not choosing to do this, then you have no understanding of the many reasons that someone may do this, which probably aren't just for money, but they obviously have to do with who you are and what you're okay with, or what's worthwhile at that time."

"So what can be done about it?" I asked.

"Basically just don't speak for other people's experiences, because obviously trafficking and coercion exist and there is all the coercion of systems. We're under capitalism and the patriarchy and the fact that it's even possible to profit off sexual and emotional labor—." She stopped short and sighed.

The social sciences have always attempted to explain the complex relationships between individuals and society. Famously, sociologist Robert Merton suggested that American culture, with its goals of financial security, career stability, marriage, and property ownership, saddled each generation with its own ambition to achieve the "American Dream." But what is the mechanism of these goals? Merton answered that, yes, our culture expects a level of success achieved through well-worn institutional paths like getting an education, which leads to a good job, which then reaps expected benefits. But the engine of these "normative" social processes is fueled by one thing: money. "Money is highly abstract and impersonal. However acquired, through fraud or institutionally, it can be used to purchase the same goods and services. The anonymity of metropolitan culture, in conjunction with this peculiarity of money, permits wealth, the sources of which may be unknown to the community . . . to serve as a symbol of status."[1]

Most providers were acutely aware of these more "meta" arguments around sex work. Society is constructed on systems: racial, gender, class, and economic systems that permeate every aspect of life, the most common system being capitalism, which, by its very nature, is coercive, and just about everyone on the planet, including sex workers, has some role to play in it. When providers say they have made a choice to become a sex worker, that choice is somehow tainted by the pressures of capitalism.

But it is odd that this is such a pervasive criticism of sex work and not just work in general. The capricious value of labor very often pushes people towards one career path and away from another. It is no coincidence that when people's material needs are provided for, they gravitate towards philosophy and art; yet when society implores us to "earn" a living, we are left with a glut of lawyers and bankers.

Penny pointed out that there is simply a fundamental lack of trust— that society believes workers are somehow unaware of the choices they are making, or ignorant of the systems that influence them. "I keep going back to the idea of false consciousness,"[2] she said with a stern shake of her head. "Because people either think that you're a victim or that you're kidding yourself. If you think that there was any choice or noncoercion involved in it, that you are basically self-victimizing. [Saying], 'Oh, you clearly don't actually know your own experience.'"

But these more existential discussions never got much traction with the workers I spoke with, because as Yvette said, people were focusing on the wrong elements when they judged the merits of sex work. She wanted people to trust the agency of providers and stand behind the knowledge that sex work can be a series of complicated choices. "A big part of the empowerment that comes along with doing sex work is that I'm able to say like, 'Do you want this? This is what you have to give me for it.' And being able to like set those terms, and being able to say, 'All right, this is what I want for what I am providing.' If I just give it out, then I'm no longer feeling as empowered, because I'm just doing it for them, and I'm doing less of it for myself." Providers understood the implications of their work from multiple perspectives, but most felt that the best way to understand their experiences was to have some kind of firsthand knowledge—and barring that, just to listen to workers.

Vivian, a twenty-nine-year-old escort, pointed out that, similarly to personal experiences with clients, the only way to help providers at a policy level would be to put those choices in the hands of workers. "Passing the microphone to people who are experiencing all these different issues is so important." For Vivian, "passing the microphone" was more than a slogan; she believed that any marginalized group needs to have representation when governments make decisions that affect them. "Sex work and sex-work laws need to be by us and for us. It's our bodies, it's our choices. You don't need to tell consenting adults what they get to do in the bedroom," she said.

The facilitation of choice that technology provided was what workers noted repeatedly. The ability to make meaningful choices is the heart of agency as an empowering concept.[3] All of the themes workers discussed—entrance, personas, risks, security—were better understood through this lens of digital agency. Though Yvette acknowledged the negatives as well as the positives of being a provider, she wanted to frame *choice* as the crucial element. "I want to highlight that despite all of those things, parts of it have shaped me, parts of it have really given me a lot of confidence that I haven't had in the past," she said.

The ability to choose affected the way providers related to their work. But that relationship was complex, and it was up to the individual to appraise its validity. Yvette ran her fingers through her long purple hair. "It's helped me find a community; it's helped me in a lot of ways that I wouldn't have been able to access without it. It's a battle in a couple of different directions."

Entrance: "I Can Deal with Dudes Being Creepy and Weird"

Isabelle tapped her fork against the side of her plate and thought for a moment. I asked her why she chose to become a provider full-time rather than stick with her vanilla job. "I would rather deal with a weird creepy dude than deal with some of these mainstream web design clients who wanna frickin' try to squeeze me as a web designer."

Prior to becoming a provider, Isabelle had worked in several settings, one as a graphic designer, but she found that workplace drama followed her wherever she went. For a time, she maintained both her jobs, doing graphic design during the week and exploring sex work online on the weekends. Isabelle had a very diverse career as a provider. She had tried most aspects of the work, from fetish modeling and dominatrixing to full escorting. She learned the distinctions between different kinds of work because of information she absorbed from the Internet.

"A lot of people mistake fetish work for the BDSM scary stuff when it's really like, putting peanut butter on my face," she said with a laugh. "Or like, revving an engine in wooden clogs. People wanna lump things into one group."

When providers first entered sex work, the overwhelming majority of them described a three-part process of recognizing a turning point in their lives, gathering information, and acknowledging (whether overtly or tacitly) how their personal characteristics factor into their level of privilege. But this process is certainly the same for any career change or major life event: a high school student choosing a college, a dating couple deciding to get married, a customer weighing which computer to purchase. People reach turning points, examine their options, and then, on the basis of their personal characteristics, decide whether a new opportunity is right for them.

And this digital model of sex work has not changed the process of entrance—instead, at each step it provides potential workers with more knowledge and resources with which to make informed choices. Previously, at least as far as Western culture would suggest, the turning point that workers would encounter would be, in essence, a final turning point. Providers were largely seen as "vulnerable" women who "turned to" sex work as a "last resort." But these providers used the Internet to assess whether or not sex work could be an appropriate choice when they were presented with a turning point.

Providers would discuss how they sought out options and found that before the advent of the Internet, these turning points would have been far more dangerous, involving many of the negative associations with sex work, like drug addiction or domestic abuse. Now the Internet has provided a safer way for workers to gather knowledge. The process is so effective at disseminating information that they can make a choice with a more realistic view, echoing both Yvette and Isabelle, rather than simply lumping sex work into one homogenous group.

Isabelle even joked that she had an advantage over other workers because of her starting career dealing with problem clients. "I like it a lot more than dealing with fucking cringey-ass web design clients. Who argue 'green is not the color I like'? Or like the whole bullshit corporate networking," she laughed. But Isabelle pointed out that if one can access the technology and learn to use it, it can pay dividends. When Isabelle thought back to the beginning of her career, she saw the Internet as a place where she could find solace. She could feel connected when she was isolated from others by an abusive relationship and a job where she did not feel compensated or appreciated. "If it wasn't for Internet sex I would never have quit a professional job," she said with a nod. "The Internet in general has maintained my faith in people."

Once providers had gathered enough information to begin to understand the depth and complexity of the work, they assessed whether the work would be right for them. This is one of the places where this new digital process differentiated itself. Like so many other aspects of social existence, the calculation of whether or not anyone's behavior is going to be rewarded or punished can be predicted on the basis of their characteristics—in essence, privilege.

Race and class privilege framed the entrance process, and technology is included in that equation. Privileged classes are exposed to new technologies first. Digital inequality is not limited to merely infrastructure and access to virtual resources; it can also include tangible issues like skill sets or level of engagement, as well as more elusive concepts like attitudes and beliefs.[4] When these characteristics are entered into the equation, workers are able to make the choice of whether or not this avenue of work will be beneficial for them.

Isabelle was able to use the experience with technology that she had gained from being a graphic designer to build a skill set that she could use on the Internet. This technological savvy, combined with her other characteristics, made her fairly confident in the choices she had made. "I can deal with dudes being creepy and weird and, you know, the Internet stalker. I am pretty darn street smart."

Persona: "That's What I'm Trying to Sell"

Roxy folded the sides of her long purple sweater across her chest, crossed her arms, and thought for a moment, before beginning. "When I had a baby, it was like an out-of-body experience. Your consciousness goes somewhere else so you can handle it," she said, tilting her head.

I asked her what she did when she put on her work persona, but did not necessarily like the client, or get along with them, or she found the experience to be unpleasant. She told me that there is a bit of compartmentalization, where she hides herself away somewhere safe. "Sometimes you just have to close your eyes and go to a happy place, man," she said with a laugh.

But she quickly walked back the comment.

"What I do day in and day out isn't unpleasant enough to take myself away, wrapped up and tucked away. For the most part I enjoy the roles I play on a daily basis," she said.

The concern for Roxy and others was not even necessarily the creation or performance of a work persona. Instead, providers said, it was that technology facilitates interactions between workers and clients, which meant more time spent on emotional labor through the performance of that work persona in digital spaces. Providers often talked about the "girlfriend experience" that happens during a client-provider session, but many of them would note that that same role has to be "put on" even between sessions to keep the clients engaged and interested.

"Generally, it's just checking in and setting up sessions. There are some that do want to try and take up your time and flirt or sext. You do have to try and manage that time wisely," she said. "Depending on who they are and how regular you see it, how long you see them. But no, I try to nip that in the bud pretty quickly."

"Why are you nipping it?" I asked.

"Well, it's my personal time. Drawing that line between personal and professional self. And, because it's not paid time. I do it a little bit to try and pique their interest, heighten anticipation, wanting them to come back," she said. "There are occasions where you will set up a certain amount of time to sext with someone and they'll pay you for it, usually via [digital transfer]. Or phone sex is also an option sometimes."

Many of the previous paradigms of sex-work research focused on the limits of client-provider interactions. But new technology has clouded the water when it comes to the ways in which providers can choose to capitalize on their labor. Most workers fostered some kind of relationship with clients, and the Internet was the prime method for maintaining these connections. They did this for a couple of reasons. First, a repeat client would not require the "up-front" unpaid labor of advertising, interacting, screening, and scheduling. This obviously increases the value of a provider's time and was a welcome way to increase their profits. Second, finding a client who is a good "fit," in terms of reliability, price, requests, and, frankly, just being someone a worker gets along with, was seen as a major benefit.

Roxy did not want to interact with just any client. She wanted to attract the right kinds of clients to her business and find a mutually beneficial balance between worker and provider. "Well, I mean, I'm a brand now to my clients. That's what I'm trying to sell, that's an idea. . . . I think continuity is very important when it comes to branding and quality control."

But Roxy pointed out that this kind of tactic is true of most jobs. "I think you could say that about any job; I think that is working. For any job you put on an alter ego." But there was another aspect of putting on a persona that most people miss: that it is the clients who are putting on personas that legitimize the interaction. "[They put on] an outside persona so that they can carry on this somewhat illicit relationship to help them feel like they're living a full life," she said.

"Is that the point, to live a full life?" I asked.

"[It's this] fantasy relationship they get to have without the negative hangups."

Exchanges with clients were a shared drama, with each person playing their assigned role, all while projecting the authenticity of the interaction. Client and provider create a space for the existence of this authentically inauthentic relationship and navigate its meaning and purpose. "So this is that little slice of them just getting to be themselves," she said.

There is an inherent contradiction between purpose and practice when it comes to client-provider interactions. Providers are creating scenarios where clients can feel like themselves while they both tacitly acknowledge that they are engaged in a business exchange. "Everyone I saw, even though it was never mentioned, there was somehow an acknowledgment of—I know I'm not the only one," she said.

For Roxy the end result for both her and her clients was a roundly positive one. "I'm giving them that sense of fulfillment they were missing in some other way and, on a personal level for them, yes, it was very satisfying for me."

Risks: "It Can Hurt Your Bottom Line"

Charlene squinted at me for a long minute. "Oh, you want my honest opinion?"

"I would absolutely love your honest opinion," I replied.

Charlene had been following a recent court case in which the United States federal government was cracking down on websites where providers advertise. "I'm watching this [website] court situation closely and I would love for them to shut that fucker down. Shut it the fuck down. I'm hoping that the attorney general comes up with a plea deal for them, like, 'shut this shit down and we'll give you immunity,'" she said through narrowed eyes.

Charlene was one of only two workers I spoke to who had been a provider before the Internet was widely used. She frequently used the technology at her disposal, and had a very nuanced view of the ways the Internet had changed the nature of sex work. She had moved from street-level work to being a digital provider advertising her escort services online and screening clients.

She watched the scene change around her, but still sees problems persist, the biggest being that someone else was taking her money, just in a new way. Charlene saw the websites' charging workers to place ads and host profiles as just a new form of control. "They have made such a vast profit off of the industry. Period—and they have really stuck their dick in this industry and fucked it raw with no Vaseline, no condoms, no lipstick, nothing. I just want the government to shut it down, just really shut it down, and maybe that'll switch up the market." Though Charlene spoke often about the procedures workers had created to improve their safety and wrest control back into their own hands, she was wary of any system that did not give complete control to providers. "They're billionaires, and they've made their money off the backs of women," she said, shaking her head.

When providers would discuss their risks, they most often spoke in general terms, but widely thought that the Internet improved security. Providers who used new technologies to screen prospective clients reported that they felt safer and had few violent or dangerous incidents to discuss during our talks. Nearly all the workers said that the resources that digital communities provide had a positive impact on security. Screening, either through referrals or gathering information firsthand, was an effective way to improve safety. But Charlene said that these new situations come with new levels of risk. Just as providers can use the Internet to gather information on prospective clients, clients can use digital lines of communication to harass workers. Charlene shared an example of a client she had to stop seeing.

"There was a point where I said, 'I'm not gonna see you anymore.' And they got really weird and stalker-ish and they, you know, kept pursuing me for a really long time," she said.

"Weird how?" I asked.

"You know, doing all kinds of really weird things. Just sending me a lot of emails and texts and stuff like that." Even though she found the behavior to be unacceptable, she admitted that a lot of her clients could have difficulty respecting her boundaries and finds that it is best to keep them at arm's length. "In those cases, I just try and keep a little bit of a distance between us without, like, alienating them, you know? I just try to do my best to regulate the relationship as best I can."

The fact that clients have more ready and immediate access to providers can create new problems of workers being threatened, either personally or for their business. More access meant more interactions—that open the door for negative or manipulative interactions. Charlene roundly dubbed behaviors that clients tried to get away with "bullshit." "When you get the 'Oh, I don't have your money. The dog ate my wallet,' that's bullshit. If I'm in the house I will probably break something. These people are idiots. They'll call you over [and agree to pay six hundred for the appointment] and you get there and then it's, 'Can you do fifty dollars?' And all this bullshit. 'Okay, well, how about I break the six hundred dollars? Where's my fucking money?'"

This new mode of working can inevitably be exploited by faithless actors. Providers told me about attempts to use technology to harm workers. A prospective client contacted Charlene, but was being evasive about screening information, so she looked up his number on a blacklist site and found that he had made multiple appointments with other providers in order to rob them at gunpoint. She shook her head as she brushed lint from her couch. "One guy called me and he didn't want to give me screening information, either. I looked at his notes [on the blacklist]; he robbed about five other bitches before trying to bring [his] ass over here. So what you think? I'm not going to deal with that."

But overall, Charlene thought the new developments in technology have helped give providers more choices. And finding the right people was the integral part of the work for Charlene. The Internet provided her with information on clients and played into whether she felt she could trust them not to give her any "bullshit." "I need to know that you're responsible to come over here and have a good time," she said, then hooked her thumb towards the door. "Act like a gentleman and keep it moving and don't be on some bullshit."

Security: "I'm in Control of What I'm Doing"

Arden exhaled a plume of smoke and squeezed one eye closed. "I get referred to some clients through other clients or through other girls and things like that, so I can easily verify somebody through word of mouth." She was explaining how technology has impacted her security protocols.

Recently, she had started using a new website that had more transparency about clients, which helps inform her choice of which clients to take. "The reason why I'm using this particular website is because the profiles on there allow me to see the interactions that they have with other providers in the area," she told me. "And I know a lot of the providers in the area because I've been doing this for like five or six years now."

Arguably, the most practical benefit providers gained from the use of technology has been improved security measures. Though communication, advertisement, and community were discussed by workers frequently, technology's impact on security was included in nearly every interaction providers described. But the security of the Internet can have contradicting effects. As often as providers recognized the value of the choice the Internet provides, workers also reported feeling isolated. Yet it is this same anonymity that gives many of them some sense of security. And the most common type of security procedure was screening: covertly gathering information on prospective clients to assess their risk. But the anonymity of the Internet can swing both ways. Clients could be lying to providers or fabricating information. "Hypothetically they could just create two new accounts and answer [from] them, and I've seen that happen before," Arden said. But providers did not simply trust the information clients gave them. They wanted the resources to verify the accuracy of the information they receive and to make an informed choice.

Providers could often describe the intricacies of their screening and security protocols, but occasionally, they pointed to "gut feelings" or intuition when assessing a client. And as vague as "intuition" sounds, workers had a long list of reliable ways to detect a bad client. Providers mentioned spelling and grammar often, complaining or insulting workers, and unclear communication as things that set off those "gut feelings." Often, intuition is seen as a vague signal or feeling, cosmic and mysterious in nature. But intuition is the culmination of experience. Providers were able to articulate its speed and effectiveness. "Feelings" played an important role in the screening procedure, and they were no less valid or reliable than other methods providers used to keep themselves safe. And they took a lot of pride in their ability to ferret out deception in new clients, even more so when their "gut" was validated. Arden managed to succinctly describe the complexity of intuition. "A lot of it's like your sixth sense and experience."

New clients can pose the largest risk, because workers have to decide how to solicit enough information from them to convince themselves that the client is safe, while also navigating interactions with a new client who may be unfamiliar with introductory protocols. And then, if those steps go well, the provider decides if they will see the new client at all. Arden explained the problem with these kinds of clients. "Then of course there are the clients that have never seen anyone at all. Sometimes they choose me as the first person they want to see. That gets a little bit hairy because then I require more personal information, and not everyone's willing to give that up. Especially if they're new." The implication here is that even though the screening process can be fraught, the space between the introduction of a new client and their first meeting, facilitated by the use of the Internet, created more choices for workers. The ease of transmitting screening information over the Internet, either in the form of referrals, employment verification, or "gut feelings," gave workers more room to breathe, increasing the space they had to decide not only if a client was safe but whether they were a good use of the provider's time.

Despite these hurdles, most providers were confident in their ability to keep themselves safe during their work. Even while gathering information, providers are making choices. They are deciding whether the information they are receiving is trustworthy and assessing how vulnerable this new situation could make them.

"I can usually detect just through the context of the conversation whether someone's full of shit or not," Arden said with a grin.

When providers combined all the different security measures, most found that they were relatively safe in their work. But Arden noted that even with all these different steps, when it really mattered, she was alone, looking across the table at a prospective client, and the choice was hers. "At that point, I look at their face and I make sure it's the same dude that I saw on Facebook."

I asked her if that made her nervous, all that responsibility resting on one decision. She lit another cigarette and said she fell back on her experience. "I'm in control of what I'm doing. I'm empowered, I'm educated, I'm aware."

Final Thoughts: "This Very Messy Place"

Jordan arched her eyebrow behind her chic square librarian glasses and gave a thoughtful nod. "How do you put one on a rung over another?" She was explaining the problem of viewing sex work hierarchically but emphasized that although sex work was a good choice for her, someone else could be coming from a different set of circumstance.

"I felt way more exploited working retail than I ever have in sex work . . . [but] for some people, sex work is way more exploitative to them than [other work]," Jordan explained, wanting a different view of sex work that acknowledged individuals' backgrounds, circumstances, and ability to make their own choices, and did not judge providers according to their type of work. She swept her blue hair out of her eyes and continued.

> There is this unspoken hierarchy . . . where you have strippers that look down on massage providers because, "Well, I don't have to touch their dicks." And then you have massage providers that look down on escorts, because, "Well at least I'm not fucking their dicks." And then you have escorts that look down on street-based workers because, "At least I'm not working the streets." Everyone's in a different position for whatever reason. It might be the hand that they were dealt. It might be how they've chosen to work in that field. But at the end of the day, we're all still sex workers.

Ultimately, after all the coffee and cocktails I had with providers from countries around the world, the message workers wanted people to hear was simple: when they have the power to make their own choices, their work is legitimate. End the stigma. Decriminalize it.

Legitimacy

"My job's awesome, that's all I can say. Best job I've ever had. My job's better than yours," Arden said with a smile. She counted on her fingers the benefits of her work. "I get paid as much as a doctor does. I have so much free time on my hands to do the things that I want to do. And I work with my best friend. And we make our own schedule. And I meet awesome people. I get to hear like professional corporate CEOs tell me like their deepest darkest fantasies and secrets. Like my job's fucking awesome."

Providers wanted people to know that their work was legitimate. But their feelings about that legitimacy could take many forms. Some wanted people to know that they enjoyed their work and that it had a positive impact, whereas others wanted to express that they felt properly remunerated for the work. Many thought that the public being more aware of the reality of sex work could increase its legitimacy. And some found that the work had deeper meaning.

"It's actually very loving work to help people explore their sexuality," Hope, a twenty-eight-year-old escort, told me. She saw that her work, overall, had a positive impact for people. Her early experiences in a fetish community taught her to be open to new things and to believe that for human beings to explore the vulnerability of their sexuality can be a worthwhile endeavor.

But part of sex work being legitimate was the fact that it is work. Being a provider required labor, both physical and emotional, and many of the workers simply compared the level of effort to that of previous jobs they had had. Bethany, a twenty-eight-year-old cam and fetish model who advertised herself as a "hot, nerdy, curvy, gamer girl," compared her current job to her previous job in retail. "It's just like working at [a big box store]. I've actually been sexually harassed more times working at [a big box store] than I have as a sex worker," she said with a shrug. "And nothing was done about it even though I reported it. So, I'm enjoying this job more than that, and getting my shit out of it."

When providers told me that their job was legitimate, often they would talk about the "behind the scenes" prep work that goes unnoticed by most people. It is the fact that sex work is work, because it actually contains work, that seems to escape the general public. In their descriptions of their work, providers could list behaviors that could be used to describe almost any business. "I spend way more time doing banal tasks like answering emails, like cleaning my toilet and fucking doing laundry than I actually do rolling in a wad of cash," Jordan told me. "There's a lot of behind-the-scene upkeep or admin work or just actual labor work that people don't realize goes into a session."

The cultural expectation is that providers throw on an outfit and show up to a session, stay the hour, and then collect their money. But the increased connectivity supplied by technology has increased the effort workers have to put in. Even beyond the administrative tasks of advertisement or scheduling, workers often spent time working out at the gym, visiting the beauty salon, purchasing clothes or other supplies, or cultivating their online presence, and all this effort needs to be factored into the cost of a session.

And when providers began to take stock of all this labor, many of them simply saw another service job, where most of them had had previous experience. Izzy, a nineteen-year-old cammer in a massive, fuzzy pink robe that spilled over her bed, echoed a lot of workers when she described the validity of sex work as stemming from the fact that it is similar to any other service work she had done, while she burrowed further into her flowing pink cocoon. "It's a job, it's real, it's valid. I see people that are like, 'Oh, you're not a doctor, you're not a whatever, like okay.' When people say you're selling your body, okay, and I'm not selling my body when I'm working at the pet store moving big bags of dog food? I'm selling physical labor either way. Honestly, this is less physical labor because I get to be in my bed."

For a worker to choose their job adds to its legitimacy. Similar to the cultural impression that workers are idle until a session, one of the most common cultural themes about providers is that they have limited agency, and ended up in sex work due to circumstances outside their control. Jordan explained, "It kills me that people out there truly believe that I'm a victim and that I have no free agency and that I have no ability to make decisions of my own. I mean, really, it's been nothing but positive for me."

Lucy, a twenty-seven-year-old cammer with a persistent smile, was more than happy to describe her work in bright, colorful detail. She never shied away from a topic and wanted people to know that her work was beneficial and that she understood that the work had problematic aspects, but a deeper understanding of the choices and processes of providers could help people understand what it was she did.

> I love doing it. When I tell a regular that I really like them, and that they're great, that's not a lie. Now, those are the girls who are trying to make your lives better, who are trying to learn as much as they can about the industry. The majority of us, at least the girls I talk to, are college educated. This is one of the best-paying industries—no, *the* best-paying industry for women. We get paid a lot more than men do in this industry. It's very feminist—being a sex worker. I mean obviously not all sex workers are feminist; being an indentured stripper is not feminist,[5] but like, that's a different issue from what I'm trying to say.

Providers viewed their work as legitimate when they were the ones making meaningful choices about where and when to work and whom to work with. And when they had that agency, often, they could find significance in their work. When the stigma, criminality, and exploitation were pulled back, some providers found that they could explore their work's deeper meanings.

Olivia, a twenty-one-year-old escort, explained, in a thick French accent, how the legitimacy of being a provider was a complex equation. At first, she found clients to be slightly hypocritical because they construct their perception of reality to frame their lives in the way that fit them best. "People tell me a lot about their lives," she said, holding a lit cigarette from the end of long, slender fingers. "They build narratives for themselves around sentimentality, how you become numb to certain things, or have this euphoria that comes back at some point."

But then she started to see these same strategies in the systems we construct for society as well. Social structures can be built with good intentions but then reinforce existing problems and inequalities. They can often have confusing and contradictory purposes, and Olivia began to notice that the same tactics clients use were baked into the majority of society.

"It helped, questioning the system," she said. "Understanding it from different points—understanding the systems and the games of power in society at a lot of different levels. At the monetary level, emotional level, sexual level." These kinds of observations were tied to Olivia's use of technology, her exploration of the Internet to find information from a variety of sources. She pulled on her cigarette and then waved it in front of her face, motioning to the outside world. "The Internet helps you have access to different points of view, and realizing you're not alone. It makes you evolve within your own point of view, and it helps you understand your position. So having access to this is amazing."

But the Internet was not a silver bullet to solve all of society's problems. It also had its own share of paradoxes. For as much as it can expose a person to new viewpoints, "it also kind of creates this very strong isolation and weight on your shoulders," she said with a very existential French sigh. "So in general, this society of taboos and judgment and guilt actually provides me with a job, because we don't have a sense of guilt or taboo with being a prostitute."

And the paradox of being stigmatized for engaging in sex work while simultaneously being insulated because of privilege was part of her realization. "I think a big one was learning about my privileges. Being young and white and pretty," she said, nodding and pointing the end of the cigarette at me.

When they called sex work empowering, most providers acknowledged their experiences in terms of positive outcomes or money. But agency is the antecedent to empowerment, the steps of the process being the choices of providers. "You're in this really compromised place where you're both deciding to own your body, and deciding what to do with it," she paused. "But on the other hand," spreading her palms, "you are self-objectifying, which can be completely the opposite. So I think being in this very messy place helps you ask yourself a lot of interesting questions."

It was these "interesting questions" that led Olivia to the realization that sex work was built on a fundamental human paradox. "What I learned mostly doing this job is not really about the job itself, it's more about—this job showed me that everybody's ultimately alone, and that it's a beautiful and extreme thing at the end of the day to do—to empathize with another person's solitude because it's so universal."

Providers saw their work as legitimate. From an internal perspective, they saw the importance of agency and choice guiding the navigation of their work. From a social perspective, they saw the paradox of communities extolling virtues like freedom or individuality while culturally stigmatizing workers. And from an existential perspective, they saw their work as desired, necessary, and even, in some cases, enlightening.

Stigma

"I didn't tell anyone about sex work for years because I was terrified as to what their reactions would be," Jordan said, looking down. "And I kind of want to go back in time and slap past me upside the head and be like, 'You can talk to people. They're gonna be okay with this,'" she smiled. "The friends that I have come out to have been really fucking cool about it."

She felt that after some time doing the work, she had not only a better perspective on how to do the job safely or feel like she is part of a community but also the clarity of self-assurance that comes with acknowledging one's choices as legitimate. "I'm providing something of value, something really meaningful, and it's not shameful," she said.

I asked her why she thinks that stigma persists.

"I think a lot of that has to do with public education. A lot of it has to do with the fact that it's portrayed in the media," she said.

Other providers agreed with her as well. Alyson, a thirty-two-year-old escort who has been a provider since 2008, saw that stigma dehumanizes workers and turns them into punchlines and that the portrayal of providers in the media has not done much to help the situation. "We're normal people. We're human beings. We're not punchlines. . . . If a TV show can get through an entire episode without making a dead hooker joke—it's sad that that's the standard we're at. You would never make jokes about killing Asian people, or killing mentally disabled people, but killing hookers, that's still ha, ha, funny, cue the little laugh track." And stigma, similar to legitimacy, seems to stem from the public having a basic misunderstanding of the choices of providers. Lucy pointed out that being forced into work would be a bad situation for anyone regardless of the person or the kind of labor, but she did not become a sex worker because of some unseen trauma or coercion and does not need to be saved.

"Being forced to do any sort of work is bad. But this isn't because I'm mentally ill," she said. "This isn't because I don't have a good life. This isn't because I haven't met my white knight to carry me off. I've met my white knight and he bought me a fucking machine," she laughed. "And that's what I would say: that we're healthy, and happy. . . . We don't— we're not trying to corrupt America. We're not trying to corrupt your children," she said. "We just wanna do what we love to do. Just because you do it behind closed doors, doesn't mean that we have to."

When it came to stigma, most providers were troubled by the fact that if a person was a sex worker, that became the only thing about that person that mattered. Providers wanted the public to have a better understanding of what it is they do, but Emma saw stigma as more of a problem for society at large. If people wanted to have opinions on her work, she thought it was incumbent on them to not be ignorant. "It's not up to me to educate you on my job; it's up to you to educate yourself about what I do, and if you don't wanna do that, then it's none of your business."

Noreen thought the concept of stigmatizing sex work was ridiculous, simply because sex is something most people do and enjoy. To her, the conflict was between her feelings of value and the commoditization of the human experience.

> There are things that define people, like responsibility or professionalism or competitiveness or expertise or whatever, but none of those things are exclusive to jobs. The only thing that makes it exclusive to a job is that you're getting some fucking cash. The idea that what defines a person is what they do for cash is one of the big faults of capitalism. That just isn't what defines a person. We've been used as muses. We've been used as connectors to spiritual enlightenment. We've been used as artistic inspiration, as political confidants, and we have a fucking purpose. We're useful. We're a useful fucking person in society. Society requires us to be around.

Noreen was pointing out that legitimacy and stigma are closely related. Providers see their work as legitimate. When their job is examined next to those in other service industries, most see more similarities than differences. The main difference seems to be that sex work is stigmatized because of its relationship to the law. Providers from countries where sex work was illegal saw decriminalization and legalization as good tactics for reducing stigma. Though there are a variety of paths to accomplish this, providers acknowledged that it would be a difficult path but saw it as a necessary one.

Lucy told me that providers wanted the legitimacy of sex work to be evident not only in the public's opinions of the work but in legal terms as well. "We don't like the stigma that we're trying to cheat the system, that we're a black-market commodity. We want to be taken seriously," she said sternly. "We want our country to know that we care, that we're patriotic, that we're citizens, you know. At least the girls I talk to."

Lucy saw that participation in conventional parts of society would help reduce the stigma of sex work and increase its legitimacy. "End the stigma. Make it better through—legalize and regulate," she said, tapping her index finger on the coffee table. "And pay taxes! What a concept," she laughed. "That would be excellent."

Decriminalization

"Legalize it," Mona said, but then waved the idea off. "They'd end up screwing that up, too," she laughed. "I think it would be a really good idea. They're trying to use this trafficking bullshit as an excuse against prostitution. 'Oh, the trafficking, the trafficking,'" she said, holding her hand to her mouth with a look of mock horror. "There's going to be trafficking whether it's legal or whether it's not legal. For being a country that is supposed to be so free, we have some real issues with sex in this country. . . . I think the attitude of denying that we're sexual creatures is really poisonous."

Mona believed that society had a tendency to turn a blind eye to topics people were uncomfortable with rather than addressing them head on. "We need to meet sex out in the open. One thing I'm really, really very pro is birth control. Birth control, people. Use it. Love it. It's good for you. I think sex is great. It's healthy." Mona could not believe that access to birth control was even something being argued about by legislators. "Even now, with the whole argument we've fallen into with legislators. The right says, 'Oh well, you sluts just use it because they want to have sex,' and then the left counters with, 'Well, it's not only used for sex,'" she said, shaking her head. "No! Screw that argument. Why don't we have the argument that sex is healthy? There's no problem to having responsible sex. Sex is good!" she yelled, exasperated.

Mona put her head in her hands and made a low groan, but a smile peeked from behind her fingers. She laughed at how ridiculous it was to have to argue that sex was a positive thing. So many of the providers I spoke to believed that stigma, laws, and regulations could be improved if only the public would place themselves in the shoes of workers. Some solutions are just more obvious after experience. "If we would have more sex and just be a little less tight-assed, maybe this world—the way I look at—my God—You know what? Experience. It's so much better than—Give me experience or a Coach purse, I'll take the experience all day long."

The Internet gave providers the opportunity to see how other countries legally navigate sex work—and discuss what policies are most effective with other providers. Workers were able to describe the details of governmental policy and legislation from places like the Nordic countries, Europe, Australia, and New Zealand. Though the specifics of decriminalization efforts are intricate, providers share a lot of the same basic ground rules they believe work best for both providers and society.

Jordan saw the advantages of a postcriminalized world. Yes, decriminalization would get rid of legal punishments for workers, but it would also open up new avenues for workers to advocate for themselves. "I really am a strong believer in decriminalization, especially if you look at New Zealand, where it is decriminalized and the parts of Australia where decriminalization has happened, what you have is workers organizing. Workers creating unions. Workers being more comfortable contacting the police when they don't feel safe. Workers feeling more comfortable to charge the rates they want to and offer the services they want to provide."

Most decriminalization discussions addressed three models: full criminalization, full legalization, and the "Nordic" model. In 1999, Sweden became the first country to pass laws criminalizing the purchasing of sex. Roughly a decade later, Norway and Iceland both adopted the same legislation. This approach was seen as a compromise between the two ends of the spectrum and focused on the clients rather than providers, and it had wide public support.[6] When the legislation passed, providers mobilized to voice their dissatisfaction. These types of laws, though seemingly well intentioned, drive sex work further underground and ostracize workers from their good, reliable, and safe clients. Jordan's voice became pointed. "When you criminalize my clients, you're just taking away the good clients and you're leaving me with the people that may not necessarily fear criminalization. They don't necessarily fear being arrested, and that's not safe for me."

Many providers were frustrated that the laws that were supposed to keep them safe actually made their lives increasingly difficult and more dangerous. Francis, a thirty-three-year-old escort, is an independent worker who is completing a PhD in gender studies. "It's just a job and criminalization makes it incredibly unsafe for a lot of people, including myself," she said. "Who, even still, is somebody who is really privileged," she noted, shaking her head.

The fact that legislators and law enforcement were either willfully ignorant or willfully blind about the differences between the choices of agentic workers and people being victimized by the atrocity of trafficking only made these debates more frustrating. "I have to worry about,

'Oh, maybe the cops are gonna book a fake call with me to come and see if I'm being trafficked.' And that pisses me off, too." Francis also noticed that many of the legal interventions by police and other law enforcement agencies simply appeared to make no sense. "Just use your fucking head. Do you really think women with professional photos and thousand-dollar websites are being trafficked, because I'm pretty sure traffickers aren't spending the money to have professional photos done. Like, get your head out of your ass. I had colleagues who got caught up and it's like four fucking police officers to one woman who's in lingerie expecting a client. And then they wonder why we don't wanna talk to them. Because that's really fucking unsafe, and cops are one of the biggest perpetrators of violence against sex workers."

Gertrude, a forty-year-old escort, agreed and echoed what many of the providers said about law enforcement not being able to recognize the difference between workers who have chosen to do sex work and trafficking victims. "We're all going 'We need full decrim!' Because . . . we're kept in the same net as traffic victims, and America is bad at that, and they're trying to eradicate the system anyway. They're not actually trying to help anyone; you can't help the victims because the police just go off on the consensual sex workers so the ones that are trafficking are just staying trafficked. Because you can't tell the difference between us." The insistence on lumping people who have chosen to be providers with victims of trafficking not only hurts workers. It confuses the efforts of law enforcement, muddles the distribution of resources, and perpetuates the difficulty of both helping victims and identifying traffickers.

Providers, by and large, wanted to make their own choices when it came to their work. When they were included in discussions of agency, legitimacy, stigma, and legality, they were hopeful that the outcomes could benefit themselves, their clients, their community, and society as a whole.

Osu, a twenty-seven-year-old escort, sat on her daybed as sun spilled over her shoulders. When she started as a provider, she took it one day at a time. She would take a moment to reflect each day on whether or not the choice to be a worker was in her best interest and if it made her happy. The strategy worked well in the beginning, so she still does it to this day, a decade later. "I do it day by day. This makes me happy today. I'll think about it tomorrow, and tomorrow, and it usually ends up being okay," she said.

I asked Osu what she would tell the world if she could let it know one thing about her job. She took a pause and then replied, "At least for me, it's empowering."

Conclusion: "Holding Space"

Roxy pulled on a straw cowboy hat and stepped into the setting sun. "So much sun, we're just a day away from the solstice," she said, pulling the brim over her eyes.

She sat on a long wooden bench that ran the length of the porch, leaned back on the gray slate, and produced her signature cigarette and lighter from her pocket. She put her foot up on a plastic deck chair, a pose straight out of a Remington painting, as American as apple pie served on a gun.

"It was really fun for me to put on a different hat every day and fill a role because it's something that I've always been good at. It's a necessary need for society, and I still, if not more now, believe the validity of that," she said. "I love the phrase, you're 'holding space' in a way for a lot of people sexually and you are letting the guy whose wife had breast cancer and her tits removed and the hysterectomy who—he still loves and has that outlet to maintain that relationship with her."

But these connections came at a price.

"[Sex work] enhanced my prior level of disconnection between mind and body. And now, I have to fix—I don't think it was necessarily bad or good for me, then, but now—to have a whole and meaningful sexual experience I have to pay attention to reconnecting those disparate parts that were probably whole at some point in my life—like a lifetime ago. But it had probably gotten here," she held up her hands, about a foot apart, measuring the distance. "And then with sex work it got to here," she said, stretching her hands another span. "And now the journey back is so much harder."

I nodded.

We paused for a moment and watched the sun slide toward the ocean.

"But was that distance worth it?" I asked.

She took a drag from her cigarette, tapped the ash on the side of the bench, and exhaled a long plume of smoke.

"Yes."

ACKNOWLEDGMENTS

This research would not have been possible without the support of many incredible people. To Dr. Jody Miller, I am eternally grateful for your patience, guidance, and encouragement. You've shown me how to use scholarship to build not only a better world but a better me. You believed in my scholarly voice before I knew I had one and encouraged me to shout when I only knew how to whisper. To Dr. Andres Rengifo, Dr. Ko-Lin Chin, Dr. Vanessa Panfil, Dr. Heidi Grundetjern, and Dr. Ange Dwyer, thank you for your thoughtful suggestions and gentle encouragement to look closer, push farther, and be better.

To NYU Press and my editing team, Ilene Kalish, Yasemin Torfilli, Alexia Traganas, and Emily Wright, thank you for encouraging me to take my scattered ideas and turn them into a story. To Kelly Ohlert, thank you for being there at the beginning and at the end and never doubting for a minute that this research is worthwhile and that I'm the right person to be doing it. To Jack Valentine, thank you for seeing beauty in me when I can't see it myself, and being the first, last, and best defense against the injustices of an indifferent universe. To the members of Mercury Radio Theater, thank you for playing music that fills my soul when it's been poured out. To Curt Wilson, thank you for teaching me that broken things can be fixed, but scars still tell an important story. To Stacey Grimes, thank you for cheering me on when progress feels like stagnation. To Tania Blackman and Mengsen Zhang, thank you for showing me that patience is the quietest of virtues and that it doesn't get the credit it deserves. To Robert Green and Allan Palombi, thank you for reminding me that good science is revision. And finally, thank you, Roxy, for being the muse that launched a thousand ships full of smiling men that sank to the bottom of an angry sea.

NOTES

INTRODUCTION: "I GOT THIS NEW JOB"

1 Middle-class sex work has gotten more attention in the last few decades. For more
   see Bernstein, 2007; Grant, 2014; Carbonero & Gomez Garrido, 2018.

2 A note on descriptive amounts: I will be using much of Miller's (2008) terminology when describing the prevalence of themes within the data. Phrases like
   "nearly all/universal/etc." describe an observation that all but a small minority
   of participants share. "Overwhelmingly" refers to more than three-quarters but
   not all of the sample, whereas "the vast majority" refers to roughly three-quarters
   of the sample. The term "most" or "the majority" is used to represent half, and
   "many" describes a sizeable minority of between a quarter and a third. Both
   "several" and "a few" will refer to a small number of participants, usually over two
   (see Miller, 2008, 235–36). However, it is important to note that relevant concepts
   in qualitative work should not be judged by quantitative metrics and a theme
   expressed by a minority of participants is no less "significant" than one expressed
   by the majority (Small, 2009).

3 Heckathorn, 2011; Woodley & Lockard, 2016.

4 Heckathorn, 1997; 2002; 2011.

5 Handcock & Gile, 2011; Heckathorn, 1997.

6 Coker, Huang, & Kashubeck-West, 2009.

7 Though these questions were not part of the interview guide, the semistructured
   nature of the conversations meant that many workers could speak to these topics
   if they felt comfortable.

8 Krefting, 1991; Lincoln & Guba, 1985.

9 England, 1994.

10 Norris, 1997.

11 Berger, 2015.

12 An example of Berger's (2015) reflexivity and being "attuned to one's own reac-
    tions" (221) occurred when I interviewed a worker who told the story of a client
    and her playing out an "abduction." I immediately perceived this to be a traumatic
    experience. Yet when I asked if she was comfortable providing more details, she
    laughed and told me how exciting it was and that it was something she had been
    wanting to try. My initial "worldview" was that workers should be respected, but
    from my perception, protection was part of respect. It was not until I discussed
    the idea of risk and safety with workers that I realized that my perception of safety

was vastly different from theirs, and not trusting workers' ability to make their own choices was a form of both bias and disrespect.

13 Kuhn, 1962.

14 Weitzer, 2011.

15 Weitzer, 2011, p. 16.

16 Chapkis, 1997, p. 29.

17 Chapkis, 1997, p. 29.

18 Marlatt, 1998, p. xii.

19 Roe, 2005, p. 244.

20 Pew Research, 2018.

21 Sampson & Laub, 1993.

22 "The terms 'sugar daddy' and 'sugar momma' generally describe older and wealthy men and women, respectively, who lavish gifts on younger men and women in exchange for their company and/or sexual favors. The term 'sugar baby' refers to a younger person who receives the gifts. Sugar arrangements are typically reliant on heterosexual relationships" (Upadhyay, 2021, p. 1).

23 Chapkis, 1997.

24 Hochschild, 1979, p. 7.

25 Ashforth & Humphrey, 1993; Morris & Feldman, 1996.

26 Bernstein, 2007.

27 Cunningham & Kendall, 2011.

28 Meta-data is "data about data," and includes many varieties: descriptive, administrative, structural, referential, etc. But this example refers to data that is not immediately visible to users but nonetheless can reveal vital information about a provider (such as geolocation data, source information, or other identifiers).

29 The term "dropping pins" refers to tagging a location with a traceable identifier— similar to using a phone with location services to check into a restaurant, bar, or other location.

30 Thukral, 2005.

31 Specific names of websites have been given pseudonyms throughout the book to ensure confidentiality. NearMart is a location-specific commercial website with an unregulated "adult services" section that many workers feel is dangerous.

CHAPTER 1. SEX WORK AND ITS FRAMES

1 DiTecco & Karaian, 2022.

2 In his 1962 book, *The Structure of Scientific Revolutions*, researcher and historian Thomas Kuhn presented the idea of a paradigm. Paradigms are framing devices that help contextualize scientific inquiry. Often paradigms contain a central thesis or concept that frames all aspects of the research (for example, astronomers switched from a geocentric model of the solar system to a heliocentric model).

3 Lister, 2017a.

4 Kipling, 1898, p. 1.

5 Weitzer, 2011, p. 16.

6 Roe, 2005.
7 Rothman, 1978; Sloan & Wahab, 2000.
8 Clarkson, 1939, p. 296.
9 Sanger, 1858, p. 17.
10 Campbell, 1991.
11 Lister, 2017b.
12 Sanger, 1858, p. 18.
13 Sanger, 1858, p. 21.
14 Clarkson, 1939; Lister, 2017a; Sanger, 1858.
15 Bindel, 2017; Bullough & Bullough, 1987; Cree, 1995; Pheterson, 1989; Roberts, 1992; Sloan & Wahab, 2000.
16 Hobson, 1990; Sloan & Wahab, 2000.
17 Addams, 1912; Sloan & Wahab, 2000.
18 Addams, 1912; Sloan & Wahab, 2000.
19 Barry, 1984; Bullough & Bullough, 1987; Decker, 1979; MacKinnon, 1985; Sloan & Wahab, 2000.
20 Barry, 1984; Farley et al., 2004; MacKinnon, 1985; Pateman, 1988; Weitzer, 2011; Wynter, 1987.
21 Wynter, 1987.
22 Barss, 2010.
23 Comte, 2014.
24 Farley et al., 2004.
25 Raymond, 1995.
26 Farley et al., 2004; Weitzer, 2013.
27 Pateman, 1988; Weitzer, 2011.
28 Grant, 2014.
29 Bindel, 2017, p. 7.
30 Barry, 1984, p. 7.
31 Barry, 1984; Bindel, 2017; Dempsey, 2010; Farley et al., 2004.
32 Dworkin, 1997; Farley et al., 2004.
33 Raymond, 2004.
34 Bullough & Bullough, 1987; Jenness, 1990; Weitzer, 1991.
35 Jenness, 1990.
36 Bernstein, 2007; Kempadoo & Jo, 1998; Pheterson, 1996.
37 During her time as an empowerment activist, Leigh was known as "The Scarlet Harlot."
38 Leigh, 1997, p. 230.
39 Leigh, 1997, p. 230; Lister, 2017b.
40 Chapkis, 1997; Delacoste, 2018; Jenness, 1990; Vanwesenbeeck, 2001; Weitzer, 2011.
41 Ericsson, 1980; Hobbes, 1651.
42 Weitzer, 2011.
43 Swendeman et al., 2015; Bernstein, 2007; Chapkis, 1997; Doezema, 2013; Weitzer, 2007.

44 Dempsey, 2019; Maher, 1997; McCarthy, Benoit & Jansson, 2014; Rosen & Venkatesh, 2008.

45 Comte, 2014.

46 Bell, 1987; Chapkis, 1997; Comte, 2014; Queen, 1997.

47 Chapkis, 1997.

48 Certeau & Mayol, 1990; Chapkis, 1997.

49 Califia, 1988; Chapkis, 1997.

50 Califia, 1988; Chapkis, 1997; Hebdige, 1979.

51 Chapkis, 1997; Paglia, 2011.

52 Chapkis, 1997; Seidman, 1992.

53 Chapkis, 1997.

54 Augustin, 1988; Kempadoo & Jo, 1998; Overall, 1992; Weitzer, 2011.

55 Bell, 1987, p. 7; Delacoste, 2018; Nagle, 1997.

56 Pajnik, Kambouri, Renault & Šori, 2016.

57 Weitzer, 2011, p. 16.

58 Vanwesenbeeck, 2001; Weitzer, 2011.

59 Weitzer, 2011, p. 18.

60 Ehrenreich & Hochschild, 2003.

61 Orchard et al., 2012.

62 Jones, 2015b.

63 Evans, 2013.

64 Barss, 2010.

65 Döring, 2009, p. 1094.

66 Bowen et al., 2011; Swendeman et al., 2015.

67 Høigård & Finstad, 1992; Maher & Daly, 1996; Maher, Dunlap, Johnson & Hamid, 1996; Thukral, Ditmore & Murphy, 2005.

68 Bernstein, 2007; Weitzer, 2007.

69 Lever & Dolnick, 2010.

70 McCarthy, Benoit & Jansson, 2014.

71 Dalla, Xi & Kennedy, 2003.

72 Sanders, 2004.

73 Brents & Hausbeck, 2005.

74 Jones, 2015b.

75 Barss, 2010.

76 Döring, 2009.

77 Tewksbury & Lapsey, 2018.

78 Thukral, Ditmore & Murphy, 2005.

79 BBC News, 2010; Joyce, 2015.

80 Sanders, Connelly & King, 2016.

81 Horswill & Weitzer, 2018; Sutherland, 1947, p. 6.

82 Capiola et al., 2014.

83 Motyl, 2013.

84 Sanders, Connelly & King, 2016.

85 Ray, 2005.
86 Jones, 2015b.
87 Grant, 2014; Twis & Shelton, 2018; Weitzer, 2013.
88 Weitzer, 2017.
89 Grant, 2014.
90 Cojocaru, 2016.
91 See also, Chin & Finckenauer, 2012.
92 Weitzer, 2013, p. 1348.
93 Farrell et al., 2009; Hickle & Roe-Sepowitz, 2017; Twis & Shelton, 2018.
94 Weitzer, 2011, p. 16.
95 Smith, 2017.
96 Abel, 2014; Benoit, Jansson, Smith, & Flagg, 2018.
97 Rekart, 2005.
98 Rekart, 2005.
99 Vanwesenbeeck, 2001.
100 Campbell, 1991; Rieder & Ruppelt, 1988; Sacks, 1996; Sloan & Wahab, 2000.
101 Lindemann, 2013; Thukral, Ditmore, & Murphy, 2005.
102 Chapkis, 1997; Vanwesenbeeck, 2001; Thukral, Ditmore & Murphy, 2005.
103 Bernstein, 2007; Chapkis, 1997; Sloan & Wahab, 2000.
104 Bailey & Figueroa, 2016: Kempadoo & Jo, 1998; Nagle, 1997; Thukral, Ditmore & Murphy, 2005
105 Boyer, Chapman & Marshal, 1993; Sloan & Wahab, 2000; Weiner, 1996.
106 Sloan & Wahab, 2000; Weiner, 1996.
107 Comte, 2014.
108 Pheterson, 1996.
109 Baratosy & Wendt, 2017; Benoit, Jansson, Smith & Flagg, 2018; Krusi et al., 2016; Shdaimah & Leon, 2018; Weitzer, 2017.
110 Goffman, 1963b, p. 14.
111 Krusi et al., 2016.
112 Benoit, Jansson, Smith & Flagg, 2018.
113 Shdaimah & Leon, 2018.
114 Koken, 2011; Shdaimah & Leon, 2018.
115 Comte, 2014, p. 206.
116 E.g., Bernstein, 2007; Chapkis, 1997; Comte, 2014; Downs, James & Cowan, 2006; O'Doherty, 2011; Oerton & Phoenix, 2001; Sanders, 2004.
117 Comte, 2014, p. 205.
118 Baratosy & Wendt, 2017; Benoit, Jansson, Smith & Flagg, 2018; Bruckert & Hannem, 2013; Krusi et al., 2016; Sanders, 2004; Shdaimah & Leon, 2018; Weitzer, 2017.
119 Turner, 1982.
120 Smith, 2017.
121 Benoit et al., 2017; Tomura, 2009.
122 Shdaimah & Leon, 2018.

123 Sanders, 2004.
124 Mimiaga et al., 2009.
125 Shdaimah & Leon, 2018.
126 Sanders, Connelly & King, 2016.
127 Panchanadeswaran et al., 2017; Sanders, Connelly & King, 2016.
128 Bernstein, 2007, p. 93.
129 Koken, Bimbi, Parsons & Halkitis, 2004, p. 5.
130 Bernstein, 2001; Döring, 2009; Motyl, 2013.
131 Arvidsson, 2005.
132 Brewis & Linstead, 2000; Hoang, 2011; Sanders, 2004.
133 Holt & Blevins, 2007.
134 Bruckert & Hannem, 2013.
135 Milrod & Monto, 2012.
136 Rekart, 2005.
137 Gall, 2007.
138 Dalby, 2008.
139 Sutherland, 1947.
140 Kuhn, 1962, p.170.

CHAPTER 2. DIGITAL STYLE AND SYMMETRY

1 Tokens and other exchange-based currencies were referenced often by digital cam providers. Their use is a tactic employed by not only adult sites but most online gambling and gaming sites. Patrons exchange money for the site's fictitious points/gold/tickets/tokens and then use them to participate in the site's games and activities.

2 The concept of tacit cultural knowledge has been used often in research on how knowledge is categorized and transferred. More recent research has looked at how these processes function and the role tacit cultural knowledge plays in constructing organization knowledge and knowledge management (Suppiah & Sandhu, 2011).

3 Milan, 2013.
4 United Nations, 2016; Pew Research, 2018.
5 Pew Research, 2018.
6 Leiner et al., 2012.
7 Bernstein, 2007.
8 Milan, 2013.
9 Ashton, 2009.
10 Leiner et al., 2012.
11 Panchanadeswaran et al., 2017.
12 Helsper, 2012.
13 Chen & Li, 2021.
14 Helpser, 2012, p. 403.
15 Ashford, 2009.

16 Hebdige, 1979, p. 17.

17 Roland Barthes, the famous semiotician, studied the recognition and interpretation of signs in a culture.

18 Hebdige, 1979, p. 18.

19 Hebdige, 1979, p. 1.

20 Ashford, 2009; Bernstein, 2007; Cunningham & Kendall, 2011; Holt & Blevins, 2007; Koken, Bimbi, Parsons & Halkitis, 2004; Lee-Gonyea, Castle & Gonyea, 2009; McLean, 2012; Minichiello, Scott & Callander, 2013; Murphy & Venkatesh, 2006; Phua & Caras, 2008; Quinn & Forsyth, 2005; Weitzer, 2005; 2011.

21 "Customs" refers to custom videos. Clients pay a premium price for workers to record scenes or scenarios that the client requests.

22 Blunt & Wolf, 2020; Musto et al., 2021.

23 Schmit, 2021.

24 Rogers, 2018.

CHAPTER 3. ENTRANCE

1 Elder, 1985, p. 17.

2 Sampson & Laub, 1993.

3 A prepaid cell phone with no additional features, only designed to send and receive calls and texts. Often also referred to as "burner phones."

4 Sutherland, 1947.

5 Drucker & Nieri, 2018; Horning, 2019; Oselin, 2014.

6 Merton, 1938.

7 Murphy & Venkatesh, 2006.

8 Cusick, Brooks-Gordon, Campbell & Edgar, 2011; Murphy & Venkatesh, 2006; Sanders & Campbell, 2007.

9 Thukral, Ditmore, & Murphy, 2005.

10 Silbert & Pines, 1982.

11 Döring, 2009; Jones, 2015b.

12 Tewksbury & Lapsey, 2018.

13 Thukral, Ditmore & Murphy, 2005.

14 Jones, 2015b, p. 567.

15 McIntosh, 1989.

16 Phua & Caras, 2008, p. 252.

17 Miller-Young, 2014, p. 8.

18 Miller-Young, 2014, p. 8.

19 Jones, 2015a; Nash, 2014.

20 Jacobs, Janssen & Pasquinelli, 2007, p. 208.

21 Mills, 1997.

22 McIntosh, 1989.

23 Mills, 1997, p. 22.

24 McIntosh, 1989, p. 33.

25 Lynn, 2019; Knox, 2014.

26 Levine & Rubinstein, 2013.
27 Fein & Spencer, 1997.
28 Cucina, Martin, Vasilopoulos & Thibodeaux, 2012.
29 Jost & Banaji, 1995.

CHAPTER 4. THE GIRLFRIEND PERSONA

 1 Refers to encounters that include features of noncommercial relationships, mimicking a "conventional" dating relationship. Bernstein (2007) argues that these relationships provide "bounded authenticity" within an "emotionally bounded erotic exchange" (p. 197). See also Milrod & Monto, 2012.
 2 Bernstein, 2007.
 3 Hochschild, 1979, p. 7.
 4 Castle & Lee, 2008, p. 109.
 5 Matthews, 2017.
 6 Parsons, Koken & Bimbi, 2004; Phua & Caras, 2008.
 7 Nayar, 2017, p. 481.
 8 Castle & Lee, 2008; Cunningham & Kendall, 2011; Jones, 2016; Lever & Dolnick, 2010.
 9 Stewart & Vache, 2010.
10 Word with Friends is a mobile gaming app that allows users to play a Scrabble-type word game with others, where each player participates autonomously via their own phone and location.
11 Koken, Bimbi & Parsons, 2010; Nayar, 2017.
12 Goffman, 1956.
13 Zickar & Carter, 2010.
14 Refers to "sexting," the act of exchanging erotic messages over messaging apps or mobile devices.
15 Horton & Wohl, 1956, pp. 215–16.
16 Koken, Bimby & Parsons, 2010, p. 213.
17 Nayar, 2017.
18 Jones, 2015a, p. 12.
19 Twigg, Wolkowitz, Cohen & Nettleton, 2011.
20 Jones, 2016, p. 230.
21 I had been a guitarist in a band for years, and Roxy had come to many of the performances.

CHAPTER 5. RISKS

 1 Benoit, Janssen, Smith & Flagg, 2018.
 2 Sandman, 1987.
 3 Minichiello, Scott & Callander, 2013.
 4 Cunningham & Kendall, 2011; Weitzer, 2011.
 5 Parson, Koken & Bimbi, 2004.
 6 Jones, 2015b.

7 "Pre-Exposure Prophylaxis (PrEP)," Centers for Disease Control and Prevention, accessed December 12, 2022: www.cdc.gov.

8 MacPhail, Scott & Minichiello, 2015.

9 Tarantino, 1994, 02:05:42.

10 Tarantino, 1994, 02:13:35.

11 "Vanilla" is a multi-use term that refers to elements within normative society and often (but not always) opposed to sex work and broader erotic culture. A "vanilla job" is socially legitimate work outside of sex work. "Vanilla sex" refers to traditional monogamous sex with no exciting or interesting elements.

12 Goffman, 1963b, p. 3.

13 Benoit et al., 2017; Krusi et al., 2016; Weitzer, 2017.

14 The stigma of sex work is not a historical constant, and research by prominent sex work historian Kate Lister shows how different societies have viewed sex work throughout time, often without the stigma imposed by Western historians and researchers (2017a).

15 Tomko et al., 2020.

16 Date-check websites are a variety of online service where one can enter a potential client's screen name, telephone number, or other vital information to see if other workers have reported them as a problem client.

17 Ashforth & Humphrey, 1993; Hochschild, 1979.

18 Cheyne & Guggisberg, 2018.

19 Belenky, Clinchy, Goldberger & Tarule, 1986.

CHAPTER 6. SECURITY

1 Blackout is a security website, also called a blacklist site, a date-check site, or bad-date site, where providers can submit data on problem clients. Providers can report vital information, such as phone numbers and screen names. MateRate is a private review site where users are given a profile page that can be rated by other users. Providers can then access these profiles for screening purposes.

2 Cunningham & Kendall, 2011.

3 Cunningham & Kendall, 2011; Minichiello, Scott & Callander, 2013; Parsons, Koken & Bimbi, 2007.

4 Thukral, Ditmore, & Murphy, 2005, p. 6.

5 Thukral, 2005.

6 Barss, 2010, p. 24.

7 Jacobs, Janssen & Pasquinelli, 2007.

8 Goldenberg, Duff & Krusi, 2015.

9 Baratosy & Wendt, 2017; Benoit et al., 2016.

10 Bernstein, 2007; Holt & Blevins, 2007; Cunningham & Kendall, 2011; Minichiello, Scott & Callander, 2013.

11 Feldman, 2014; Jones, 2015b.

12 Sullivan, 1999; 2010.

13 Koken, Bimbi & Parsons, 2010.

14 The act of surreptitiously taking off a condom without the provider knowing, increasing the worker's risk of contracting an STI and violating the trust of the worker.

15 BetterDate is a different review site that Kelly explains is trustworthy.

16 A safe call is a call made by a provider to a friend or partner during a session to confirm that they are safe and the session went as planned. During these calls providers will often have a set of code words to discreetly indicate whether they are safe or in danger (Weitzer, 2009a).

17 Ashforth & Humphrey, 1993; Hochschild, 1979.

18 Bernstein, 2007.

19 James et al., 2016.

CHAPTER 7. A NEW MODEL

1 Merton, 1938, p. 675.

2 A concept laid out by Friedrich Engels in his 1893 letter to Franz Mehring describing the misconception that thoughts and perceptions are solely the construct of the individual, rather than a mélange of elements influenced by history, society, and culture.

3 Bandura, 2001.

4 Chen & Li, 2021.

5 "Indentured stripper" is a play on the term "indentured servant" to describe a person trapped in a labor situation with little recourse to exit.

6 Benoit, Jansson, Smith & Flagg, 2018.

REFERENCES

Abbot, S. (2010). Motivations for pursuing a career in pornography. In R. Weitzer, ed., *Sex for sale: Prostitution, pornography, and the sex industry*, 47–66. New York: Routledge.

Abel, G. (2014). A decade of decriminalization: Sex work "down under" but not underground. *Criminology & criminal justice*, 14(5), 580–92.

Addams, J. (1912). *A new conscience and an ancient evil*. New York: Macmillan.

Arvidsson, A. (2005). Brands: A critical perspective. *Journal of consumer culture*, 5(2), 235–58.

Ashford, C. (2009). Queer theory, cyber-ethnographies, and researching online sex environments. *Information & communications technology law*, 18(3), 297–314.

Ashforth, B. E., & Humphrey, R. H. (1993). Emotional labor in service roles: The influence of identity. *Academy of management review*, 18(1), 88–115.

Ashton, K. (2009). That "internet of things" thing. *RFID journal*, 22(7), 97–114.

Augustin, L. (1988). *Sex at the margins: Migration*. New York: St. Martin's.

Bailey, A., & Figueroa, J. P. (2016). A framework for sexual decision-making among female sex workers in Jamaica. *Archives of sexual behavior*, 45(4), 911–21.

Bakehorn, J. (2010). Women made pornography. In R. Weitzer, ed., *Sex for sale: Prostitution, pornography, and the sex industry*, 91. New York: Taylor & Francis.

Bandura, A. (2001). Social cognitive theory: An agentic perspective. *Annual review of psychology*, 52, 1–26.

Baratosy, R., & Wendt, S. (2017). "Outdated laws, outspoken whores": Exploring sex work in a criminalised setting. *Women's studies international forum*, 62, 34–42.

Barry, K. (1984). *Female sexual slavery*. New York: NYU Press.

Barss, P. (2010). *The erotic engine: How pornography has powered mass communication, from Gutenberg to Google*. Toronto: Doubleday Canada.

BBC News. (2010, March 8). Internet access is "a fundamental right." *BBC News*, 1–24.

Belenky, M. F., Clinchy, B. M., Goldberger, N. R., & Tarule, J. M. (1986). *Women's ways of knowing: The development of self, voice, and mind* (vol. 15). New York: Basic Books.

Bell, L. (1987). *Good girls/bad girls: Sex trade workers and feminists face to face* (vol. 123). Ontario: Canadian Scholars Press.

Benoit, C., Jansson, M., Smith, M., & Flagg, J. (2018). Prostitution stigma and its effect on the working conditions, personal lives, and health of sex workers. *Journal of sex research*, 457–71.

Benoit, C., Smith, M., Jansson, M., Magnus, S., Flagg, J., & Maurice, R. (2017). Sex work and three dimensions of self-esteem: Self-worth, authenticity, and self-efficacy. *Culture, health & sexuality*, *55*(4–5), 1–15.

Benoit, C., Smith, M., Jansson, M., Magnus, S., Ouellet, N., Atchison, C., . . . & Shaver, F. M. (2016). Lack of confidence in police creates a "blue ceiling" for sex workers' safety. *Canadian public policy*, *42*(4), 456–68.

Berger, R. (2015). "Now I see it, now I don't": Researcher's position and reflexivity in qualitative research. *Qualitative research*, *15*(2), 219–34.

Bernstein, E. (2001). The meaning of the purchase: Desire, demand, and the commerce of sex. *Ethnography*, *2*(3), 389–420.

Bernstein, E. (2007). *Temporarily yours: Intimacy, authenticity, and the commerce of sex*. Chicago: University of Chicago Press.

Bindel, J. (2017). *The pimping of prostitution*. London: Palgrave Macmillan.

Blunt, D., & Wolf, A. (2020). Erased: The impact of FOSTA-SESTA and the removal of Backpage on sex workers. *Anti-trafficking review*, *14*, 117–21.

Bowen, K., Dzuvichu, B., Rungsung, R., Devine, A. E., Hocking, J., & Kermode, M. (2011). Life circumstances of women entering sex work in Nagaland, India. *Asia Pacific journal of public health*, *23*(6), 843–51.

Boyer, D. K., Chapman, L., & Marshall, B. K. (1993). *Survival sex in King County: Helping women out*. Seattle, WA: Women's Advisory Board.

Brents, B. G., & Hausbeck, K. (2005). Violence and legalized brothel prostitution in Nevada: Examining safety, risk, and prostitution policy. *Journal of interpersonal violence*, *20*(3), 270–95.

Brewis, J., & Linstead, S. (2000). "The worst thing is the screwing" (1): Consumption and the management of identity in sex work. *Gender, work & organization*, *7*(2), 84–97.

Bruckert, C., & Hannem, S. (2013). Rethinking the prostitution debates: Transcending structural stigma in systemic responses to sex work. *Canadian journal of law & society/La revue Canadienne droit et société*, *28*(1), 43–63.

Bullough, V., & Bullough, B. (1987). *Women and prostitution: A social history*. New York: Prometheus.

Califia, P. (1988). *Sapphistry: The book of lesbian sexuality*. Tallahassee, FL: Naiad Press.

Campbell, C. (1991). Prostitution, AIDS, and preventive health behavior. *Social science & medicine*, *32*(12), 1367–78.

Capiola, A., Griffith, J., Balotti, B., Turner, R., & Sharrah, M. (2014). Online escorts: The influence of advertised sexual orientation. *Journal of bisexuality*, *14*(2), 222–35.

Carbonero, M. A., & Gómez Garrido, M. (2018). Being like your girlfriend: Authenticity and the shifting borders of intimacy in sex work. *Sociology*, *52*(2), 384–99.

Castle, T., & Lee, J. (2008). Ordering sex in cyberspace: A content analysis of escort websites. *International journal of cultural studies*, *11*(1), 107–21.

Certeau, M. d., & Mayol, P. (1990). *The practice of everyday life: Living and cooking* (vol. 2). Minneapolis: University of Minnesota Press.

Chapkis, W. (1997). *Live sex acts: Women performing erotic labor*. New York: Routledge.

Chen, W., & Li, X. (2021). Digital inequalities in American disadvantaged urban communities: Access, skills, and expectations for digital inclusion programs. *Information, communication & society*, 25(13), 1916–33.

Cheyne, N., & Guggisberg, M. (2018). Stalking: An age-old problem with new expressions in the digital age. In J. Henricksen & M. Guggisberg, ed., *Violence against women in the 21st century: Challenges and future directions*, 161–90. Hauppauge, NY: Nova Science.

Chin, K., & Finkenauer, J. (2012). *Selling sex overseas: Chinese women and the realities of prostitution and global sex*. New York: NYU Press.

Clarkson, F. A. (1939). History of prostitution. *Canadian Medical Association journal*, 41(3), 296–301.

Cohen, B. (1980). *Deviant street networks: Prostitution in New York City*. Lexington, MA: Lexington Books.

Cojocaru, C. (2016). My experience is mine to tell: Challenging the abolitionist victimhood framework. *Anti-trafficking review*, (7), 12–38.

Coker, A. D., Huang, H.-H., & Kashubeck-West, S. (2009). Research with African Americans: Lessons learned about recruiting African American women. *Journal of multicultural counseling and development*, 37(3), 153–65.

Comte, J. (2014). Decriminalization of sex work: Feminist discourses in light of research. *Sexuality & culture*, 18(1), 196–217.

Cree, V. (1995). *From public streets to private lives: The changing task of social work*. Farnham, UK: Ashgate.

Cucina, J., Martin, N., Vasilopoulos, N., & Thibodeuax, H. (2012). Self-serving bias effects on job analysis ratings. *Journal of psychology*, 146(5), 511–31.

Cunningham, S., and Kendall, T. (2011). "Prostitution 2.0: The changing face of sex work." *Journal of urban economics*, 69(3), 273–87.

Cusick, L., Brooks-Gordon, B., Campbell, R., & Edgar, F. (2011). "Exiting" drug use and sex work: Career paths, interventions, and government strategy targets. *Drugs: Education, prevention, and policy*, 18(2), 145–56.

Dalby, L. (2008). *Geisha*. Berkeley: University of California Press.

Dalla, R. L., Xia, Y., & Kennedy, H. (2003). "You just give them what they want and pray they don't kill you": Street-level sex workers' reports of victimization, personal resources, and coping strategies. *Violence against women*, 9(11), 1367–94.

Davis, N. (1971). The prostitute: Developing a deviant identity. In Henslin, J., ed., *Studies in the sociology of sex*, 297–322. New York: Appleton-Century-Crofts.

Decker, J. (1979). *Prostitution: Regulation and control*. Littleton, CO: Rothman.

Delacoste, F. E. (2018). *Sex work: Writings by women in the sex industry*. New York: Simon & Schuster.

Dempsey, M. M. (2010). Sex trafficking and criminalization: In defense of feminist abolitionism. *University of Pennsylvania law review*, 158(6), 1729–78.

Dempsey, M. M. (2019). Prostitution. In L. Alexander & K. Ferzan, ed., *The Palgrave handbook of applied ethics and the criminal law*, 599–622. London: Palgrave Macmillan.

DiTecco, D., & Karaian, L. (2022). New technology, same old stigma: Media narratives of sex robots and sex work. *Sexuality & Culture, 26*(6), 1–31

Doezema, J. (2013). *Sex slaves and discourse masters: The construction of trafficking.* London: Zed.

Döring, N. (2009). The Internet's impact on sexuality: A critical review of 15 years of research. *Computers in human behavior, 25*(5), 1089–1101.

Downs, D. M., James, S., & Cowan, G. (2006). Body objectification, self-esteem, and relationship satisfaction: A comparison of exotic dancers and college women. *Sex roles, 54*(11–12), 745–52.

Drucker, J., & Nieri, T. (2018). Female online sex workers' perceptions of exit from sex work. *Deviant behavior, 39*(1), 1–19.

Dworkin, A. (1979). *Pornography: Men possessing women.* New York: Penguin.

Dworkin, A. (1997). *Life and death.* New York: Free Press.

Ehrenreich, B., & Hochschild, A. R. (2003). *Global woman: Nannies, maids, and sex workers in the new economy.* Basingstoke, UK: Macmillan.

Elder, G. H. (Ed.). (1985). *Life course dynamics: Trajectories and transitions, 1968–1980.* Ithaca, NY: Cornell University Press.

England, K. V. (1994). Getting personal: Reflexivity, positionality, and feminist research. *Professional geographer, 46*(1), 80–89.

Ericsson, L. (1980). Charges against prostitution: An attempt at a philosophical assessment. *Ethics, 90*(3), 335–66.

Evans, J. V. (2013). Seeing subjectivity: Erotic photography and the optics of desire. *American historical review, 118*(2), 430–62.

Farley, M., Cotton, A., Lynne, J., Zumbeck, S., Spiwak, F., Reyes, M. E., . . . & Sezgin, U. (2004). Prostitution and trafficking in nine countries: An update on violence and posttraumatic stress disorder. *Journal of trauma practice, 2*(3–4), 33–74.

Farrell, A., McDevitt, J., Perry, N., Fahy, S., Chamberlain, K., Adams, W., . . . & Wheeler, K. (2009). *Review of existing estimates of victims of human trafficking in the United States and recommendations for improving research and measurement of human trafficking.* Washington, DC: Humanity United.

Fein, S., & Spencer, S. J. (1997). Prejudice as self-image maintenance: Affirming the self through derogating others. *Journal of personality and social psychology, 73*(1), 31.

Feldman, V. (2014). Sex work, politics, and the Internet: Forging local and translocal political communities through the blogosphere. In C. Showden & S. Majic, ed., *Negotiating sex work: Unintended consequences of policy and activism*, 243–66. Minneapolis: University of Minnesota Press

Gall, G. (2007). Sex worker unionisation: An exploratory study of emerging collective organisation. *Industrial relations journal, 38*(1), 70–88.

Goffman, E. (1956). *The presentation of self in everyday life.* New York: Random House.

Goffman, E. (1963a). Stigma and social identity. In T. L. Anderson, ed., *Understanding deviance: Connecting classical and contemporary perspectives*, 256–65. New York: Routledge, 2014.

Goffman, E. (1963b). *Stigma: Notes on the management of spoiled identity*. New York: Simon & Schuster.

Goldenberg, S. M., Duff, P., & Krusi, A. (2015). Work environments and HIV prevention: A qualitative review and meta-synthesis of sex worker narratives. *BMC public health*, *15*(1), 1–15.

Grant, M. G. (2014). *Playing the whore: The work of sex work*. New York: Verso Books.

Handcock, M., & Gile, K. (2011). Comment: On the concept of snowball sampling. *Sociological methodology*, *41*(1), 367–71.

Hebdige, D. (1979). *Subculture: The meaning of style*. New York: Routledge.

Heckathorn, D. (1997). Respondent-driven sampling: A new approach to the study of hidden populations. *Social problems*, *44*(2), 174–99.

Heckathorn, D. (2002). Populations, respondent-driven sampling II: Deriving valid population estimates from chain-referral samples of hidden populations. *Social problems*, *49*(1), 11–34.

Heckathorn, D. (2011). Snowball versus respondent-driven sampling. *Social methodology*, *41*(1), 355–66.

Helsper, E. J. (2012). A corresponding fields model for the links between social and digital exclusion. *Communication theory*, *22*(4), 403–26.

Hickle, K., & Roe-Sepowitz, D. (2017). "Curiosity and a pimp": Exploring sex trafficking victimization in experiences of entering sex trade industry work among participants in a prostitution diversion program. *Women & criminal justice*, *27*(2), 122–38.

Hirschi, T. (1972). The professional prostitute. In R. Bell and M. Gordon, ed., *The social dimensions of human sexuality*, 249–67. Boston: Little, Brown.

Hoang, L. A. (2011). Gender identity and agency in migration decision-making: Evidence from Vietnam. *Journal of ethnic and migration studies*, *37*(9), 1441–57.

Hobbes, T. (1651). *Leviathan*. London: Routledge.

Hobson, B. M. (1990). *Uneasy virtue: The politics of prostitution and the American reform tradition*. Chicago: University of Chicago Press.

Hochschild, A. R. (1979). *The managed heart*. Berkeley: University of California Press.

Hodson, R. (2004). A meta-analysis of workplace ethnographies: Race, gender, and employee attitudes and behaviors. *Journal of contemporary ethnography*, *33*(1), 4–38.

Høigård, C., & Finstad, L. (1992). *Backstreets: Prostitution, money, and love*. University Park: Pennsylvania State University Press.

Holt, T. J., & Blevins, K. R. (2007). Examining sex work from the client's perspective: Assessing johns using on-line data. *Deviant behavior*, *28*(4), 333–54.

Horning, A. (2019). Quitting the sex trade: Keeping narratives inside the debates on prostitution policy and legislation. *Victims & offenders*, *14*(5), 533–39.

Horswill, A., & Weitzer, R. (2018). Becoming a client: The socialization of novice buyers of sexual services. *Deviant behavior*, *39*(2), 148–58.

Horton, D., & Richard Wohl, R. (1956). Mass communication and para-social interaction: Observations on intimacy at a distance. *Psychiatry*, *19*(3), 215229.

James, S. E., Herman, J. L., Rankin, S., Keisling, M., Mottet, L., & Anafi, M. (2016). *The report of the 2015 U.S. transgender survey*. Washington, DC: National Center for Transgender Equality.

Jenness, V. (1990). From sex as sin to sex as work: COYOTE and the reorganization of prostitution as a social problem. *Social problems, 37*(3), 403–20.

Jones, A. (2015a). For black models scroll down: Webcam modeling and the racialization of erotic labor. *Sexuality & culture, 19*(4), 776–99.

Jones, A. (2015b). Sex work in a digital era. *Sociology compass, 9*(7), 558–70.

Jones, A. (2016). "I get paid to have orgasms": Adult webcam models' negotiation of pleasure and danger. *Signs: Journal of women in culture and society, 42*(1), 227–56.

Jost, J., & Banaji, M. (1995). The role of stereotyping in system-justification and the production of false consciousness. *British journal of social psychology, 33*(1), 1–27.

Joyce, D. (2015). Internet freedom and human rights. *European journal of international law, 26*, 493–514.

Kempadoo, K., & Jo, D. (1998). *Global sex workers: Rights, resistance, and redefinition*. London: Psychology Press.

Kipling, R. (1898). *On the city wall*. Philadelphia: Henry Altemus.

Knox, B. (2014, July 2). Tearing down the whorearchy from the inside. *Jezebel*, 1–3.

Koken, J. (2011). Independent female escorts' strategies for coping with sex work related stigma. *Sexuality & culture, 16*(3), 209–29.

Koken, J., Bimbi, D. S., & Parsons, J. (2010). Male and female escorts: A comparative analysis. In R. Weitzer, ed., *Sex for sale: Prostitution, pornography, and the sex industry*, 2nd ed., 205–32. New York: Routledge.

Koken, J. A., Bimbi, D. S., Parsons, J. T., & Halkitis, P. N. (2004). The experience of stigma in the lives of male Internet escorts. *Journal of psychology & human sexuality, 16*(1), 13–32.

Krefting, L. (1991). Rigor in qualitative research: the assessment of trustworthiness. *American journal of occupational therapy, 45*(3), 214–22.

Krusi, A., Kerr, T., Taylor, C., Rhodes, T., & Shannon, K. (2016). "They won't change it back in their heads that we're trash": The intersection of sex work–related stigma and evolving policing strategies. *Sociology of health and illness, 38*(7), 1137–50.

Kuhn, T. (1962). *The structure of scientific revolutions*. Chicago: University of Chicago Press.

Laub, J. H., & Sampson, R. J. (1993). Turning points in the life course: Why change matters to the study of crime. *Criminology, 31*(3), 301–25.

Lee-Gonyea, J. A., Castle, T., & Gonyea, N. E. (2009). Laid to order: Male escorts advertising on the Internet. *Deviant behavior, 30*(4), 321–48.

Leigh, C. (1997). Inventing sex work. In J. Nagle, ed., *Whores and other feminists*, 223–31. London: Routledge.

Leiner, B., Cerf, V., Clark, D., Kahn, R., Kleinrock, L., Lynch, D., . . . & Wolff, S. (2012, October 1). *Brief history of the Internet*. Retrieved August 22, 2017, from Internet Society: www.internetsociety.org/.

Lessig, L. (2009). *Code: And other laws of cyberspace*. New York: Basic Books.

Lever, J., & Dolnick, D. (2010). Call girls and street prostitutes: Selling sex and intimacy. In R. Weitzer, ed., *Sex for sale: Prostitution, pornography, and the sex industry*, 187–203. New York: Routledge.

Levine, R., & Rubinstein, Y. (2013). *Smart and illicit: Who becomes an entrepreneur and does it pay?* National Bureau of Economic Research. (No. w19276).

Li, X., & Chen, W. (2021). Core tech support networks and digital inequalities in American disadvantaged urban communities. *Journal of computer-mediated communication, 26*(2), 91–107.

Lincoln, Y., & Guba, E. (1985). *Naturalistic inquiry*. Thousand Oaks, CA: Sage.

Lindemann, D. J. (2013, August 31). Health discourse and within-group stigma in professional BDSM. *Social science & medicine, 99*, 169–75.

Lister, K. (2017a, June 26). The oldest profession in the world? Sex work stigma in historical research. *Whores of Yore*. Retrieved December 26, 2022, from https://www.thewhoresofyore.com/katersquos-blog/the-oldest-profession-in-the-world-historical-stigma-around-sex-work.

Lister, K. (2017b, October 5). Sex workers or prostitutes? Why words matter. Retrieved July 1, 2018, from *News: The essential daily briefing*: https://inews.co.uk.

Lynn, F. (2019, February 12). The new age of whorearchy. *Medium*, 1.

MacKinnon, C. (1985). Pornography, civil rights, and speech. *Harvard civil rights law review, 20*, 1–70.

MacPhail, C., Scott, J., & Minichiello, V. (2015). Technology, normalization, and male sex work. *Culture, health & sexuality, 17*(4), 483–95.

Maher, L. (1997). *Sexed work: Gender, race, and resistance in a Brooklyn drug market*. Oxford: Clarendon.

Maher, L., & Daly, K. (1996). Women in the street-level drug economy: Continuity or change? *Criminology, 34*(4), 465–92.

Maher, L., Dunlap, E., Johnson, B., & Hamid, A. (1996). Gender, power, and alternative living arrangements in the inner-city crack culture. *Journal of research in crime and delinquency, 33*(2), 181–205.

Mann, S. (2013, September 24). Just say no: Why you shouldn't study sex work in school. Retrieved October 4, 2017, from Autocannibal: https://autocannibalism.wordpress.com.

Marlatt, G. A. (Ed). (1998). *Harm reduction: Pragmatic strategies for managing high risk behaviors*. New York: Guilford Press.

Mathews, P. W. (2017). Cam models, sex work, and job immobility in the Philippines. *Feminist economics, 23*(3), 160–83.

McCarthy, B., Benoit, C., & Jansson, M. (2014). Sex work: A comparative study. *Archives of sexual behavior, 43*(7), 1379–90.

McIntosh, P. (1989). White privilege: Unpacking the invisible knapsack. *Peace and Freeedom*, July/August.

McLean, A. (2012). New realm, new problems? Issues and support networks in online male sex work. *Gay and lesbian issues and psychology review, 8*(2), 70.

Merton, R. K. (1938). Social structure and anomie. *American sociological review*, 3(5), 672–82.

Milan, S. (2013). *Social movements and their technologies: Wiring social change.* Toronto: Palgrave Macmillan.

Miller, J. (2008). *Getting played: African American girls, urban inequality, and gendered violence.* New York: NYU Press.

Miller-Young, Mireille. (2014). *A taste for brown sugar: Black women in pornography.* Durham, NC: Duke University Press.

Mills, C. W. (1997). *The racial contract.* Ithaca, NY: Cornell University Press.

Milrod, C., & Monto, M. A. (2012). The hobbyist and the girlfriend experience: Behaviors and preferences of male customers of Internet sexual service providers. *Deviant behavior*, 33(10), 792–810.

Mimiaga, M. J., Reisner, S. L., Tinsley, J. P., Mayer, K. H., & Safren, S. A. (2009). Street workers and Internet escorts: Contextual and psychosocial factors surrounding HIV risk behavior among men who engage in sex work with other men. *Journal of urban health*, 86(1), 54–66.

Minichiello, V., Scott, J., & Callander, D. (2013). New pleasures and old dangers: Reinventing male sex work. *Journal of sex research*, 50(3–4), 263–75.

Morris, J. A., & Feldman, D. C. (1996). The dimensions, antecedents, and consequences of emotional labor. *Academy of management review*, 21(4), 986–1010.

Motyl, J. (2013). Trading sex for college tuition: How sugar daddy dating sites may be sugar coating prostitution. *Penn State law review*, 117, 927–57.

Murphy, A. K., & Venkatesh, S. A. (2006). Vice careers: The changing contours of sex work in New York City. *Qualitative sociology*, 29(2), 129–54.

Musto, J., Fehrenbacher, A. E., Hoefinger, H., Mai, N., Macioti, P. G., Bennachie, C., . . . & D'Adamo, K. (2021). Anti-trafficking in the time of FOSTA/SESTA: Networked moral gentrification and sexual humanitarian creep. *Social sciences*, 10(2), 58.

Nagle, J. (Ed.). (1997). *Whores and other feminists.* New York: Routledge.

Nash, Jennifer C. (2014). *The black body in ecstasy: Reading race, reading pornography.* Durham, NC: Duke University Press.

Nayar, K. I. (2017). Working it: The professionalization of amateurism in digital adult entertainment. *Feminist media studies*, 17(3), 473–88.

Norris, N. (1997). Error, bias, and validity in qualitative research. *Educational action research*, 5(1), 172–76.

O'Doherty, T. (2011). Criminalization and off-street sex work in Canada. *Canadian journal of criminology and criminal justice*, 53(2), 217–45.

Oerton, S., & Phoenix, J. (2001). Sex/bodywork: Discourses and practices. *Sexualities*, 4(4), 387–412.

Orchard, T., Farr, S., Macphail, S., Wender, C., & Young, D. (2012). Sex work in the forest city: Experiences of sex work beginnings, types, and clientele among women in London, Ontario. *Sexuality research and social policy*, 9(4), 350–62.

Orchard, T., Vale, J., Macphail, S., Wender, C., & Oiamo, T. (2016). "You just have to be smart": Spatial practices and subjectivity among women in sex work in London, Ontario. *Gender, place & culture, 23*(11), 1572–85.

Oselin, S. S. (2014). *Leaving prostitution: Getting out and staying out of sex work.* New York: NYU Press.

Overall, C. (1992). What's wrong with prostitution? Evaluating sex work. *Signs: Journal of women in culture and society, 17*(4), 705–24.

Paglia, C. (2011). *Sex, art, and American culture: Essays.* New York: Vintage.

Pajnik, M., Kambouri, N., Renault, M., & Šori, I. (2016). Digitalising sex commerce and sex work: A comparative analysis of French, Greek, and Slovenian websites. *Gender, place & culture, 23*(3), 345–64.

Panchanadeswaran, S., Unnithan, A. M., Chacko, S., Brazda, M., & Kuruppu, S. (2017). What's technology got to do with it? Exploring the impact of mobile phones on female sex workers' lives and livelihood in India. *Gender, technology, and development, 21*(1–2), 152–67.

Parsons, J. T., Koken, J. A., & Bimbi, D. S. (2004). The use of the Internet by gay and bisexual male escorts: Sex workers as sex educators. *AIDS care, 16*(8), 1021–35.

Parsons, J. T., Koken, J. A., & Bimbi, D. S. (2007). Looking beyond HIV: Eliciting individual and community needs of male Internet escorts. *Journal of homosexuality, 53*(1–2), 219–40.

Pateman, C. (1988). *The sexual contract.* Cambridge: Polity Press.

Pew Research. (2018, February 5). Internet broadband factsheet. Retrieved from Pew Research Center: www.pewinternet.org.

Pheterson, G. (1989). *A vindication of the rights of whores.* Seattle: De Capo Press.

Pheterson, G. (1996). *The prostitution prism.* Leiden: Leiden University Press.

Phua, V. C., & Caras, A. (2008). Personal brand in online advertisements: Comparing white and Brazilian male sex workers. *Sociological focus, 41*(3), 238–55.

Queen, C. (1997). *Real live nude girl: Chronicles of sex positive culture.* San Francisco: Cleis.

Quinn, J. F., & Forsyth, C. J. (2005). Describing sexual behavior in the era of the Internet: A typology for empirical research. *Deviant behavior, 26*(3), 191–207.

Ray, A. (2007). Sex on the open market: Sex workers harness the power of the Internet. In K. Jacobs, M. Janssen & M. Pasquinelli, ed., *"C'lick me": A netporn studies reader,* 45–68. Amsterdam: Institute of Network Cultures.

Raymond, J. (1995, December 11). Perspective on human rights: Prostitution is rape that's paid for; The U.S. military must have zero tolerance for this exploitation of women and children, at home and abroad. *Los Angeles times.*

Raymond, J. G. (2004). Ten reasons for not legalizing prostitution and a legal response to the demand for prostitution. *Journal of trauma practice, 2*(3–4), 315–32.

Rekart, M. (2005). Sex-work harm reduction. *Lancet, 366*(9503), 2123–34.

Rieder, I., & Ruppelt, P. (1988). *AIDS: The women.* San Francisco: Cleis Press.

Roberts, N. (1992). *Whores in history: Prostitution in western society.* New York: HarperCollins.

Roe, G. (2005). Harm reduction as paradigm: Is better than bad good enough? The origins of harm reduction. *Critical public health*, 15(3), 243–50.

Rogers, K. (2018, December 17). Tumblr's algorithm thinks vomiting unicorns, raw chicken, and boot cleaners are porn. *Vice*, 1–3.

Rosen, E., & Venkatesh, S. A. (2008). A "perversion" of choice: Sex work offers just enough in Chicago's urban ghetto. *Journal of contemporary ethnography*, 37(4), 417–41.

Rothman, S. M. (1978). *Woman's proper place: A history of changing ideals and practices, 1970 to the present.* New York: Basic Books.

Sacks, V. (1996). Women and AIDS: An analysis of media misrepresentations. *Social science & medicine*, 42(1), 59–73.

Sampson, R., & Laub, J. (1993). Turning points in the life course: Why change matters to the study of crime. *Criminology*, 31(3), 301–25.

Sanders, T. (2004). The risks of street prostitution: Punters, police, and protesters. *Urban studies*, 41(9), 1703–17.

Sanders, T., & Campbell, R. (2007). Designing out vulnerability, building in respect: Violence, safety, and sex work policy. *British journal of sociology*, 58(1), 1–19.

Sanders, T., Connelly, L., & King, L. J. (2016). On our own terms: The working conditions of Internet-based sex workers in the UK. *Sociological research online*, 21(4), 1–14.

Sandman, P. M. (1987). Risk communication: Facing public outrage. *Environmental Protection Agency journal*, 13, 21–22.

Sanger, W. (1858). *History of prostitution.* New York: Harper & Brothers.

Schmit, T. (2021, May 26). The continued neutering of the Internet. *Philadelphia weekly*, 1–7.

Seidman, S. (1992). *Embattled eros: Sexual politics and ethics in contemporary America.* London: Routledge.

Shdaimah, C., & Leon, C. (2018). Whose knowledges? Moving beyond damage-centred research in studies of women in street-based sex work. *Criminological encounters*, 1(1), 19–30.

Silbert, M. H., & Pines., A. M. (1982). Entrance into prostitution. *Youth & society, 13(4), 471–500.*

Sloan, L., & Wahab, S. (2000). Feminist voices on sex work: Implications for social work. *Affilia*, 15(4), 457–79.

Small, M. L. (2009). How many cases do I need? On science and the logic of case selection in field-based research. *Ethnography, 10*(1), 5–38.

Smith, E. M. (2017). "It gets very intimate for me": Discursive boundaries of pleasure and performance in sex work. *Sexualities*, 20(3), 344–63.

Spradley, J. (1979). *The ethnographic interview.* Philadelphia: Harcourt Brace Jovanovich College Publishers.

Stewart, P., & Vache, J. (Eds.). (2010). *Julie; or, The new Heloise: Letters of two lovers who live in a small town at the foot of the Alps* (vol. 6). Lebanon, NH: University Press of New England.

Sullivan, B. (1999). Prostitution law reform in Australia: A preliminary evaluation. *Social alternatives, 18*(3), 9–14.

Sullivan, B. (2010). When (some) prostitution is legal: The impact of law reform on sex work in Australia. *Journal of law and society, 37*(1), 85–104.

Suppiah, V., & Sandhu, M. S. (2011). Organizational culture's influence on tacit knowledge-sharing behaviour. *Journal of knowledge management, 15*(3), 462–77.

Sutherland, E. (1947). *Principles of criminology.* Chicago: Lippincott.

Swendeman, D., Ali, S., Collins, M., George, S., Ghose, T., Fehrenbacher, A. E., Dey, B. (2015). "Whatever I have, I have made by coming into this profession": The intersection of resources, agency, and achievements in pathways to sex work in Kolkata, India. *Archives of sexual behavior, 44*(4), 1011–23.

Tarantino, Q. (Director). (1994). *Pulp fiction* [Motion Picture].

Tewksbury, R., & Lapsey, D. (2018). It's more than just a big dick: Desires, experiences, and how male escorts satisfy their customers. *Deviant behavior, 39*(1), 126–35.

Thukral, J. (2005). Behind closed doors: An analysis of indoor sex work in New York City. *Siecus report, 33*(2), 3.

Thukral, J., Ditmore, M., & Murphy, A. (2005). *Behind closed doors: An analysis of indoor sex work in New York City.* New York: Urban Justice Center.

Tomko, C., Nestadt, D. F., Rouhani, S., Silberzahn, B. E., Haney, K., Park, J. N., . . . & Sherman, S. G. (2020). Confirmatory factor analysis and construct validity of the internalized sex work stigma scale among a cohort of cisgender female sex workers in Baltimore, Maryland, United States. *Journal of sex research, 58*(6), 1–11.

Tomura, M. (2009). A prostitute's lived experiences of stigma. *Journal of phenomenological psychology, 40*(1), 51–84.

Turner, J. (1982). Towards a cognitive redefinition of the social group. In H. Tajfel, ed., *Social identity and intergroup relations,* 15–40. Cambridge: Cambridge University Press.

Twigg, J., Wolkowitz, C., Cohen, R. L., & Nettleton, S. (2011). Conceptualising body work in health and social care. *Sociology of health & illness, 33*(2), 171–88.

Twis, M., & Shelton, B. (2018). Systematic review of empiricism and theory in domestic minor sex trafficking research. *Journal of evidence-informed social work, 15*(4), 1–25.

United Nations. (2016). *The state of broadband 2016: Broadband catalyzing sustainable development.* New York: United Nations.

Upadhyay, S. (2021). Sugaring: Understanding the world of sugar daddies and sugar babies. *Journal of sex research, 58*(6), 1–10.

Van Doorn, N., & Velthuis, O. (2018). A good hustle: The moral economy of market competition in adult webcam modeling. *Journal of cultural economy, 11*(3), 177–92.

Vanwesenbeeck, I. (2001). Another decade of social scientific work on sex work: A review of research, 1990–2000. *Annual review of sex research, 12*(1), 242–89.

Weiner, A. (1996). Understanding the social needs of streetwalking prostitutes. *Social work, 41*(1), 97–105.

Weitzer, R. (1991). Prostitutes' rights in the United States: The failure of a movement. *Sociological quarterly, 32*(1), 23–41.

Weitzer, R. (2005). New directions in research on prostitution. *Crime, law, and social change, 43*(4–5), 211–35.

Weitzer, R. (2007). Prostitution: Facts and fictions. *Contexts, 6*(4), 28–33.

Weitzer, R. (Ed.). (2009a). *Sex for sale: Prostitution, pornography, and the sex industry.* New York: Routledge.

Weitzer, R. (2009b). Sociology of sex work. *Annual review of sociology, 35,* 213–34.

Weitzer, R. (2011). *Legalizing prostitution: From illicit vice to lawful business.* New York: NYU Press.

Weitzer, R. (2013). Sex trafficking and the sex industry: The need for evidence-based theory and legislation. *Journal of criminal law and criminology, 101,* 1337–70.

Weitzer, R. (2017). Resistance to sex work stigma. *Sexualities, 21*(5–6), 3–13.

Woodley, X. M., & Lockard, M. (2016). Womanism and snowball sampling: Engaging marginalized populations in holistic research. *Qualitative report, 21*(2), 321–29.

Wynter, S. (1987). Whisper: Women hurt in systems of prostitution engaged in revolt. In F. Delacoste, ed., *Sex work: Writings by women in the sex industry,* 266–70. New York: Simon & Schuster.

Zickar, M. J., & Carter, N. T. (2010). Reconnecting with the spirit of workplace ethnography: A historical review. *Organizational research methods, 13*(2), 304–19.

INDEX

Abbot, Sharon, 46
abolitionist feminists, 40–41, 50–51,
    173–74
abortion, sex work stigma compared with,
    161
academia, sex work research and, 35–37
accommodation of clients, of Liz, 135–36
active workers: omission of active workers
    from, 42; perceptions of, 41
activism on sex work, universities and, 37
activist groups, for sex workers, 42, 58
adaptive ability, of sex workers, 45, 84
Addams, Jane, 40
added value, emotional labor as, 113
additional screening steps, Kaley on, 195
administrative tasks, of sex workers, 172–
    73, 215–16
adult gambling sites, 15
advertisement of services, 126, 201–2;
    Hannah on, 125; Internet use of, 48–49,
    97, 169, 209; Janine on, 69; male sex
    workers and, 112
advertising study, of Phua and Caras,
    99–100
aesthetics of sex work process, Roxy on,
    200
affective life, Rousseau on, 116
African gray parrots, 86–87
agency, perceived lack of, 142, 216
agency, sex work and, 43, 54, 173–74, 204,
    216; Olivia on, 218
agentic contractarian idea, 43
ahuienime, differing translations of, 39
AIDS epidemic, 53

algorithms, 81
Alyson (study participant), 104–5, 116; on
    availability, 114–15
American client, Charlene on, 178
American criminal justice system, Char-
    lene on, 83
American culture, Merton on, 202–3
American Dream, Merton on, 203
angler fish costume, of Lucy, 70–71
anonymity, of Internet, 163, 212
anti-prostitution activists, of early twenti-
    eth century, 40
antisocial interactions, frequency on
    Internet of, 82
app, repurposing of, 81–82
appointment process, Alyson on, 114–15
architecture, of digital spaces, 81–82
Arden (study participant), 126–27, 132–33,
    166–67, 175–76; on benefits of sex work,
    214; black book of, 168; on screening,
    197, 198, 211–13
art, sex work as, 15
Asia, Vivian and, 88
assault, by clients, 155
assumptions about sex work, change of, 12,
    33–34, 95
atmosphere, of Kill Time Club, 2
attraction with unattractive clients, Nor-
    een on, 133–34
attractive parts of clients, focus on, 134
Australia, 177, 222
Australian approach to problem clients,
    American contrasted with, 177–78
Australian providers, police and, 178

ABOUT THE AUTHOR

Kurt Fowler is Assistant Professor of Criminal Justice at Penn State Abington. He received his PhD in Criminal Justice from Rutgers University and a master's degree in Criminology from the University of Pennsylvania. His research focuses on the intersection of technology and deviance.